Technique and Interpretation on the Harpsichord and Clavichord

Technique and Interpretation on the Harpsichord and Clavichord

RICHARD TROEGER

INDIANA UNIVERSITY PRESS

Bloomington
&
Indianapolis

This book was brought to publication with the assistance of a grant from the Andrew W. Mellon Foundation.

Manufactured in the United States of America

Library of Congress Cataloging-in-Publication Data
Troeger, Richard.
  Technique and interpretation on the harpsichord and clavichord.
  Bibliography: p.
  Includes index.
  1. Harpsichord—Instruction and study. 2. Clavichord—Instruction and study. 3. Music—Interpretation (Phrasing, dynamics, etc.) I. Title.
MT252.T76   1987   786.3'0421   85-42830
ISBN 0-253-35835-3
ISBN 0-253-20408-9 (pbk.)

1 2 3 4 5 91 90 89 88 87

To Paulette

 Contents

Foreword

One of the obstacles to our understanding of Baroque performance practice is the paucity of explanatory information for professionals. Most treatises of the period (Couperin's *L'Art de toucher le clavecin*, for example) were compiled for children, students, or amateurs, while most other printed accounts sought to inform (or influence) the general public, as they still do. Writing an instruction book for those who supposedly know what to do and how to do it might reasonably be considered superfluous, but it is actually the practicing performers, conductors, improvisers, and editors who realize how much help is needed once the basics have been mastered.

In *Technique and Interpretation on the Harpsichord and Clavichord* Richard Troeger has written a guide for professionals and advanced students in the practical application of historical advice, especially that relating to the technique of playing keyboard instruments. He has tapped his own resources as a player and educator to give us a thorough and analytical approach to harpsichord and clavichord technique. Like Mr. Troeger, I am not a believer in "technique" as separated from the control, facility, and freedom needed to express one's thoughts, or those of others, but it is often necessary to analyze the body's actions to ensure that efficiency and not energy waste prevails.

Mr. Troeger's work is praiseworthy in many respects. Perhaps most extraordinary is his determination to analyze aspects of performance many performers would rather not think about or cannot articulate. *Technique and Interpretation* will take its place as an unusual and valuable reference tool.

KENNETH COOPER
New York, 1986

Introduction

The practical matters of playing the harpsichord and the clavichord are the subject matter of this volume. Its aim is to outline the techniques and musical resources of these instruments by discussing their scope and relationships. *Technique* in the full sense of the word embraces all that is involved in conveying music through a given medium; this book considers the physical aspects of playing the harpsichord and the clavichord and the manipulation of their sounds in relation to musical interpretation. The variables of music and its performance will always leave a discussion of this kind open-ended. However, I hope to have covered the essentials and to have represented sufficiently the possible variations in approach to start a newcomer toward the formation of his or her own technique, or at least to increase the reader's awareness of his or her own musical purposes and means of realizing them. Music can be projected in many ways; my intent is to indicate points of departure rather than to define one specific approach or to make prescriptions of taste.

A basic knowledge of music theory and keyboard playing will be useful to the reader. Some commentary is directed to adult beginners who have chosen the early keyboard instruments, but the text is intended primarily for players with some proficiency, including those who are accomplished players on another keyboard instrument but are newcomers to the harpsichord or the clavichord. A background in early performance practices will also be helpful, since most of the repertory dates from the sixteenth through the eighteenth century. The focus of the text is musical projection and the manipulation of keyboard sound, but these are intimately tied to historical matters of fact and conjecture. Source materials are quoted extensively on such fundamental issues as keyboard touch, articulation, and time stresses. More peripheral and/or controversial subjects such as *notes inégales* and overdotting are touched on only in reference to their larger musical aspects. The performance practices of a single early school can provide material for volumes, and even representative documentation on these matters would repeat material that is already available elsewhere as well as overburden the text and lose sight of its main intent. Therefore, historical issues are defined briefly as they arise and/or a relevant authority is cited to focus the discussion and incidentally to suggest starting points for the reader's independent research. The discussion of dance in chapter 5, for instance, is intended only to show the range and importance of the topic, to suggest guidelines for investigation, and to relate it to the chapter's main discussion of tempo, rhythm, and meter. Ornaments, rhythmic alteration, and other facets of performance practice are discussed in terms of their musical functions. The reader is referred to the sources and the secondary books and articles listed in the Bibliography for historical information; I suggest that each quotation be located in its source, both as a spur to further reading and as a means of seeing the quoted excerpts in their original contexts.

The many short musical illustrations in the text are drawn mainly from readily accessible repertory; thus the context of an example can be located easily if the reader requires it. The comments made on each example are not meant to be prescriptive; the examples are presented only to show possible applications of the points made in the text. The reader should develop alternative approaches to each example. The examples are notated in accordance with modern usage regarding clefs, accidentals, note shapes, etc.; however, when the rhythmic notation of the original incorporates incompatible values (such as "extra" beams to indicate rhythmic sharpening in certain figurations), the original has been followed.

The sequence of chapters moves from fundamental matters of instruments and finger technique to musical expression and its relationship to instrumental sound. Chapter 1 considers the harpsichord and the clavichord in regard to their tonal characteristics and the way tonal and mechanical variations affect the player. Among the early harpsichords and clavichords, individual instruments, even from the same country and period, vary sufficiently that they can require different approaches. The opening chapter outlines the nature of some of these differences; the reader is referred to the section on instruments in the Bibliography for specialized organological information. Chapter 2 discusses the fundamentals of touch on the harpsichord and the clavichord and the ranges of attack possible on each, depending on the individual hand and instrument. Attack is basically a technical issue and is in some ways independent of articulation. Different touches are often required on different instruments to produce equivalent styles of articulation. Therefore, the technical aspect of sound production is treated on its own, albeit with some reference to articulation, and the musical use of different levels of articulation is discussed in a subsequent chapter. Chapter 3 continues the technical exposition with a discussion of fingering. Appropriate fingerings for certain standard figurations are described, historical fingering as practiced in various times and places is briefly outlined, and some commentary is devoted to the subtle relationships between fingering and articulation.

Chapter 4, on articulation* and legato, and chapter 5, on timing, form the heart of the book. Chapter 4 explores ways of varying the sound through linking and separating notes and stressing the textural variations composed into the music. Together with the subtleties of timing outlined in chapter 5, these techniques supply a varied palette of dynamic realization and implication for the harpsichordist and reinforce the dynamic expressivity of the clavichord. Chapter 5 endeavors to describe the time frame in which music operates and the interrelationships of its various facets. This chapter also gives some attention to the relationships among articulation, timing, texture, and dynamics; this topic is too dependent on musical circumstance for extended discussion, but some basic considerations have been included. Chapter 6 considers the musical functions of ornamentation and embellishment, particularly in reference to their dynamic, rhythmic, and accentual effects. In this sense, it extends the discussion of the preceding two chapters. It also examines some aspects of ornamentation and embellishment that characterize particular early schools of keyboard writing. The account of continuo playing in chapter 7 is intended to introduce the newcomer to the scope of the field, supplying some practical guidelines to the realization of accompaniment textures and outlining some of the continuo styles of different countries in the seventeenth and eighteenth centuries. The subject is also important for the understanding that first-hand continuo experience can provide regarding the nature of textural variations in solo keyboard works. Harpsichord registration is the subject of chapter 8. Aspects of registrational color are discussed, but the thrust of the chapter is toward choosing registration that complements articulatory requirements. Chapter 9 describes some representative temperaments and considers variations in temperament from the standpoint of varying musical needs. Appendix 1 discusses mechanical aspects of keyboard facility and includes some exercises, both for practice and to illustrate lines on which the reader can devise exercises for individual problems.

Many minutiae regarding specific fine points of performance are included in the course of the main presentation of each topic. These details are brought in for their own sake as well as to follow up and sometimes illustrate the main points. Others could be added, but many tangential observations could obscure the main lines of discussion. I have tried to indicate some useful points of departure and the mutual influences of the many factors of interpretation, as well as suggest the many possible varieties of approach and emphasis. Even so, there is a strong danger of sounding simplistic when

---

*Although in ordinary usage the noun *articulation* applies broadly to the entire gamut from detached to overlapping tones, the verb *to articulate* is often used only in the narrower sense of separating notes. For the sake of clarity, this book employs both the noun and the verb in reference to detached notes only.

describing so complex a subject as musical performance. My intent has been to open avenues, not to close them off: to show approaches, not "solutions." No overall "method" is outlined. Circumstance as a deciding factor is often stressed; and in addition to the variations of approach necessitated by specific musical textures, instruments, rooms, auditoriums, and styles and periods of composition, each player has an individual inclination to certain expressive means, tonal qualities, rhythmic styles, and so forth. Any perspective on performance, past or present, must take such variables into account. As far as interpretation itself is concerned, the book's focus is on ways of implementing instrumental techniques in projecting an interpretation rather than on interpretive choices *per se*, although the latter subject is necessarily introduced on occasion.

The performer's relationship with the instrument involves thinking in terms of the musical ideal—what is perceived imaginatively in the inner ear—and at the same time in terms of what can be produced through the instrumental medium, given the kinds of circumstance just enumerated. The player must weigh what can be fully realized on the instrument against what can be implied on it to transcend its actual capabilities for singing tone, dynamic flexibility, sustaining a fabric of parts, or even suggesting orchestral or ensemble forces. In this area of tonal illusion and suggestion, many performance devices are described; for example, certain ways of articulating textures or inflecting time. It is important that the use of such techniques originate in instinctive responses to musical needs instead of being consciously applied. The player's modulations of sound should stem from hearing and automatically reacting in terms of the instrument. Although such fine adjustments are often instinctive to begin with, it is useful for the player to examine them intellectually, then allow them to sink back into unconscious reflex responses. By understanding such processes, the player can gain greater control and more readily reproduce what happens in inspired performance (when instinct is especially productive).

I have given very little attention to differences between early keyboard techniques and those of the modern piano or the organ. Rather, I have described harpsichord and clavichord techniques as thoroughly as possible in their own terms. Obviously, there are immediately apparent differences between early and modern instruments in tone, feel, and appearance, even down to the material covering the keys. The harpsichord and clavichord sound thin, soft, and even brittle to ears accustomed only to the modern piano or to the organ, and the newcomer may not at first perceive the nuances made available by their transparency of tone. Their actions, too, are light, although it is just as necessary to "feel bottom" on these instruments as on heavier keyboards. The clavichord's touch particularly seems to be lighter than it really is. Control of the tone occasionally demands use of certain kinds of weight, but weight in either harpsichord or clavichord playing is quite different from weight on the piano or organ, and the pianist or organist approaching the early instruments must be prepared to develop new ways of using the hands and fingers. These new techniques will not confuse those techniques acquired for other instruments but will only increase one's versatility, even on accustomed keyboards.

Subtler and more difficult than adapting one's touch is developing new ways of hearing and thinking about music so as to bring out the most from the early instruments and to become used to the dynamics implied by changing textures in the early repertories. The organ's sustained tone and the piano's powerful sound and comparatively wooly attack (to say nothing of the interpretation of later repertories) develop habits of timing and articulation that are not always appropriate on the harpsichord or the clavichord. To be sure, a pianist will want to make full use of the clavichord's flexible dynamics. On the other hand, an organist may tend at first to play too articulately and inflexibly on the harpsichord, reluctant to exploit the instrument's resources of *legatissimo*, since the organ's sustained tone blurs so easily when notes overlap.

In many respects harpsichord and clavichord techniques are distinct from one another, yet there are several reasons for including the two instruments in this study. For the most part they share a common literature; and both their techniques, although individual, involve light actions, clear and decaying sounds, and general use of the fingers alone. The clavichord, on whose technique very little has appeared in modern times, was regarded during the Renaissance and Baroque periods as the ideal training instrument for the other keyboards, as well as being prized as an instrument in its own right. Often both instruments were cultivated by players in earlier times; each instrument sheds its own light on one and the same piece of music.

The relation of finger to key on the harpsichord is often quite different from what it is on the clavichord, although it has frequently been pointed out that control of the clavichord improves control of the harpsichord. Musically, the two instruments have many points in common, in that the players must deal with their tonal clarity and decaying tone. Of the three basic elements in musical expression available to the performer, both the harpsichord and the clavichord utilize adjustments of timing and are highly sensitive to niceties of articulation. The third element, expression through dynamic nuance, can be fully realized only on the clavichord. The harpsichord can usually only imply this element, apart from register changes (not usually open to graded effects) and dynamic variation built into the musical texture. With respect to dynamics, then, the two instruments often require different treatment to yield similar musical results. The harpsichordist must use somewhat different musical devices to imply or sketch what the clavichord can often fully realize. The ways that both instruments may be manipulated to a given musical end is the concern of most of this volume.

I have been fortunate in receiving comment and opinion from players of many viewpoints. For reading the manuscript and making valuable observations I am grateful to Kenneth Cooper, Miriam Duncan, Miriam Graff, Charles Gunn, Marilyn Keiser, Joanne Koonce, Mark Kroll, Karyl Louwenaar, Ronald McKean, Gavin Williamson, and Marie Zorn. I owe special thanks to Anthony Newman, who has discussed many points with me, and to Jeffrey Gaynor, who was generous with time and suggestions when this book was still in the planning stages. To my wife, Paulette Grundeen, my gratitude for advice, support, and assistance during every stage in the preparation of this volume.

Technique and Interpretation on the Harpsichord and Clavichord

Instruments

THE TERMS *HARPSICHORD* AND *CLAVICHORD* cover many types of instrument. From their first appearance in the early Renaissance until they were gradually replaced by the piano in the late eighteenth century, the harpsichord and the clavichord appeared in many forms. At any one time, different European nations showed diverse approaches to the construction and musical qualities of these instruments. Further variations appeared from one local center to another and even among instruments by the same builder. This chapter briefly outlines the development of each instrument and discusses the ways some of their constructional and musical variables affect the player. For detailed information on the design of early keyboard instruments, see the section on instruments in the Bibliography.

❧ The Harpsichord

The harpsichord family includes the wing-shaped harpsichord proper, as well as rectangular, polygonal, and even upright forms: virginal, spinet, and clavicytherium respectively. Virginals and spinets were popular in various forms as household instruments during the sixteenth through the eighteenth century. Normally they possessed a single keyboard and a single register at 8′ or, more rarely, 4′ pitch. (Stops on the harpsichord use the same pitch designations as those on the organ, which are derived from pipe lengths for C [two octaves below middle C, or c¹]: 8′ pitch is normal pitch level, a stop an octave higher is said to be at 4′ pitch, that an octave lower at 16′ pitch.) The harpsichord most often had a single keyboard and two stops (both at 8′ or one each at 8′ and 4′ pitch) until the early seventeenth century, when larger instruments and more complex dispositions began to appear: a second 8′ as well as a 4′; auxiliary stops such as the front-plucking lute; and the 16′ in eighteenth-century Germany. Two-manual instruments apparently developed in the first half of the seventeenth century.[1]

Two basic tendencies appear in the acoustic design of historical harpsichords. The first to develop appeared in both Continental and English harpsichords until some time in the seventeenth century and continued as the basis of Italian and, apparently, Iberian harpsichords throughout the eighteenth century. This approach features short string scaling: c^2, an octave above middle C ($c′$), usually ranges between 9″ and 12″ in length. Case walls tend to be thin, often $\frac{3}{16}$″ in Italian instruments of cedar or cypress and marginally thicker in some northern instruments, with case walls often of oak or walnut. The entire case participates in tone production; the sound tends to be bright and very clear, with a well-marked, sometimes almost explosive pluck. The other tendency developed from the early seventeenth century, notably with the Ruckers family of builders in Antwerp; their influence dominated later seventeenth- and eighteenth-century building practices in northern Europe. This approach uses longer scales (c^2 typically 13″ to 14″), heavier case sides ($\frac{1}{2}$″ to $\frac{3}{4}$″), and case and framing in soft woods such as pine and poplar. Tonally such design tends to produce instruments with a less accentual pluck, longer-lasting tone, and a slower initial rate of tonal decay. Stemming from either of these two basic tendencies, each country had its own approach to harpsichord construction. National styles became more pronounced after the middle of the seventeenth century, although many cross-currents remained. Some rough generalizations about tonal characteristics can be made: for instance, eighteenth-century French harpsichords tend to produce a complex, voluptuous tone in the bass, which complements and explains the frequent low-range writing of French composers. Some eighteenth-century German harpsichords yield a plainer tone than do the French, and often of longer duration; Italian instruments usually sound clear and dry and show rapid tonal decay. However, every harpsichord is musically individual, and words are a notoriously poor means of conveying tonal characteristics. The reader should play and hear as many historical and modern instruments as possible.

Tone quality obviously influences the way a player manipulates a particular harpsichord, but perhaps more important than tonal beauty (or lack of it) are the various factors of attack, decay rate, and variation of timbre across the range of any single stop or combination. An instrument that is initially unimpressive may prove to be more flexible than one with a richer sound, depending on the relationships among these qualities. Harpsichord tone is characterized by a minute drop in pitch at the start of each note. The string is stretched as the plectrum contacts and releases it; it resumes normal tension and pitch as it settles into vibration. This phenomenon is not immediately perceptible, but it has much to do with the color of attack in an instrument. Equally important to the tone are the speed with which a note attenuates and the length and position of its plateau of sustained quality in relation to the first decline in volume. Instruments with long scales and tight strings tend to have a longer, more sustained tone with a less incisive attack. Harpsichords with shorter, slacker strings often have a more explosive attack and a sharper curve of attenuation. Variations in attack and sustain on different harpsichords, as well as variations in quality from bass to treble, may require different means of articulation and legato to achieve comparable musical results and often render an instrument more suitable for some styles and textures than for others.

An instrument's overall resonance can be affected by the way it is set up for damping. There are a few indications that the quick and immediate damping usually preferred today was not always an eighteenth-century preference. Old instruments with two choirs of 8' strings often show the close pairs of strings pinned very close together on the nut and the bridge. To prevent the dampers from touching their adjacent strings, they must be cut so short that when the register is retired (i.e., in "off" position, so that its quills do not pluck its strings) the dampers fail to engage their own strings. Thus, sympathetic resonance of the undamped strings occurs when one 8' is turned off and the other played upon. William Dowd, describing a single-manual, 2 × 8' French harpsichord with such close pinning, comments:

> That the close pairs are so close together (2mm) indicates that a register did not damp when disengaged or "off." In a double [-manual] harpsichord with standard French disposition [i.e., a single 8' stop on each keyboard, a 4' on the lower keyboard, and a manual coupler] this would not be important, for the lower 8' would only be off when the player wished to play the upper 8' with the undamped lower 8' sounding sympathetically, or on those occasions when a solo 4' was desired. With a single, however, the conditions are different. If the pairs are this close, one can never play a solo 8' without the other one sounding sympathetically, a carillon effect which inhibits articulation. Obviously they either liked this effect or simply did not care, for in an instrument without a 4' choir there is no need to crowd the close pairs.[2]

In such cases, to prevent the ends of the 8' dampers from jamming against their strings instead of riding smoothly back into place on top of them, the dampers must be cut with a rounded, sloping lower edge: ⊃. rather than ⊐. The former is depicted in a plate from Diderot's *Encyclopédie*.[3] That such a cut for dampers should be illustrated in a general account of harpsichord construction suggests that close pinning and its effect on damping were common in eighteenth-century France, and that the cut was often necessary.

Sympathetic vibrations are also encountered on a harpsichord by J. C. Fleischer (Hamburg, 1710, now in Berlin's Musikinstrumenten-Museum).

This instrument, with a single manual and 1 × 8′, 1 × 4′ disposition, has no provision for dampers on the 4′ jacks. The strings ring sympathetically to increase the resonance of the 8′ stop when the 8′ is used alone, and only the string contact made by the 4′ plectra upon descent damps the 4′ strings when that stop is employed. The lack of 4′ damping is an entirely atypical feature of early harpsichords but suggests, like the close pinning of 8′ strings, that the added luster of sympathetic vibration was often regarded as desirable.

Both touch and tone can be affected by the order of plucks in the key descent. (The plucks of different stops take place successively in a consistent order in any well-regulated harpsichord action, as may be found by depressing a key slowly. Precisely simultaneous plucking of all stops, as found in some early twentieth-century harpsichords, adds excessive resistance to the touch.) The order usually followed in the twentieth century has the 4′ sounding first as the key is depressed, followed by the 8′ stop located furthest from the player (the back or lower-manual 8′). The front or upper-manual 8′ sounds next, and the 16′, if present, sounds last. The arrangement with the 4′ on top has definite advantages. The 8′ notes, plucking lower in the key descent, can be reiterated without raising the key all the way to its original position, thus allowing easier and more connected repetition of notes, rather like the double escapement in a piano action. Also, it is more natural to the mechanics of the action for the 4′ to sound first, because its plectra and strings normally offer less resistance than those of the 8′ stops. Delaying the 4′ until a more resistant 8′ stop has sounded can crowd the plucks together near the bottom of the key descent, adding an unnecessary feeling of weight to the touch.

The staggering order depends on the relative lengths of the jacks. They are adjustable in most modern harpsichords but not in early instruments. Evidence on the staggering of antique actions is slight because of the deterioration of the original plectra and cloth key linings and changes made during restorations. Dowd has found a double-manual French harpsichord (by Blanchet, 1733) in seemingly original condition whose action adjustment unmistakably places the staggering order "uniformly and evenly lower 8′ first, then upper 8′, and 4′ last."[4] When one or both 8′ stops are employed with the 4′, this plucking order places more emphasis on the 8′, fundamental components of the ensemble than on the 4′, whose main function is to reinforce the octave overtone of the 8′ stops. Staggering with the 4′ first yields a lighter tone quality because the ear perceives the 4′ as more dominant. Dowd observes that "the discovery of one instrument with a plucking order regulated in this way does not prove it to have been a common practice of the eighteenth century."[5] Mechanical and historical evidence suggest both options; and a harpsichordist should adjust the staggering as well as the fine voicing of the instrument to suit particular needs or preferences in touch and tone.

The voicing of the instrument—the way the plectra are cut and their resistance to the strings—is of course a major influence on touch, tone, and volume. Historical accounts mention both heavy and light quilling. Voicing decisions depend on the player's requirements concerning absolute volume, the relative strengths of different registers (see chapter 8, pp.201–202), and the resonance of the harpsichord itself.

At one point in the revival of historical harpsichords there was a tendency among some builders and players to stress very light quilling and to suggest that it is not in the nature of the harpsichord to have a powerful tone. It is true that some instruments are not resonant enough to accommodate a strong pluck, and in any case it is clear that the voicing should stop short of the rasping effect of too strong a quill. However, many old instruments and modern reproductions can handle all the resonance imparted by a strong pluck. Indeed, some harpsichords seem to require strong voicing to bring out their full tonal qualities. Others are highly efficient, in that a light pluck produces a full, resonant tone. In either case, an advantage of loud voicing is that it brings out the dynamic variations of musical textures. On a loud harpsichord in comparison to a soft one, there is an appreciably greater difference in volume between an interval of two notes (sounding from two to six strings on a three-choir instrument) and a chord of eight notes (sounding eight to twenty-four strings).

A strong plucking action is by no means limited to the twentieth century. To be sure, light actions were to be found (see Burney's comment that weak quilling was prevalent on eighteenth-century French instruments[6]). However, such diverse authors as Diruta (1593), Saint Lambert (1707), Quantz (1752), and C. P. E. Bach (1753) all mention the occasional necessity to raise the fingers or to strike firmly so as to ensure that all the plucks take place. Diruta remarks that the harpsichord should be evenly quilled and pluck easily, but comments:

> But the organist, wishing to play dances [on the harpsichord], needs to observe the rules [of organ playing], yes, except, however, in regard to leaping and striking with his fingers. This is conceded him for two reasons; first, because the quilled instruments must be struck in order for the jacks and quills to play better; second, to play the dances with grace in that style, the organist wishing to play dances is permitted to strike with the fingers, just as any other player.[7]

Saint Lambert comments that for accompanying a singer with a loud voice "it is necessary to employ all the harpsichord's stops and strike the chords vigorously, just so one does not hear the noise of wood."[8]

Speaking of instruments generally, C. P. E. Bach remarks,

> The action of the harpsichord must not be too light and effeminate; the keys must not fall too deep; the fingers must meet resistance from them and be raised again by the jacks. On the other hand, they must not be too difficult to depress.[9]
>
> In accompaniments, just as much as in solos, a constant playing on the surface of the keys must be avoided; rather they should be depressed with definite force. This will not occur unless the hands are raised somewhat. Provided this is not done in the manner of a woodchopper, the raised hands are not only not wrong, but necessary and good, in that they provide a simple way of indicating the tempo to the other performers and make it possible to strike the keys with proper weight so that the tones will sound clear, in accord with the rules of good performance.[10]

According to Quantz,

> Experience shows ... that if two musicians play the same instrument, one produces a better tone than the other. The reason for this must be the touch peculiar to each person. In this regard it is necessary that each finger strikes the key with equal force and emphasis, and with the proper weight; that the strings are given sufficient time to make their vibrations unhindered; and that the fingers are not depressed too sluggishly, but are rather given, through a snap, a certain force that will make the vibrations of the strings longer in duration, and sustain the tone longer. In this fashion you will obviate as much as possible the natural weakness of the instrument, which is that the tones cannot be joined to one another as upon other instruments.[11]

The use for which an instrument is intended of course affects voicing decisions: a harpsichord meant for the private music room or to accompany one or two instruments can be more gently adjusted than one intended for public use and the accompaniment of large forces. The eighteenth-century notice for the sale of the deceased Handel's harpsichord states that the instrument "has a powerful tone and is well calculated for concerts."[12] Handel's famous improvisations in his operatic accompaniments, which so enraged Mattheson, were doubtless projected to the full limits of the composer's instrument.

The touch is further influenced by the position of the balance point (the fulcrum) of the keys. Some harpsichords, such as Italian and seventeenth-century Flemish instruments, balance the keys just behind their playing surfaces. This creates a somewhat heavier touch than is produced by a more retired balance point, but it allows a shallower key dip and a crisp, rapid feel to the action. These instruments sometimes require a more positive attack than, for example, eighteenth-century French harpsichords, in which the keys are usually balanced farther to the rear. The front ends of French keys are often carved out underneath, so that the forward weight is reduced in proportion to the rear. The key return is therefore rapid, as in a more forward-balanced instrument, but the rearward balance point requires less effort to depress the keys. Almost the entire resistance of the action lies in the weight of the jacks and the contact between the strings and plectra. Such actions are very responsive and allow the keys to be caressed more gently than do forward-balanced actions. Heavy or light, a good action allows rapid repetition of notes and complements sensitive tonal qualities by allowing a wide range of articulations.

Antique double-manual harpsichords use several methods to couple the manuals in order to employ upper- and lower-manual stops together. Many eighteenth-century Flemish doubles, and most if not all English doubles of the same period, permanently couple the upper 8′ to the lower by means of a "dogleg" jack that is operated from both keyboards. This device has the disadvantage that independent 8′ stops on separate manuals are unavailable unless the nasal "lute" register, often found on the upper manual of these instruments and independent of the lower keyboard, is present. Its usefulness in dialogue with the robust lower 8′ is limited. Some antique German doubles use a dogleg jack that can be disengaged from the lower manual by sliding the latter toward the player. When the coupler is disengaged, the jack works only from the upper manual. When the coupler is employed, the lower manual carries only the weight of the extra jack, whereas the French coupler involves carrying the weight of the upper-manual key as well: the key end is shoved up by a slim shank of wood ("coupler dog") affixed to the lower manual key. The French system, which is most often encountered today, can work lightly and efficiently, but the advantage of the German system is obvious. It is especially desirable if strong voicing and/or extra stops are present, with the resulting heavier action.

Keyboard dimensions vary significantly among historical keyboard instruments from different eras and countries. Octave spans vary from 6″ for some seventeenth-century French instruments to 6½″ for some Italian harpsichords; the octave on many others is typically 6¼″. Players tend to prefer an octave span that suits their own hands, but other dimensions are perhaps more important than the lateral distance. Other factors being equal, two instruments with identical octave measurements will feel different to the player if the depths of the key descent differ. The length of the natural keyheads in relation to the height of the accidentals strongly affects the comfort with which one negotiates some figurations. The shorter the natural keyheads the lower should be the accidentals, for otherwise the hand has too little room to negotiate the two levels: the keyboard feels too "steep." (However, the accidentals should never be so low that they descend below the surface of the naturals when depressed.) It is usually advantageous for the accidentals to narrow slightly from base to playing surface. J. S. Bach is said to have preferred them made that way. He also favored short keys, feeling that properly curved fingers did not require long keys.[13] The keys on many late eighteenth-century instruments, particularly on German clavichords and fortepianos, are noticeably longer than those on earlier instruments. The natural keyheads are not especially extended, but the accidentals are much longer than previously, possibly reflecting a change in playing technique, with the fingers more frequently extended. The increase in passages lying among the accidentals, resulting from the wider modulatory range of much *galant* music, could also help to explain this development.

The harpsichord was the first historical instrument to receive attention when the revival of interest in early music began in the late nineteenth century. The desire was generally for an instrument suitable for the music of J. S. Bach and his contemporaries, and insofar as earlier and later repertory was considered, most builders of this period tried to develop an all-purpose instrument. To be sure, a few individual restorers, builders, and players were closely involved with historical instruments, and a few fairly accurate reproductions were built. However, the mainstream of endeavor went toward "modernizing" the harpsichord, usually on lines derived from modern piano technology. This attitude regarded departures from historical models as a continuation of the harpsichord's natural development.

The instruments built during the first decades of the revival exhibited perhaps as many diversities as the entire corpus of antique harpsichords. They generally departed from historical precedent in regard to overall geometry; heaviness of case, soundboard, bridges, and stringing; complexity and heaviness of action; complexity of disposition (stop-changing pedals, 16' and lute registers, placement of the 4' on the upper manual); and, above all, in tone quality. The transparent sound of early instruments was generally lacking. The new builders were seeking a long-sustained tone and a variety of registrational colors; their instruments lacked the well-blended ensemble of registers, the diversity of color across the range, and the attenuating tones that allow flexible articulation and legato on the old instruments. These comments are not meant to denigrate the sincerity of effort among many of this century's first builders and players, who included some craftsmen and musicians of preeminent abilities; and it should be noted that some of the "revival" harpsichords inspired important modern works and were the foundation of several schools of playing during the first half of the twentieth century. The differences between such harpsichords and their historical predecessors have been aptly summed up by the British restorer and builder John Barnes:

> Traditional harpsichords, whatever their period, are rather like sports-cars: light to handle, exactly designed for a particular, well-understood purpose, and brought to a state of great efficiency by ruthless competition. Whereas the modern concert harpsichord is more like a family vehicle, designed to provide comfort and distraction during long journeys to its assorted occupants and a feeling of familiar solidarity to its driver.[14]

Once the move to greater authenticity was under way, the place of the typical revival harpsichord was taken by the now ubiquitous eighteenth-century, French-style two-manual instrument, and it is only in recent years that builders and performers have looked more seriously at the instruments developed in other European centers. The same development is going on regarding the earlier forms of the clavichord. Larger instruments, harpsichord or clavichord, are not necessarily louder or better sounding than the smaller varieties; and the latter are more economical of space, money, and maintenance and are preferable for some repertory.

The revival style of instrument will receive little specific attention in this book. Even with the restriction to historical harpsichords and clavichords, one is confronted with a wide variety of instruments, all of distinct tonal characteristics and musical response, and most of them probably best suited to a specific repertory. Although the variations among different periods and schools of early keyboard building are often considerable, they resemble the differences among shades of grey rather than between black and white. Both a small, light Italian harpsichord and a heavy, late English Kirckman or Shudi will exhibit a certain precision of attack, decaying tone, feel of plucking the strings, and so forth. The quality of each of these features is, of course, different, and suggestions made in this book concerning such factors must be adapted to the individual instrument and the music at hand. There is no standard, invariable approach to harpsichord or clavichord technique.

Since the first revival of interest in the performing techniques of early music, choice and style of instrument have naturally received a great deal of attention. In the keyboard realm, there have been arguments over such matters as the preferability of early or modern instruments generally; the allocation of a specific type of instrument for particular works or collections (a famous instance being the question of whether J. S. Bach's *Well-Tempered Clavier* was intended for harpsichord or clavichord); and the choice of a particular national style of instrument for corresponding repertory. In the last regard, it often makes sense to find out what style of harpsichord or clavichord might have been known to a given school of composers. For a sonata by Antonio Soler, for instance, a small, fretted Iberian clavichord would probably be much closer to the instruments known to the composer than would a large, unfretted German clavichord of the same period. Such relationships between instruments and repertory can be fascinating and musically revealing, but they entail practical difficulties, apart from the limitations of available historical information. Few players have the time, money, or inclination to amass and keep in playing order a wide range of instruments of different styles; and such restrictions are hardly unique to the twentieth century.

In any case, most pieces reveal new and different features on different instruments. Professionals and amateurs of all periods have played whatever music came to hand on whatever instrument was available. Harpsichords by Flemish and Italian makers were exported to places throughout Europe during most of the Baroque period (some even came to the New World), so most composers of prominence would have been acquainted with them. Some European nations showed a distinct preference for the harpsichord or the clavichord; for example, in France, England, and Flanders the harpsichord was in far more general use than the clavichord, while the latter was more often favored in Italy, the Iberian peninsula, Scandinavia, Germany, and Austria.

Whatever the features of a particular style of harpsichord, the tonal advantages of the instrument are immediately apparent: its brilliance, rhythmic authority, and textural clarity are unique among keyboard instruments. Although greatly overemphasized by early twentieth-century builders and players, its timbral variety is also attractive and can be musically useful. Its powers of blending with any kind of ensemble are well known, and properly used it provides a subtle but powerful rhythmic support. Above all, the harpsichord possesses an extremely refined palette of articulatory shading.

The limitations of the harpsichord are to a large extent the natural corollaries of its best qualities. The instrument lacks dynamic shading: variations in attack on the keys make little or no difference in volume. (Note, however, that such superficial dynamic rigidity can give energy to fast movements and brilliance to well-executed ornaments.) Nor is the harpsichord possessed of the true legato natural to stringed instruments or to the voice, in the sense of one note being sustained at full volume into the next. Its tonal decay, however, can be used to great advantage with varying articulation and legato. The harpsichordist's musical expressivity depends on timing and on the many inflections of articulation and legato that the clarity and decay rate of a fine instrument afford.

In view of these characteristics, it is not surprising that those who come newly to this instrument and find its briskness stimulating in a brilliant movement are frustrated when they attempt to perform slower, gentler pieces. Since most instruments are dynamically expressive, the newcomer to the harpsichord will find it necessary to express musical nuances in somewhat unaccustomed terms, to cultivate rhythmic and articulatory sensitivity in a more complete way.

🌺 The Clavichord

The clavichord is inherently less open than the harpsichord to superficial variations in construction, such as the choice of different dispositions of registers, and the instrument's action generates so little energy that its only resonating part is the soundboard; the case does not participate in tone production. Therefore, most variations in design are concentrated in the scaling, the geometrical layout, and the arrangement of strings, bridge, and soundboard. (The late eighteenth century saw the development of several mechanical attachments for the clavichord. These were essentially extrinsic to the design of the instrument and never entered common use, nor are they required by any extant literature.)

The earliest clavichords, known from fifteenth- and early sixteenth-century descriptions and pictures, were constructed with the soundboard below the keyboard level, unlike the arrangement that became normal later. The bridge had to be very high to receive the strings, reminiscent of the bridge on a violin or viol, and its height may have inhibited the resonance of the instrument. The earliest extant clavichord (1543) already shows most features of the typical later arrangement with a light, shallow bridge and the soundboard on the keyboard level.

All clavichords from the fifteenth through most of the seventeenth century, regardless of design, were fretted. In a fretted instrument, each string (actually, pair of strings) produces two to four different pitches by serving two to four adjacent keys. The tangent on each key marks off the sounding length of the strings and also sets them into vibration. Thus, tangents striking at different points produce different pitches; and for any group of notes fretted together, only one can sound at a time. Certain intervals are impossible with the fretting patterns of three and four adjacent notes that were standard until later in the seventeenth century, and literature intended for the clavichord often avoided simultaneous sounding of those intervals.

Early clavichords were often made with the same distribution of fretted notes. The layouts of several fifteenth- and sixteenth-century designs have been published by Ripin.[15] They are essentially congruent with one another and with the patterns used in later instruments. In the chart below, the dotted lines indicate that the first two groups of notes occur in both fretted and unfretted forms. (For mechanical reasons, the lowest notes cannot be fretted.)

c ¦	c♯ ¦	d	
e♭ ¦	e ¦	f	f♯
g	g♯	a	
b♭	b	c′	c♯′
d′	e♭′	e′	
f′	f♯′	g′	g♯′
a′	b♭′	b′	
c″	c♯″	d″	
e♭″	e″	f″	f♯″
g″	g♯″	a″	
b♭″	b″	c‴	

Fretted groups
of notes

It should be noted that this fretting pattern is not consistent among all octaves; and similar inconsistencies appear in the fretting of clavichords at least through the end of the seventeenth century, although patterns with octave consistency also appeared before 1700. Many patterns, using different combinations of duple, triple, and quadruple fretting, appeared during the sixteenth and seventeenth centuries. During the seventeenth, pairwise (duple) fretting came into use and is typical of eighteenth-century fretted clavichords. Duple fretting considerably increases the harmonic possibilities of the clavichord, for only certain semitones are fretted. Instruments with duple fretting are generally arranged with the following paired notes: C/C♯, E♭/E, F/F♯, G/G♯, and B♭/B. (Iberian clavichords are sometimes fretted so as to leave E and B, rather than D and A, unfretted.) Duple fretting continued in use into the nineteenth century.

Fretted clavichords present somewhat of a challenge in that they restrict overlapping legato between notes fretted together and require special care to produce a connected effect. This limitation is rarely a problem with duple fretting, because the tonalities normally employed in the literature hardly ever require that the fretted notes be played together or in succession. The instrument is thus essentially unfretted within the usual range of keys. Playing in remote tonalities was probably unusual on fretted instruments. It can be managed if the tangents' positions are set for reasonable intonation, but one must exercise care when playing consecutive fretted notes (see chapter 2, p.34).

In the sixteenth and seventeenth centuries, fretted instruments of similar design but from different countries possessed their own tonal characteristics. German clavichords tended to sound bright and rich in overtones, while Iberian instruments usually stressed the fundamental and had a darker sound. Many of these earlier clavichords possess a shorter sustain than do eighteenth-century instruments. As with some virginals, the beauty of the tone is often concentrated in the attack and the time immediately following.

Completely unfretted clavichords, with an independent pair of strings for each key, were in common use before the middle of the eighteenth century and may have appeared in the last decades of the seventeenth. This design allows unrestricted freedom to play in all tonalities and apparently developed as the repertory more habitually employed remote keys.[16] Unfretted instruments became increasingly popular in Germany, Austria, and Scandinavia through the eighteenth century, and by the last decades some very large instruments were being made, with ranges exceeding five octaves. Fretted instruments continued to hold their own against the larger, unfretted models. Each type has certain advantages. If other factors in the acoustic design are carried out properly, the smaller number of strings borne by a fretted instrument (as opposed to the many independent pairs of strings in an unfretted instrument) create less tension on the soundboard and allow a freer development of tone. The narrower string band also allows keys of nearly equal length and thus a more sensitive, uniform touch. The range is usually limited to C in the bass, as an increase in bass range and its added strings would cancel the advantage gained by fretting in the higher registers. Unfretted clavichords are governed by no such considerations; they can carry the full range of keys necessary for much *galant* and classical literature as well as accommodate the distant tonalities often explored in that music.

The musical differences between the late fretted and unfretted clavichord styles are similar to those found in fortepianos of the late eighteenth century: those of the Stein school of building have a bright, silvery, rather brittle quality while those of Walther's design exhibit darker tones. The fretted instruments tend to be bright, highly touch-responsive, and of good tonal balance across the range. Some specimens, like earlier fretted models, are at their best in a median dynamic range; they do not make especially impressive large-scale dynamic inflections very well. The large, unfretted instruments possess a deeper resonance; fine specimens yield a hazy luster—a veiled, singing quality on each note. They usually produce vibrato more readily than the less yielding fretted instruments and excel at large-scale dynamic contrasts. Unfortunately, many of the large instruments are poorly balanced from bass to treble, being weak in the upper registers. The player can compensate to some degree for this imbalance. These instruments are characterized by more variation of timbre across the range than on fretted clavichords, and those with a good balance between treble and bass can yield a wide variety of effects. Leopold Mozart enthusiastically describes such an instrument in a letter to his son:

> Further, he [the instrument's owner] has a clavichord also in mahogany, which he would not sell for 200 gulden, as he says that this instrument simply has not got its equal; that the descant sounds like a violin being played softly and the bass notes like trombones.[17]

Both fretted and unfretted clavichords had their limitations and advantages, and for this reason both were cultivated throughout the eighteenth century.

Several aspects of construction and musical response are applicable to any style of clavichord. The touch is strongly affected by several factors: the balance point of the keys, the distance from the tangents to their strings, the tension of the strings, and the presence or absence of a pressure bar. The first two are closely related and affect the key dip, the volume, and the ease of playing the instrument. The feasible variations in the distance the tangents must travel to the strings are slight but they can powerfully affect the clavichord's response. If they are too close to the strings, the tangents cannot build up enough momentum to bring out a full range of volume. If they are set too low, the key dip increases uncomfortably and the action becomes difficult to control because the tangents are more likely to bounce on and off the strings than remain in constant contact with them. (This response is often termed *chucking*; it produces a hoarse, spitting sound.) The tangents require a median level that allows the fullest dynamic variation compatible with ease of playing; unfortunately, the tangents are not easily adjusted in most instruments. The setting of the tangents usually tapers from bass to treble, being deeper in the lower ranges. The balance point of the keys also influences the tendency to chuck. A forward balance point, just behind the keys, is typical of many historical clavichords and allows a readier response than a retired fulcrum, but it increases the danger of chucking.

The pitch to which a clavichord is tuned affects its string tension, and hence its tonal quality and touch sensitivity. A clavichord, like any instrument, will resonate best at a particular pitch level. (Historical pitch varied widely, and this state of affairs is mirrored in many modern reconstructions of early instruments.) That level may or may not be compatible with the most manageable touch, but very slight variations in pitch level can sometimes make noticeable changes in the feel of an instrument. The touch can be further affected by the presence of a pressure bar, a strip of wood padded underneath that latches into the case and bears down on the muted portion of the strings to the left of the row of tangents. Pressure bars are found in many historical clavichords and depictions of them, but they were by no means a universal feature of the early instruments. The bar makes possible a more uniform touch and a higher level of volume than would be otherwise available by countering the upward movement of the strings as the tangents raise them. Some instruments require this adjustment; and some yield different but equally useful results with and without this device. It tends to create a brighter sound and a crisper touch; it inhibits the use of vibrato and certain other tonal shadings that are encouraged by less resistance from the strings.

Since the tangents remain in contact with the strings as long as the keys are depressed, the player is responsible for tone quality not only at the beginning of a note but throughout its duration. This involves smooth tonal production without chucking as well as pure intonation. Excessive pressure forces the strings out of tune. Although the early styles of clavichord are far less prone to pitch distortion than some modern reconstructions, one must learn to play in tune on this instrument and even to assist intonation when necessary. Some intervals can be brought into better accord by raising the pitch of one of the notes. A sharp major third can be made sweeter by sharpening the lower note; an excessively flat fifth can be adjusted by applying extra pressure to the upper tone.

The clavichord is famous, and deservedly so, as the most expressive of keyboard instruments. A fine specimen combines the clarity and articulatory sensitivity of the harpsichord with a dynamic range that is, on its own terms, comparable to that of the modern piano: although the level of the clavichord's top volume is low, its softest *pianissimo* is proportionately softer than that of the piano in relation to its greatest volume. The famous vibrato (*Bebung*), too, is unique to this keyboard. The clavichord's main limitation is its volume, and that is a limitation of performing site rather than musical use. Although the clavichord is mainly a solo instrument, it can be successful in accompanying delicate voices or soft solo instruments, such as the Baroque flute. C. P. E. Bach mentions the clavichord in this connection, and he is not alone among eighteenth-century authorities in recommending it in this capacity:

> The pianoforte and the clavichord provide the best accompaniments in performances that require the most elegant taste. Some singers, however, prefer the support of the clavichord or harpsichord to the pianoforte.[18]

❧ Conclusion

In dealing with the harpsichord or the clavichord, or indeed any instrument, the player must assess how much of the musical idea can actually be realized (particularly in regard to dynamics and sustained tones) and how much must be suggested. These factors must be kept in balance; if the level of implication is overwhelmed by one actual extreme of realization (for example, a dramatic change of harpsichord registration that undermines the dynamic aspects of timing and articulation), then the musical image will be thrown out of proportion. The clavichord and particularly the harpsichord frequently accomplish as much, or more, by implication than by direct statement, and the player will find his musical responses subtly reshaped by often suggesting, rather than fully realizing, the music's dynamic flow. The extent to which a piece is "fully realized" on the harpsichord depends on a number of factors. The varied textures written into a work can manipulate the instrument's flat dynamic surface into varied levels of intensity or actual volume. The needs of a specific work or individual passage, too, may be more or less dependent on dynamic flux, whether written into the texture or implied (or felt necessary) by the performer. Whatever the musical requirements and the balance between implication and realization, the player must strive to extract as much from the instrument as possible; this means accepting the limits of the instrument and allowing it to guide the shaping of musical utterance by its inherent qualities. The importance of accommodating one's playing to the instrument at hand, without permitting it to limit one's imagination, can hardly be overemphasized. A particular instrument may suggest or demand something new—a different direction—in the player's interpretation. A new approach is profitable for the player and need not limit the fullness of expression, only the means. The player's awareness of what an instrument can and cannot do will help to maximize the expression of musical thought, which must, finally, be independent of the instrumental medium.

2

Approach to the Keys

🌺 Preliminaries: Harpsichord and Clavichord

THE HEIGHT, FIRMNESS, AND POSITIONING of the player's chair are very important. A change in the height of the seat can make a dramatic difference in the ease of playing. The height that allows the fingers to flex in the middle of their range of movement is usually best. (Authors from the sixteenth through the eighteenth century advocate high or low seating and wrists high, low, or level with the arm and hand: preferences probably stemming from the writers' personal requirements.) For most players, the forearm, hands, and first joint of the fingers should all lie in one plane. For some, higher seating, which causes a slight downward slope of the forearm, is advantageous; for others, the reverse is true. The chair or bench should be level and unyielding to changes in body position. The player should be centered at the keyboard, the feet firmly on the floor so as to support the body, and the spine comfortably erect. As with the seat height, different distances from the keyboard should be tried until one allowing optimal flexibility is found. (François Couperin recommended turning slightly to the right.) The elbows should be near the rib cage, with the arms free enough to reach comfortably to any area of the keyboard. At a two-manual harpsichord, one should be able to reach the upper manual easily, but the main positioning should be made relative to the lower manual because it is likely to receive more use. The distance between keyboards varies from harpsichord to harpsichord; some players find it helpful to use a higher seating at some two-manual instruments than at a single keyboard.

There should be no element of discomfort in any aspect of the player's basic posture. One should experiment with seating to find the most comfortable and flexible position possible.

In earlier centuries, small, portable harpsichords and clavichords were often placed on a table when used. Some seventeenth-century Flemish instruments had very high stands and the player stood. Modern reproductions occasionally follow these practices. High stands should be proportioned to the player: average height is now greater than it was several hundred years ago, and a high stand of the original proportions may induce a cramped position for today's player. The same care should be exercised in choosing a table of the proper height for sitting or standing. The keyboard level should allow a more or less level arm for uninhibited movement of the wrists and fingers. Since body weight is distributed differently in sitting and standing postures, the standing player must find a relaxed but supple position.

✿ The Harpsichord

The diversity of finger attack that is useful on most harpsichords is fairly wide. The various factors include speed and pressure of attack and release, amount of hand or arm weight (if any), height of the fingers above the keys or upon them, and position of the hands and fingers. Some instruments respond to a much wider range of attack than others, and hands of differing strength and facility (not always the same thing) may find use for a wider or narrower range of attacks. Certainly, a sizable proportion of the attacks described below are exceptions to the usual requirements.

The basic touch of the harpsichord consists in playing from the fingers alone, with relaxed wrists and the arms lightly supporting themselves. The arms should not be tensed, but capable of easy movement, without directing any weight or tension into the hands. Weight is occasionally necessary but should be employed by choice; the basic touch should be free of weight. All motions should be made with as little tension as possible. The wrist, most of all, must remain relaxed and fluid in its motions. Its suppleness and flexibility allows easy movement in the fingers and absorb whatever arm weight is employed (see below) or is inescapable. Overly deliberate restraint of arm weight must be avoided because it can create tension and stiffness in the arm and wrist.

The fingers should be curved so that their tips fall more or less into a line. Whether the line is straight or slightly curved depends on the relative lengths of the different digits. In any case, the thumb and the little finger must not hang off the keyboard. Players with short thumbs may have to turn their hands slightly outward in order to position all the fingers on the keys. The longest fingers will have to be curved more than the rest; and no finger should lose its convex curve entirely. The end joints of the fingers must not collapse when depressing a key. It is usually best on the harpsichord, as on the clavichord, to play as much as possible at the near ends of the keys. This approach allows maximum leverage, which is especially important when the instrument has a forward balance point and/or a heavy touch. It is also advantageous to maintain the hand in a closed, compact position as much as possible and to center it well over the keys immediately required. This technique allows greater strength with less effort on heavy harpsichord actions and is a foundation of clavichord technique (see pp.30-31). In this area, as in many others, the clavichord will instill good habits in the harpsichordist.

Players new to the harpsichord sometimes develop unnecessary tension in the hands as a result of several, often related, factors. The harpsichord action affords the player a vivid awareness of the plectrum's contact with the string and of the moment the resistance between the two is overcome. This very precision, especially if coupled with minute irregularities in the instrument's adjustment, often leads one to adopt a heavy and/or tense touch for the sake of a false sense of control. This tendency is strongest with players who have difficulty adjusting to the lightness of the harpsichord action after being long accustomed to the heavier keyboards of many pianos and organs. Until the newcomer has learned to respond to the lightness, rapidity, and precision of the plucking action, practice should be confined to a single 8′ stop. Its unvarying sound is in any case a good point of departure for learning to be expressive on the instrument. Working with a single stop allows one to assimilate the proper touch more readily, without having to cope with the increased plucking resistance of additional registers, which can also lead to a tense touch. The action should be evenly regulated, and the voicing strength should be light for a beginner.

Early authorities on keyboard technique recommend that the fingers play from the surface of the keys or at the most from just above it. Although Diruta and Saint Lambert mention striking the keys in some contexts (see p.5 above), it is generally best for the fingers to fall onto the keys rather than hit them. There are three basic modes of attack: from just above the surface of the keys; from the surface, i.e., with the fingertips in contact with the keys before pressing them; and with the fingers resting on the keys so closely that their respective plectra are already in contact with the strings. The last is a particularly useful technique for immediacy of attack, as one is in precise control of the moment of plucking and can combine gentleness of touch with great rhythmic control; on-string attack should be given preference whenever possible. However, playing from just above the keys is generally best for a beginner, as it requires somewhat less finger control and accentuates the feeling of using only the fingers. Also, the closer the finger position, the more easily can one develop the habit of tensing the wrist and/or fingers, as the fingers perform their operations within a smaller latitude. In training the fingers for free motion, it is often useful to allow them a broader range of play than is found in immediate key contact. Exaggeration of physical movements is often a sure way to gain awareness of their nature. Newcomers may find it helpful to practice slow scales and simple figurations with the fingers relaxed and raised well above the keys until the simple finger stroke is under control. (This motion is recommended as an exercise, not as a normal mode of playing.) Two approaches to a high finger attack are possible: with the wrist in the position it assumes for normal key contact and the fingers raised; and with the entire wrist and hand slightly raised. The latter is preferable when it preserves lightness of movement; the former is likely in some cases to create tension in the wrist and fingers.

Of the three modes of attack enumerated above, the first, playing from just above the surface of the keys, is suited to a variety of situations, most particularly in dealing with excessively heavy or clumsy actions. In such cases the fingers should be kept light and supple in their motions; the longer finger descent will assure that the pluck takes place without tensing the hand, wrist, or arm. Alternatively, a carefully regulated degree of arm weight can be directed into the motions of the fingers. Both approaches have their uses. Regardless of an instrument's action, a higher finger position or independently moving, weightless fingers are sometimes best for clean negotiation of single-line passage work or detached articulation. Weight is preferable for passages that involve many held notes and consequent close application of the fingers. Playing in close, on-string contact with the keys is frequently desirable for delicate adjustments of legato, because the player is in immediate contact with attacks and releases. The close approach to the keys and the longer note durations allow less impetus to the fingers, so some use of weight is often helpful. Rameau's comments on seat height and a clinging, legato touch seem to suggest some use of weight:

> When one feels that the hand has been trained, one reduces little by little the height of the seat, until the elbows are placed slightly below the level of the keyboard; this causes the hand to cling as if glued to the keyboard, and this lends the touch all the legato [*liaison*] that can be put into it.[1]

Players with a slight build and light arms can usually apply weight more freely than those of solid physique. In any case, all weight employed must flow freely from the arms and be susceptible of continual adjustment. Deadweight or any tendency to press from the shoulder or body must be avoided. Often the weight of a relaxed forearm or even the hand's weight from a relaxed wrist is sufficient, but this kind of usage should not create stiffness in the shoulders or upper arm. One common fault is a tendency to push from the elbow or shoulder and to tense the wrist as a counteractive measure so that the fingers still retain some freedom of movement. Whatever its origin, weight is applied for relaxation and certainty of control, not for the attack itself, which must always be governed by the finger alone and originate in it.

An attack led from the elbow or wrist is a sign of insufficient relaxation and poor technique in general.

A touch that is firmer than usual is sometimes necessary when the fingers drop onto the keys from different heights. This situation is to be avoided, but for some hands it can hardly be obviated because of the demands of certain sustained passages and configurations.

Use of the fingers alone and without tension is difficult for some newcomers to the instrument, especially those with weak fingers or those accustomed to using weight from the shoulder of body, as is often the case in playing the piano. On the harpsichord, however, the arm often does nothing but guide the freely operating fingers, whose movement should be based in the center of their range of free play. To some newcomers, untensed use of the fingers alone seems to be a completely foreign concept. The following procedure can be very successful in overcoming this problem: Allow the arm to hang limply from the shoulder, dangling toward the floor. When thus completely relaxed, move from two to five fingers in a rapid, to-and-fro motion, while the arm remains limp. Then, with the fingers continuing their loose movement, raise the forearm to the level of the keyboard. The relaxed feeling in the hand and the free motion of the fingers should be preserved at the keyboard. An exercise derived from this procedure is very helpful in freeing and speeding up recalcitrant trills: Beginning with a dangling arm as before, raise the hand well above the keyboard and then lower it with two fingers "trilling" freely. Slowly lowering them onto the keys and lifting them off again, paying no attention to the moments of contact and departure, suggest the feeling that should be pursued when playing an actual trill.

It is inevitable that a certain degree of tension will enter into the hands when one is faced with certain difficulties. The phrase "relaxed technique" actually refers to carefully regulated interplay between tension and relaxation in the muscles of the hand, wrist, and arm. Maximum use must be made of a state of minimum tension; such tension as is necessary must be released as quickly as possible. Of course, muscles are employed in merely holding up the arms or moving the fingers, but any stiffness is unnecessary, energy wasting, and inimical to freedom of motion.

The newcomer must bear in mind that an increase in sound activity requires proportionately a much smaller increase in energy on the harpsichord than on the piano. Movement in general should be as economical as possible. As Rameau advised, "Never make the greater motion when the smaller one will suffice."[2]

There are two approaches to the finger stroke itself. The modern tendency is usually a simple down-and-up motion, which is useful in some contexts. The other has been aptly if crudely characterized as "chicken scratching." The finger depresses the key and then, instead of rising, withdraws toward the palm. Forkel, at second hand from C. P. E. Bach, describes J. S. Bach as playing in this manner; and Quantz, who saw Bach perform on at least one occasion, confirms Forkel's account:

> Whether you strike one finger more forcefully than another is ... very important. This may happen if you have accustomed yourself to curve some fingers inwards while extending others straight forward, a habit that not only causes inequality in the force of your playing, but is also obstructive to the round, distinct, and agreeable execution of quick passage-work. As a result many persons sound as it they were literally stumbling over the notes if they have to produce a run of several step-wise notes. If you accustom yourself at the very beginning to curving all the fingers inwards, each one as far as the others, you are less likely to make this mistake. In the performance of these running passages, however, you must not raise the fingers immediately after striking the key, but rather draw the tips of the fingers back towards yourself to the foremost part of the key, until they glide away from it. Running passages are produced most distinctly in this manner. I appeal here to the example of one of the greatest of all players on the keyboard, who practiced and taught this way.[3]

In his index, Quantz identifies this player as J. S. Bach.

Finger withdrawal is also described by Tomás de Sancta María:

> When the right hand plays an ascending run, two fingers are usually used, 3 and 4. Each time the third finger plays a key it should be raised more than the fourth. The fourth, however, should not be raised more than enough to release it from the key, so that it appears to drag over the keys. Moreover, the fourth finger should play the tip of the key while the third plays more to the inside. The second finger is held somewhat contracted and higher than the third finger, to which it is joined. This way the hand has the strength needed to play ascending runs perfectly.[4]

(The author goes on to say the same thing for descending scales in the right hand and for left-hand scales.)

The motions of finger withdrawal need not be exaggerated or self-consciously applied. They come very naturally with the third variety of attack listed above, that involving preliminary contact with the string. This approach can be described as "squeezing the keys." Finger withdrawal is also helpful in smooth rendition of early-style finger crossing in conjunct passages, the context in which Tomás describes it. This is apparently the same relationship Quantz is describing, for finger crossing was still used in the mid-eighteenth century (see chapter 3, pp.54-57). Both authors find finger withdrawal to be the smoothest approach for this style of fingering.

Different hands have different needs and preferences, but both kinds of finger stroke should be cultivated for the different articulatory results they assist and for additional flexibility in dealing with different styles of harpsichord action. This is not meant to suggest that types of articulation are inevitably linked with types of attack, but only that certain types of passage and articulation can often benefit from different attacks. For instance, a strong attack, perhaps from slightly above the key, is sometimes helpful in detached, aggressive passages, although this approach should not become habitual. A basically relaxed hand should be cultivated for detached playing, as for other styles. Conversely, with stiff or heavy actions, one should be able to combine a firm attack with various shadings of legato. In Italian and early Flemish instruments the keyboard's balance point is generally right behind the nameboard; this forward location of the fulcrum results in a direct and crisp touch that often requires a more definitive finger motion than do the comparatively retired balance points of other instruments. The best French eighteenth-century actions are notable for their comparatively smooth feel combined with rapid response. On such a keyboard one may often glide effortlessly, and variations in attack may be unnecessary or far more restricted than on a more resistant action, although yielding as wide or wider a range of articulation.

Regardless of the types of touch employed, it is essential that the force exerted on the keys be at all times sufficient to press the quills past their strings at the precise moment intended. A harpsichord voiced to absolute equality of touch is a rare item, and one must be sure that one's touch is strong enough to overcome any discrepancies in key resistance. However light the action and the player's touch, a good follow through past the pluck to the bottom of the key descent is necessary at all times. Care in this regard assists clean and uniform finger action and avoids any delay in the pluck. Few things musical are less attractive than a weakly played harpsichord whose plucks are not controlled by the player; under such circumstances, all effects of rhythmic finesse are lost. On the other hand, a touch that roughly thrusts the keys down will produce extraneous noise from the action and will fail to control fine grades of rhythm, legato, and articulation. The golden mean between these extremes must be found for any instrument and registration employed. All motions, all kinds of touch, should be based on a circular movement, with follow through not only to the bottom of each key but from one finger motion into the next, in a continual stream. The ear and fingers should already be aware of the release of each note when beginning it, and conduct the finger motion accordingly. Thus all movements are coordinated, preparing and making way for one another.

The variety of attack that is useful on a good harpsichord will be readily apparent to the player who is willing to experiment and to listen objectively to the effects produced by different approaches. Sensitivity to different kinds of attack will help the player produce a wide range of articulation and legato under varying circumstances: with different registrations, acoustics, types of harpsichord, musical configurations and textures, and technical difficulties. The variables involving touch on the instrument include the factors just named, as well as the action, the style of quilling, the player's posture and control of tension, the occasional use of weight, and varieties of finger position and withdrawal.

Especially for players accustomed to the piano or the clavichord, it is natural to associate certain finger motions with dynamic qualities, but on the harpsichord such cause and effect is largely illusory. To be sure, full textures played with several registers require more energy than thinly written passages on a single stop; but on a strongly voiced instrument, even delicate *piano* effects may require a firm attack while with light quilling the most violent effects may not necessitate more than an easy touch. The player must not give in to unwarranted associations of touch and tone, which can produce unsure attack in the former case and excessive heaviness in the latter.

Closely textured, velvety pieces (F. Couperin's "La Garnier" or his famous "Baricades mistérieuses," for instance), whether slow or rapid in tempo, are usually best played with the fingers in close, "squeezing" contact with the keys. The touch using on-string contact is usually the most flexible for achieving a variety of legato or articulatory effects, including staccato, which depends not on speed of attack but on speed of release. On the face of it, this suggests that attack affects release, but they are independent factors, except to the extent that a close contact with the keys also affords the most precise control over duration. The sense of intimate contact with the instrument that a close touch affords and the consequent range of implied or even realized dynamics constitute one of the harpsichordist's greatest assets. The prime requisite of any kind of attack is that it permit the player to sound and quit each note at the precise moment desired, and a variety of attacks may be necessary for this end. Some hands require less variation than others.

The sensitive player will constantly search for new refinements of touch. With very occasional use of arm or hand weight, many permutations are possible among the factors of wrist level, degree of finger curve, raising or drawing in of the fingers, level of attack, and variations between striking and gently pressing the keys. Some of these factors, alone or together, minutely influence the actual quality and quantity of tone. Much more importantly, the player must seek the type of touch best suited to any specific fingering, texture, registration, or type of articulation or legato.

Slight variations in tone are sometimes possible by modifications of pressure and attack alone. Dynamic variation through force of attack is more characteristic of the softer types of leather plectra than of the more generally used Delrin. Natural bird quill, properly cut, is also a little more sensitive than a synthetic quill. Quantz, as quoted above (p.6), suggests that a stronger attack produces a more sustained tone. François Couperin mentions that too forceful an attack draws a harsh sound from the string. Under certain circumstances the harsher and slightly louder tone can be desirable. (The stronger sound possibly results from a change in the relationship between the string and the quill during a rapid pluck. Normally the string rolls off the quill as the quill bends. If the quill is driven past rapidly, there is little time for their mutual yielding; the quill, with less bending, displaces the string further than is normal and a slightly stronger, harsher tone results. Also, when several stops sound together, the tone may be affected by the speed with which the plucks, staggered in the action, approach simultaneity.) Some harpsichords are more sensitive in this regard than others, and some do not respond to different strengths of attack at all. The effect, if present, is apparent only in low registers (perhaps because of the slacker strings) and with several stops or notes sounding, rather than with single notes or strings. If the instrument is responsive, a springy attack can benefit phrases that begin with a single resonant note or chord (Example II-1). The finger(s) may start from slightly above the key and must attack firmly. The tonal variations from different attacks on a full chord can be quite startling on a sensitive instrument. The opening of the *Italian Concerto* is most resonantly attacked (if the instrument responds to changes of attack) with a loose wrist and a small, heavy drop onto the keyboard. No arm weight is employed, and banging must be eschewed at all times. The extra jangle sometimes incidental to such an attack can be obviated by minutely spreading the chord. It must be stressed that heavy attacks are useful, if at all, only for isolated notes or chords, never for ongoing passages.

EXAMPLE II-1.
a. J. S. Bach, *Italian Concerto* [Allegro], m.1-2.
b. Scarlatti, Sonata in D, K. 400, m.1-2.

Unless dynamic variations are possible, and they are rare, heaviness in playing must always be avoided. Another exception may be suggested: if the fingering and/or articulation or even the physical difficulty of a passage warrant it, strike as firmly as is necessary, but *always from the level of the keys.*

Another touch of limited application involves playing very lightly, with a high wrist and the fingers extended as far as is compatible with their reaching the keys more or less evenly. (Details of this technique and associated wrist angling are discussed in Appendix I.) The raised, relaxed wrist allows wide play to the fingers, which should receive as free a movement as possible; the feeling is that of playing on the extreme ends of the finger-tips. Such a skimming touch is useful in fast, light, fairly regular figurations, especially those played with a light registration. Some players have difficulty in ridding themselves of the false sense of control associated with an overly tight hand and wrist, as opposed to the real control allowed by a more normal interplay of tension and relaxation. However, the lack of encumbrance by tension can actually assist accuracy as well as velocity. This touch is well suited to passages that do not require many nuances of touch, but perhaps only a clean legato or a lightly detached style. Obviously, there are many levels of touch between this extreme and other basics described above. Most pieces require frequent or constant adjustment of the levels of legato and articulation and of the precise way the fingers are applied to the keys.

The speed with which the key is released requires attention on some harpsichords and in some musical contexts. In the right circumstances, a slowly released note lasts just discernibly longer than one released briskly. The difference is minute but can be useful. Whether a slow or a rapid release makes any appreciable difference depends on the tone and resonance of the instrument, the damping material, the adjustment of the dampers and the extent to which they are worn, the distance the plectra project beyond their strings, the registration employed, and the pitch of the note. High notes are less likely to linger with slow damping; on many instruments, however, little or no difference can be found throughout the range. Worn or soft dampers often allow more variety of release than dampers of new or firm material. A highly resonant instrument is more likely to be sensitive to varied release speeds than one that is comparatively dead or quiet.

Action noise is a danger with slow releases, for the descending quill touches the vibrating string ahead of the damper. If the descent is too slow and/or the quill projects an appreciable distance beyond the string, a buzzing sound will replace effects of gently diminishing tone. Lighter voicing is better for this technique, and even then the correct speed of key release must be found to avoid buzzing. Use of a single stop is best, for slow release of two or more registers together is likely to provide more buzzing than sustaining.

If the speed of release makes any difference on the particular harpsichord, a fast release is better for simple legato, as there is less chance of action noise to interfere with the sound of one note following another. Slow releases are better for overlegato, in some circumstances, and for tones that cannot be sustained by the hand but should, ideally, ring on. (See, for instance, the low notes in Example II-2.) Slow releases are generally feasible only in slow movements.

EXAMPLE II-2.
J. S. Bach, *Italian Concerto*, Andante, mm.33-34.

A very rapid release can be managed on a springy keyboard by adding pressure and suddenly releasing the keys. This technique causes the keys to rise more rapidly and makes the least noise when one is releasing the last chord of a movement or section.

❦ The Clavichord

The harpsichord and the clavichord have little in common in the matter of touch. For players accustomed to modern keyboards the touch of both instruments appears light and often startlingly rapid in response, but these resemblances are fairly superficial. The clavichord's dynamic sensitivity and the tangent's continued contact with the strings allow a far more limited range of motions than does the harpsichord's action. For this reason the clavichord's touch is generally more demanding than the harpsichord's, although different clavichords can vary as much as harpsichords do in the feel of their keyboards. Many of the finest clavichords are harder to control than less-sensitive instruments; their greater expressive and tonal range calls for greater command by the player.

The clavichord, unlike any other keyboard instrument, makes the player responsible not only for the balance and interrelationships of tones and dynamic levels but also for the basic tone quality. The effect of a tangent ricocheting from its strings ("chucking") is feeble and rasping, similar in a general way to harp strings buzzing against the player's fingers or to lute or guitar strings too weakly stopped on the frets. Unfortunately, most clavichords with reasonable volume and sensitivity are prone to some degree of chucking, most conspicuously in the treble. Some sensitive instruments show little tendency to chuck and yield a full tone to a light although necessarily pliant touch. The player will find that on responsive clavichords prone to chucking, this tendency is related to the instrument's overall sensitivity. Nonetheless, a clavichord that chucks at the slightest provocation is a poorly designed instrument.

Almost without exception, the clavichordist plays with the fingers in close contact with the keys. The action often creates a distinct sensation of pressing the strings into vibration rather than striking them, and the player should do nothing to interfere with that basic sense of contact. Rather, one should be guided by it, for the clavichord will quickly tell the player when the touch is inappropriate. Exceptions to close finger application are very rare, perhaps occurring only in some cases of extreme *fortissimo*; nearly every passage can sound at full volume when the fingers are kept in close contact with the keys.

Even more than with the harpsichord, extraneous tension must be avoided. Since the tangent remains in contact with the strings for as long as the key is down, the player's touch must not slacken or a partial release of at least one of the two strings may occur, creating unmusical noise and inhibiting the sustaining power of the note. (The sustain is affected by pressure, regardless of the constancy of the string contact, as will be shown.) The harpsichordist's finger can and should be relatively relaxed after the key has reached the bottom of its descent, however much energy that descent required. But on the clavichord, pressure must be maintained evenly. The attack itself must be sure and unhesitant, particularly when playing soft or detached (especially staccato) notes, for these are most prone to chucking. Even the lightest, most fleeting touch must grasp the strings cleanly. A supple, fluid touch is necessary; there must be a sense of constant movement, from the attack through contact with the string, its release, and progress to the next note. The circular, streaming flow of movement described above regarding the harpsichord is even more important with the clavichord.

This supple touch is essential in all situations, and many textures can be played with a very light attack based only on fluid movement of the fingers. Particular fluidity is needed for passages that change hand position frequently or require an open hand (with consequently less support for the fingers). Passages consisting of several sustained parts may require maintenance of a high level of pressure on the keys. The player must develop all possible pliancy of touch so that such passages will not tire the hands or suffer tonally.

Playing at the ends of the keys with the fingers well curved increases one's control. Tomás de Sancta María (1565) likens this curved hand position to a cat's paw and recommends playing at the ends of the clavichord keys for greater leverage and a more powerful sound. He advises that the fingers be arched above the level of the hand and should not attack from much above the surface of the keys; that the palms remain in one place when the fingers move to attack; and that one maintain pressure on the keys to sustain the tone.[5] Since sustained pressure is often required on the clavichord, the strength that a curved position lends the fingers is even more important than on the harpsichord. The hand position described by Tomás has received exaggerated interpretation from some modern commentators, but the precise degree of curve to the fingers and angle to the wrist of course depend on the individual hand, particular musical figurations, and so forth. The point of Tomás's directions is maintenance of a compact hand and good leverage.

It will be evident from these considerations that the touch of the clavichord, although superficially quite light, often demands a certain weight in a way foreign even to heavy harpsichord actions. Such pressure as is needed in addition to the strength gained through a curved, compact hand position can be suppled from the weight of the hand itself, hanging into the fingers from a loose wrist, or from arm weight, guided through a relaxed wrist into the fingers. The wrist can be kept below the finger level, as Tomás suggests, but this is not suited to all hands. The wrist should be positioned so as to allow the fingers to move with the greatest freedom, and different figurations often require different positions. Weight, conducted through the wrist, can help the hand achieve both power and relaxation. It should never originate in a tense back or in tight shoulders and arms; and it should not go into the attack, which is left to the fingers, but into the sustaining of notes. Weight must always be carefully regulated so as never to force the strings and strain the pitch. Whether hand weight or arm weight is employed, a raised wrist sometimes helps to conduct it, and the fingertips thereby receive a sense of greater power in controlling the action. Again, the raised wrist position is only feasible in certain musical figurations.

The lightness and delicate response of the clavichord action together with the pressure it often requires can induce even experienced players to clench their hands and create unnecessary tension, or to play from a tight, crouching posture. This may happen when one is working on fine dynamic control or the sustaining of complicated textures. It is advisable to take frequent short rest periods when practicing if these tendencies develop. The player should be careful to sit with the shoulders well back and allow the fingers and hands to balance themselves on the keys. Perhaps more than any other keyboard player, the clavichordist must strive for maximum results from minimum effort.

As mentioned, the sustaining quality of the tone is closely connected with maintaining pressure on the keys after pressing them. The energy of the vibrating strings is imparted back to the key as readily as to the bridge and soundboard. A more massive key than is usual in clavichords would be less receptive to such vibrations, but the finger and hand, by offering firm support to the key, can effectively deaden its response. Experiment will readily confirm that on most instruments, a tone struck and sustained by a firm finger lasts appreciably longer than a tone of the same initial volume but sustained by minimal pressure.

Control of the softer levels can only be achieved by careful practice, beginning with the simplest of textures so that the fingers need not deal with too many elements at one time. There are few shortcuts to this kind of control, although some musical contexts allow adjustments. If sufficient time is available, lowering a key partway in advance of sounding its strings will cause the tangent to rise with less momentum; this device is very successful in repetition of soft notes and in opening a movement softly. (In a way, it is the clavichord's equivalent of the on-string attack at the harpsichord.) The player who could habitually play with fingers so close upon the keys as to raise the tangents partially, when necessary, before pressing them to the strings would possess superb dynamic control. Such a technique is so subtle as to be scarcely feasible in any but simple and moderately paced movements; it is an extreme end of the spectrum of attacks. In a loud or median attack, the tangent strikes the strings; in softer attacks it presses them; and in the realm of lowest tangent velocity, the fingers can be trained to a slow, pressing attack that abridges some of the distance that the tangent must travel.

In respect to both dynamic and tone control, it is useful to consider the advantages and disadvantages of each finger (see also chapter 3). Differences among fingers can be pronounced on the clavichord, and weaknesses will be mercilessly exposed. Careful work can minimize weaknesses and inequalities among the fingers, but their natural differences cannot be wholly eliminated, and a player can turn these to advantage. (This is the basis of much early fingering and was as well the foundation of Chopin's piano technique.)

For clavichord playing, the most important point to consider is how well each digit is supported by the hand, for those with the best support produce a clear, sustained tone most easily. The middle finger has an advantage in this regard; it is mounted at the center of the hand and, being the longest digit, it is curved the most in the basic hand position. Some hands possess greater natural uniformity in finger form, strength, and support than others, but the little finger will usually require some special attention. When extended from the hand it can readily lose support, to the great detriment of its tone control; its curve must be retained whenever possible. Therefore, the hand should maintain a closed position as often as is feasible, keeping the fingers laterally together. Whether the hand position must be extended or not, the middle finger's natural sense of central balance should be transferred to whatever fingers are momentarily in use. Often this can be accomplished with the slightest of wrist rotations. In a way scarcely noticeable to an observer, such rotation can move the hand's center of balance to the fingers in need of reinforcement. (For increased freedom of movement, this technique is equally useful on other keyboard instruments.) Awkward stretches and fingerings must be avoided; beginners' exercises should not require much, if any, opening of the hand from a convex positioning of all five fingers. (The advantages of early-style finger crossings become obvious from this perspective.) In music of normal complexity, changes of hand position must be fingered for maximum smoothness. When jumps and stretches are unavoidable, the leaping or extended finger should be placed in position before contact is actually made with the key.

Tomás de Sancta María comments on the need for a closed hand position, keeping fingers 2, 3, 4, and 5 together as much as possible, and 1 and 5 well flexed. "This position contributes greatly toward playing with smoothness and sweetness. . . . Good playing is not possible if the fingers, particularly the thumb and fifth, are scattered apart from each other, because the hands are then obstructed, and lack force and power, as if they were tied."[6]

Forkel, deriving his information from C. P. E. Bach and perhaps also from Quantz, describes the clavichord playing of J. S. Bach:

> Seb. Bach is said to have played with so easy and small a motion of the fingers that it was hardly perceptible. Only the first joints of the fingers were in motion; the hand retained even in the most difficult passages its rounded form; the fingers rose very little from the keys, hardly more than in a trill, and when one was employed, the other remained quietly in its position. Still less did the other parts of his body take any share in his playing, as happens many whose hand is not light enough.[7]

Forkel also describes the gliding motion of finger withdrawal in the same terms used by Quantz. This action is as applicable to the clavichord as to the harpsichord. The clavichord does not respond to, or require, such diversity of attack as was described for the harpsichord. Its considerable diversity of musical resource is achieved from the same basic touch, a fluid motion of fingers sometimes backed by weight and constantly making minute adjustments of position in accordance with the requirements of the musical texture and the topography of the keyboard (see also chapter 3, pp.49-50).

On some harpsichords, as mentioned, a slow release of the key may be of occasional use. On the clavichord, however, regardless of musical context or style of articulation, a rapid release of the key is essential to avoid the buzzing of the strings against the tangents. It is particularly important in the lower registers, where the strings are relatively slack, and for any keys whose strings are released one after another rather than simultaneously. Non-simultaneous release by the tangent can be caused by minute irregularities in the string levels, wrapping of the muting cloth, or surface of the tangent. These factors can create buzzing noises so that a slow, "soft" release of the key defeats its own purpose.

Some sustained notes, if not reiterated, can only be made to last by sounding them at a dynamic level somewhat above that which they would otherwise receive. This means can be effective in producing a sustained texture and is often worth the occasionally excessive accent of the strong initial attack. Careful timing of the accented note can obviate some of the dynamic stress, but the effect must be used sparingly and always differently if it is employed several times in the same piece. Otherwise, it easily stands out as a mannerism and detracts from the musical expression (as can be true of many a performing device). In the bass register, a dying note can often be partically renewed by slackening pressure on the key (not releasing the strings) and then restoring it. Apparently the abrupt change in tension disturbs the pattern of string vibrations and jars the strings into new life. This technique is only marginally related to vibrato and portato (discussed below).

A sustained, warmly glowing tone is in some ways more difficult to achieve on the clavichord than on the harpsichord because of the clavichord's percussive action and overall restricted resonance. Its achievement depends on careful balancing of dynamic levels and tonal control. The problems already cited in controlling the action can lead the player to concentrate only on the moving lines of the musical fabric, but sustained notes must receive their due in dynamic emphasis and sustained pressure. Even advanced players may find it advisable to practice simple, conjunct patterns, first without sustained notes and then with various notes held through the others, to develop control of notes sustained against moving parts. Players new to the clavichord, even if advanced on other keyboards, should begin by developing a supple touch through two-part music with conjunct lines before working with textures that place more than one line in each hand.

In comparison to other dynamically sensitive keyboard instruments, the clavichord creates dynamic variation only by slight modifications of the pressure on the keys. For this reason and because of the frequent difficulty of controlling the softer levels, it is easy to fall into the error of playing the clavichord too loudly, i.e., playing with little dynamic inflection and near the peak of its volume. Two approaches are possible. As with any instrument, the dynamics should usually be centered in the middle of the instrument's capabilities. Much *galant* and classical repertory requires all extremes of volume, which are best proportioned to the instrument's natural median range. (On the clavichord, as on the piano, it is possible to suggest very low dynamics for a whole phrase when actually rendering only certain crucial notes at an extreme of softness that might not be successfully controlled for the entire passage. The most remote levels of the clavichord's softer range can lend magical perspectives to a phrase, even if only a few notes are so rendered.) On the other hand, some works require only a narrow dynamic range, and they can often be played from a *forte* level.

The instrument's limited power allows a relatively higher sustained volume than would be successful on the piano. If a piece's overall dynamic range is limited, one can play more loudly than if it is wide. Either way, small-scale dynamic inflections are still available for phrasing; only the large-scale dynamics have a different point of departure. Tomás speaks of cultivating a full, vigorous sound, and a style of limited dynamic contrast is often suitable for much sixteenth- and seventeenth-century repertory. For other styles, notably *galant* and and classical music, one must utilize all levels of volume and reserve the loudest for musical emphases. Whatever the point of departure for dynamics, whether centered in the instrument's range or in its higher reaches, subsidiary parts (accompanying chords, etc.) should never be played with unwarranted strength for the sake of the overall dynamics. A proper balance among parts according to musical requirements will produce an effect of greater volume than will distorted levels that are in fact louder. Proportion is all-important.

VIBRATO AND PORTATO

The clavichord uses two forms of pitch modification, which have often been described in early and modern accounts of the instrument. *Vibrato* (*Bebung*, literally "trembling"), the more frequently used of the two, is also the more versatile. It can be rendered in degrees from the slightest coloring of sound to long, wailing tones. Variations in speed and degree of pitch modification are of course up to the player, as is discretion to avoid its overuse. *Portato* (*Tragen der Töne*) takes the form of a single, sharp inflection of the pitch after the note has been sounded. (Charles Burney's famous reference to the "cry of sorrow and complaint" that C. P. E. Bach drew forth so expressively from his clavichord may well be as much to this effect as to *Bebung*.[8]) It should be noted that the clavichord really admits of only a half vibrato, as one cannot go below, only above, the usual pitch of the note. Both vibrato and portato are effected by vertical, not lateral, motion of the key; the player produces the movement from the base of the finger. Eighteenth-century clavichords are often more susceptible to *Bebung* than earlier styles of instrument, but each individual clavichord has its own capabilities.

Bebung is most readily achieved with the three central digits. The thumb, with its more laterally based movement, and the little finger, which has weaker support, are usually less fluent in this motion. Practice can to some extent overcome these disadvantages, which will naturally vary from player to player. Vibrato can be most easily achieved on an extended thumb or fifth finger by vibrating the entire wrist.

Vibrato is sometimes difficult to produce when the notes involved are of short duration or a change of hand position must immediately follow the vibrato. In the latter case, when possible, the passage should be divided between the hands, thus allowing the vibrato to persist until the sounding of the next note.

Bebung and *Tragen der Töne* were indicated with some frequency in the latter part of the eighteenth century (see chapter 6). They were notated as ornaments by sign and require a noticeable vibrato. These instances do not limit use of the effect, however. More frequent and flexible use of vibrato involves coloration of the overall tone quality: scarcely noticeable variations of pitch on notes and whole chords, which enhance the sheen of the sound or absorb the impact of a *fortissimo* attack without drawing attention to themselves. (More extreme use of vibrato on chords is also possible.) Experiment will constantly suggest new uses for vibrato.

FRETTED CLAVICHORDS

Fretted clavichords are discussed in chapter 1 (pp.11-13). Since many consecutively played notes will be fretted together on triply and quadruply fretted instruments, the player must be careful to avoid the unpleasant metallic noise produced when one of two fretted keys is depressed before the release of its mate or when two are struck simultaneously. Tomás de Sancta María's description of a clean touch (see chapter 4, p.69) is surely connected with the problem of negotiating fretted notes, but to claim a uniform nonlegato as the necessary meaning of his account is a rather crude interpretation. Overlapping legato is out of the question, but a clean link between fretted notes is fully accessible, and it is even possible to trill with a fretted pair. Some instruments are more amenable than others to smooth connections between fretted notes: the string tension and immediacy of tonal response have much to do with variations among instruments in this respect. Indeed, on some specimens a clean, rapid change between fretted notes produces an extra luster in the sound that more than glosses over the lack of an actual legato. The care necessary for clean traversal of fretted notes is simply another facet of the art of playing the instrument.

As C. P. E. Bach recommended, it is to every player's technical and musical advantage to study both the harpsichord and the clavichord. The clavichord develops touch sensitivity and finger control in a way taught by no other keyboard instrument and increases the player's delicacy of touch and nuance on the harpsichord. The clavichord's dynamic sensitivity also increases the player's awareness of the effects implied on the harpsichord. The different means by which the two instruments create nuance stimulate the player's musical imagination and bring out different aspects of any style or individual composition.

3

Fingering

Correct employment of the fingers is inseparably
related to the whole art of performance.

—C. P. E. BACH

THE IMPORTANCE OF GOOD FINGERING
is stressed by all early authorities on keyboard technique. The subject encompasses general consistency of finger patterns with standard musical figurations as well as particular subtleties of musical expression. At the beginner's level, good and consistent fingering is necessary for well-ordered and economical motion and reliable assimilation of basic figurations. At the level of fine artistry, much finesse of rhythm, articulation, and legato depends on balancing subtle interrelationships among the fingers. One may work out fingerings for comfort and facility, for musical effect, or, ideally, for both. These perspectives interrelate more than they remain independent.

Early and modern fingerings often differ in their approaches to the relative strengths and weaknesses of the various digits. Early fingerings accept these differences and try to use each finger to its best advantage. However, starting in the mid-eighteenth century and with strong emphasis during the nineteenth, modern keyboard playing often seeks to minimize the differences among the fingers. While it is of obvious advantage to develop each finger as far as possible, the natural capacities of different digits should be taken into account. Independence of fingers is distinct in some ways from finger strength. The capabilities of different digits and the relationship of fingering to musical expression are difficult to describe in general terms without appearing to make wholesale attributions of physical advantage or articulatory and rhythmic effects, but it is hoped that some aspects of these delicate relationships are made clear in the course of this chapter.

✿ Basic Principles

Economy of motion is a basic goal of good fingering, whether the player uses an early or a modern technique or some aspects of both. Fingering designed to assist particular musical emphases will sometimes depart from the most economical motion, but the starting point should be smooth movement of the fingers and smooth changes of hand position. Jerky changes from one finger or position to another should be avoided unless they are deliberately employed for a particular articulation or timing.

A fundamental rule for economical and relaxed finger motion is to press the key with the finger nearest it, but this principle is subject to many exceptions in view of both musical and technical requirements. A more complex fingering than the simplest one that lies under the hand may better utilize certain finger strengths or better relate the hand and fingers to the topography of the keyboard. Also, choices of fingering and changes in hand position are largely reciprocal in their requirements. Certainly, musical textures often necessitate expansion or contraction of the hand, but careful fingering can help to preserve a closed hand as much as possible. This technique helps the fingers to retain their curve and the hand to concentrate its power. While a loose, open hand is often useful on the harpsichord and is necessary for many widely spaced figurations, some players may find it advantageous to cultivate the closer formations of the hand whenever possible. This approach is important to clavichord technique (see p.30 above). When working with a more or less closed hand, the fingering should be gauged to preserve it and to make smooth transitions from one area of the keyboard to another. Finger crossing is often useful in this regard. At times, a relatively awkward shift may assist an articulation or other stress.

Hand position may be changed gradually or suddenly. In either case the musical effect may be smooth or articulated, depending on the context and the player's intentions. The literature does not often require long stretches of legato, and it is often musically effective and most comfortable technically to change position by phrase or subphrase. (This can also help one to retain a closed hand position.) Smooth shifts can often be made by adjustments of fingering (see Example III-24 and the discussion on p.48 below) or at articulations between phrases. More sudden shifts can produce minor or major articulations. (The shift to the thumb on the Bb in the right hand in Example III-1 and the fingering shown in Example III-2 are illustrative. More pronounced articulations are suggested by the beaming of notes in Example III-3, which suggests a plunge of the left hand to the 8–5 diad on C.) Some shifts are made suddenly but are smooth in effect because of a detached style (see the suggested fingering and articulations marked in Example III-4).

Depending on musical context, adjustments of fingering and hand position are more meaningful for some hands than for others. For a player with a heavy, powerful hand and fingers of fairly equal length, different fingerings may produce less variation in effect than for a person with a lean hand

EXAMPLE III-1.
J. S. Bach, *Italian Concerto,* Presto, mm.151-53.

EXAMPLE III-2.
Scarlatti, Sonata in a, K. 175, mm.1-4.

EXAMPLE III-3.
Girolamo Frescobaldi, Toccata 10, Book 1, mm.2-3.

EXAMPLE III-4.
J. S. Bach, Partita in D, Ouverture, m.66.

and fingers of markedly varied lengths. The former type of hand gives better, more uniform support to the fingers.

The topography of the keyboard is an important consideration. The contours of some hands make them especially sensitive to the advantages and disadvantages of leverage provided by the different levels of the naturals and accidentals. For any hand, however, the relationship of the accidentals to the naturals should be used to advantage in fingering. Because of varying patterns of accidentals and naturals, sequences should not always receive the same fingering on successive pattern statements. The feel of accidentals involved in different statements can vary considerably. In very long sequences or long patterns of any sort, changes of fingering are advisable anyway, to avoid pattern blindness.

Early authorities usually prohibit placement of the first or fifth finger on accidentals except when it is unavoidable, but exceptions often occur in original fingerings contained in actual music. The intent of the rule is to avoid displacement of the hand from its usual positions; it was obviously not ironclad, in the past any more than now.

🌺 Basic Figurations

The scale fingerings normally taught in modern piano and organ technique are based on passing the thumb under the other fingers and passing the other fingers over the thumb. (This distinction is noteworthy, but the general procedure will be referred to as "thumb under technique" throughout this book.) The technique was known in earlier times (sixteenth-century Spain, for instance), but early scale fingerings show some variety, usually involving pairwise crossing of fingers, as in 3 over 2 descending or 3 over 4 ascending in the right hand. This maneuver often strikes modern players as clumsy and unnecessarily complicated but it has many advantages. Finger crossings apply to conjunct lines in general as well as to lengthy scales *per se* and allow a wide latitude in changes of hand position and variations of emphasis, articulation, and, on the clavichord particularly, handweight. The early fingering patterns, like modern ones, often require adjustment according to the particular musical detail and the requirements of individual hands. It is helpful to be fluent in both finger crossing and thumb passing.

Glissando rendition of scales is sometimes indicated by a slur or verbal directions. *Glissandi* can assist both the brilliance and timing of scales such as those in Example III-5. The accurate and facile execution of scales in parallel and especially contrary motion is greatly helped by using finger crossings or thumb transfers in both hands at the same time, as shown in Example III-6.

The beaming of runs and flourishes in original scores often shows that they were to be divided between the hands. This division allows fuller control both rhythmically and in regard to facility and brilliance. The changeovers from one hand to another usually occur on offbeats (see Example III-7). In divided scales, the simplest changeover and the one least likely to disturb the line is for 2 or 4 to begin in one hand where the other left off.

Arpeggios are another basic aspect of keyboard technique. They appear frequently in eighteenth-century repertory, but less often in earlier styles. Just as scales form, in part, an abstract of many conjunct passages for practice purposes, so arpeggios are useful practice material for disjunct figura-

EXAMPLE III-5.
J. S. Bach, Concerto in C for two harpsichords,
Allegro, mm.122-23.

EXAMPLE III-6.
J. S. Bach, Partita in G, Praeambulum, mm.63-64.

EXAMPLE III-7.
J. S. Bach, Fantasia in a, m.105.

EXAMPLE III-8.
Arpeggio fingerings.

tions. The fingering of standard arpeggio patterns does not present as much
variation as do scale figures; Example III-8 shows some typical fingerings
and alternatives. However, in the diversity of real musical contexts, the fingering of disjunct motions offers many variations of articulatory stress

EXAMPLE III-9.
Possible fingerings for a disjunct passage.

EXAMPLE III-10.
D. Scarlatti: a. Sonata in g, K. 190, mm.33-34.
b. Sonata in A, K. 181, mm.36-38.

EXAMPLE III-11.
F. Couperin, Prelude in C, mm.1-4.

through choice of fingering. Example III-9 is one illustration of an infinitely varied practice.

Parallel chords are often best played with consecutive fingers (Example III-10a) or the same fingers (Example III-10b).

Use of the same finger to play successive long, sustained tones is found in sources from Tomás de Sancta María to J. S. Bach and later. The rhythmic placement of held tones and general ease in playing is usually more important than the "connection" of already dying sonorities, and the involved fingering often necessary for such connections is not usually worth the extra effort involved. However, context must always be the deciding factor. François Couperin shows fingerings for the legato binding of long notes (see Example III-11).

Repeated notes are usually best played with a change of finger toward the thumb, i.e., 3–2–1 rather than 1–2–3. This rule applies both to long passages of repeated notes, such as abound in Scarlatti's sonatas (sometimes bearing the direction *mutandi i detti*, "changing the fingers"), and to single reiterations, as in dotted rhythms. Finger change for repetitions appears at least as early as the virginalist repertory and is advocated by C. P. E. Bach for the greater smoothness it affords. On the harpsichord, repetition by the same finger is occasionally useful, but it often imparts a clumsy accent and it can leave gaps in an otherwise smooth line. For a smooth negotiation of Example III-12, finger change is almost indispensable. On the clavichord, however, certain repeated notes can be managed more smoothly with a single finger, especially in soft passages. In such a case, the key need not be raised fully between repetitions, and the consequent closer proximity of the tangent to the strings allows finer dynamic control.

EXAMPLE III-12.
J. S. Bach, English Suite in F, Prelude, mm.2-4.

Virtuosic strings of repeated notes can be fingered with various combinations, such as 3-2-1-3-2-1, 3-1-3-1-3-1, 2-1-2-1-2-1, 4-3-2-1-4-3-2-1, etc. Rhythmic groupings and leaps between repeated groups will determine some choices. For instance, ♪♪♪♪♪♪ may be heard in pairs or as one unit of six notes more readily than ♪♪♪♪♪♪, which may be heard as two units of three notes. Samuel Scheidt (1624) shows 3-2-3-2 (right hand) and 2-1-2-1 (left hand) for repeated notes. Repeated notes and patterns often benefit from a closed pattern, as shown in Example III-13.

Rapidly repeated chords will generally use the same fingers. In a passage such as Example III-14, careful use of the rebound of a loose wrist is

EXAMPLE III-13.
D. Scarlatti, Sonata in G, K. 455, mm.18-22.

EXAMPLE III-14.
D. Scarlatti, Sonata in G, K. 324, mm.43-45.

important. From a level close to the keys, the wrist can reiterate the chords in rhythmic groups. The player may find it comfortable to extend the fingers slightly.

Often one must hold a key down while the hand shifts position and substitute one finger for another. A different fingering should be sought if substitution in a particular passage is clumsy or difficult. The technique can cause needless complication and should not be used to excess.

Substitutions may use consecutive or nonconsecutive fingers. They should be made lightly and smoothly, and never so as to affect the rhythm. Some modern approaches substitute on rhythmic subdivisions of the sustained note, as in ♪♪, but this technique can lead to heaviness of touch or rhythm. Substitutions should be made fluently and freely, performed as unselfconsciously as the negotiation of standard figurations. This technique does not appear until the eighteenth century, when it is mentioned by F. Couperin, Jacques Duphly, and J. P. Kirnberger, among others. It was quite possibly used in previous periods, but no evidence has survived.

Parallel thirds, sixths, and octaves usually occur for the sake of brilliance. At least through the seventeenth century, parallel intervals were often played with the same pair of fingers, lending a sparkling quality to passages like those in Example III-15. A relaxed wrist, perhaps held low, is necessary for this kind of execution. Properly prepared, such passages can be played in large impulses of perhaps up to six notes.

François Couperin disliked what he called the "old" manner of playing parallel thirds, as it allowed no legato. His examples of the "old" and "new" styles of fingering appear in Example III-16. Certainly many passages with parallel thirds and sixths require as much finesse in articulation as do single lines, and various patterns of fingering should be cultivated.

EXAMPLE III-15.
a. J. P. Sweelinck (?), *Balletto del granduca*, Var. 5, mm.1-4.
b. D. Scarlatti, Sonata in C, K. 548, mm. 83-86.

EXAMPLE III-16.
F. Couperin, "old" and "new" styles of fingering
parallel intervals.

Octave passages are rare in the harpsichord literature and are poorly suited to the clavichord. Large hands can slur octaves in pairs or even larger groups. When playing parallel octaves, the thumb must be kept fluid and mobile and it should glide as much as possible from one key to the next, if a smooth rendition is sought. In some cases, especially from accidental to natural, the entire hand can slide or at least approximate actual legato. Even when playing detached octaves, stiffness should be avoided, particularly in the wrist.

The technical difficulty of executing ornaments is often more illusory than actual. Understanding an ornament as an integral part of the line, especially comprehending its rhythmic role, facilitates its absorption into both the musical flow and the player's fingers. Ornaments vary as much in their speed and rhythmic realization as any other facet of music and should never be treated as though they are external to the music. (Musical and technical aspects of ornaments are considered in chapter 6 and Appendix 1.)

The fingering of ornaments sometimes varies with the rendition intended: a rapid, snapped trill or mordent often receives a different fingering than a slow, languishing one. Early treatises or fingered sources generally show right hand 3–2 and 4–3 and left hand 1–2 and 2–3 for trilling, but it is best to have as many combinations as possible at one's command. Right hand 2–1, 3–2, 4–3, 5–4, and 5–3 and left hand 1–2, 2–3, and 3–4 are all useful in various situations. Changing finger pairs in the course of a trill is often useful, depending on the context and musical intent. There are several types of generally applicable finger change:

1. As in standard piano technique, long sustained trills will often be more even and less fatiguing when fingered with the alternation of one digit, such as 3–2–3–1–3–2–3–1.

2. Short, aggressive, even trills can be produced by alternation of finger pairs: right hand 2–1–3–2, 3–2–4–3; left hand 2–3–1–2. This scheme is of limited application, as it is not flexible in its rhythmic impetus. It can be very effective in a suitable context and is mechanically reliable, once mastered. The same kind of snap can be produced in a turn or in the turned termination of a trill, as in right hand 4–3–2–1.

3. When playing a trill against another part in the same hand, a change of finger can improve clarity and ease the difficulty (see Example III-17).

EXAMPLE III-17.
J. S. Bach, Fugue in b, *WTC* II, mm.18-21.

4. Double trills, so admired by François Couperin, are sometimes facilitated by alternating inner and outer pairs of fingers, as in Example III-18a. For many players this motion is more easily controlled than parallel motions among the fingers. For some hands, reversal of digits in single trills can be efficacious when the different levels of naturals and accidentals are otherwise a hindrance (Example III-18b).

EXAMPLE III-18.
a. Fingering of double trills. b. J. S. Bach, *Goldberg Variations,* Var. 28, mm.15-16.

5. The player should be able to negotiate mordents of all varieties: fast and slow, even and uneven. Fast mordents particularly can benefit from finger change: right hand ♫, left hand ♫ , for example.
6. Finger change on repeated notes in executing ornaments is important for a graceful performance, ornaments usually being heavily legato. François Couperin discusses this point in regard to fingering the *port de voix* (see Example III-19).

EXAMPLE III-19.
F. Couperin, fingering for the *port de voix.*

Fingering can sometimes assist rhythmic control. Just as the changes from 2–3–4 to 1–2–3 in Example III-7 aid clarity, often a certain smoothness can be gained by changes of finger while the hand remains in a constant position. The perfect evenness (if evenness is desired) of so simple a passage as the left hand in Example III-20 can be assisted by the fingering shown.

EXAMPLE III-20.
J. S. Bach, Fugue in C♯, *WTC* II, m.22.

Division of lines between the hands has been described above in regard to scale passages. The same principle can be applied to many types of passage, whether for smoothness or for subtle emphases. Dividing a passage even when it lies under one hand often affords greater rhythmic control and is especially useful when first stating a fugue subject with a strong rhythmic profile, as in Example III-21. (The opening of a fugue, with no counterpoint or rhythmic interplay, is often the most resistant to a convincingly rhythmic rendition. Obviously, one must be able to manage without subdivisions in the course of a piece, but easy control at the beginning can help to initiate rhythmic impetus.) Division of this sort is also helpful in some contexts for producing vibrato on the clavichord, as mentioned in chapter 2.

EXAMPLE III-21.
J. S. Bach, Fugue in D, *WTC* I, mm.1-2.

Redistribution of notes between the hands can also facilitate rapid playing. Scarlatti's Sonata in G, K. 348, for instance, is marked *prestissimo* and is clearly intended as a brilliant stream of tone. It can be negotiated by playing the notes of each hand as they are divided between the staves on the page, but divisions such as those shown in Example III-22a allow a less tiring, more easily fluent performance. Stronger articulations result if the hands play the notes as divided by the staves. Whether such articulations are the intent of this and similar cases is open to question. Composers rarely indicated fingering and hand position and perhaps often preserved linear

EXAMPLE III-22.
D. Scarlatti, Sonata in G, K. 348. a. mm.6-10.
b. mm.30-32.

continuity in the notation regardless of technical considerations. In the case of the first excerpt from K. 348, analogous sixteenth-note passages can be played with complete smoothness by one hand (Example III-22b), and similar smoothness might be desirable in Example III-22a and similar passages. The meaning of the notation in this and like instances must be decided by the player, who should be cognizant of the effect of redistribution of notes on articulation and whether articulations created by the way a figuration lies under the hand are intentional or accidental (i.e., a technical difficulty to be overcome).

Clavichord Fingering

The preceding discussion applies equally to the harpsichord and the clavichord, but clavichord fingering requires some special consideration. On the clavichord, any lack of control is immediately apparent in distorted tone quality, dynamics, or pitch level; fingering must be chosen carefully to provide security and solidarity. Again, the natural inequality of the fingers, if not minimized, must be turned to the player's best advantage.

Clavichord fingering should avoid awkward shifts and allow the fingers to stay in unconstrained, close proximity to the keys. A closed hand position should be maintained as much as the musical textures allow. If the hand is spread out, the fingers that are least supported by the body of the hand, particularly the little finger, will have difficulty controlling the tone and the dynamics. (See chapter 2.) A closed position is generally useful on the harpsichord, but its prevalence is far more important on the clavichord. Fingering should be devised with that in mind; for instance, the way a middle voice is divided between the hands can often be helpful in retaining the closed position.

A good point of departure for clavichord fingering is illustrated by the fingering that has survived with J. S. Bach's Praeludium and Fughetta in C, the original version of the first prelude and fugue from Book 2 of the *Well-Tempered Clavier*. The fingering is in a copy of the piece made by Johann Caspar Vogler, a pupil of Bach's at Weimar, but perhaps reflects Bach's own technique.[1] In any case, the fingering is of interest, being especially suggestive of the requirements of clavichord technique. It stresses a closed hand position and often centers the hand over whatever fingers are employed. Changes of position are achieved as much by multifarious forms of finger crossing as by pivots on the thumb.

For maximum flexibility in changing position and to preserve a closed hand, every finger, as much as possible, should be able to cross its neighbor or slide beneath it. The thumb, of course, is the foundation for pivoting in modern keyboard technique, although its use in this capacity is part of earlier techniques as well. Until the middle of the eighteenth century the thumb was, at most, on a par with the other digits used in crossing. Some of the many types of finger crossings found in the Praeludium and Fughetta are shown in Examples III-23 and III-24. They include right hand ascending 1–1, 2–3–4–3, 4–2; descending 5–4–5, 1–1, 5[–4–3]–5, 5–5–3–5, 1–3, 4–5; left hand ascending 2–1–2–1, 4–5; descending 1–2–1, 1–2–3–4–2. For many of these sequences, smooth execution can be considerably assisted by using the technique of finger withdrawal as described by Quantz (see p.22 above). Note the frequent movement of the thumb and fifth finger from one note to its neighbor; the second note is usually on an accented beat. These motions suggest structural legato (see chapter 4) or small articulations.

EXAMPLE III-23.
J. S. Bach, Praeludium in C. a. m.4. b. mm.9-12.
c. mm.15-16.

EXAMPLE III-24.
J. S. Bach, Fughetta in C. a. m.10. b. m.24. c. m.18.

The thumb is by nature so strong and, in some positions, so lacking in lightness, that its use as a pivot can induce unwanted accents, especially on the clavichord's light and dynamically sensitive action. Hence, whereas modern usage might finger the passage in Example III-24c as indicated in brackets, the original fingering changes position gradually rather than all at once, allowing greater fluency. This is not to say that a smooth rendition is impossible with modern fingering, but that the original makes virtually automatic what the other accomplishes only with effort.

The left-hand fingerings for the second beat of m.8 and the fourth beat of m.13 in the Praeludium (Example III-25) are calculated to balance the hand for maximum control. In both cases the fingering is based on the third finger (the central one and the best supported) and the thumb (the strongest), which play the most important roles. The descent to G♯ in m.8 places 3 on the arrival point, and the preceding sixteenth notes are fingered so that the hand is compacted. As far as the musical lines allow, the hand is kept closed in m.13 as well. The fingering given for these passage allows a full, sonorous tone without effort. These fingerings, like others in the Praeludium and Fughetta, may look peculiar to a modern player, but their basic principles may be adapted to individual preferences. Flexibility is the essential feature, allowing the closed hand to focus its position directly above each motion on the keys.

A single finger may often be transferred smoothly from one key to another, creating an essentially unbroken effect. This technique is very useful on the clavichord, but sliding a finger from an accidental to a natural is not

EXAMPLE III-25.
J. S. Bach, Praeludium in C. a. m.8. b. mm.13-14.

descending right-hand scale figures; Buchner uses 3 crossing over 2 for ascending left-hand scales, while Ammerbach shows 4–3–2–1 sequences and occasionally 4–3–4 ascending left-hand figures. An organ piece given full fingering by Buchner shows consistent patterns; the fingering keeps the hand well centered over the notes it is playing.

An important Italian figure was Girolamo Diruta, a pupil of Claudio Merulo and author of *Il Transilvano* (1593/1607), a treatise on keyboard playing. Diruta regards 2 and 4 as "good" fingers falling on metrically accented notes. However, the finger crossings he advocates are quite different from those of Buchner and Ammerbach. In right-hand conjunct passages, 3 crosses over 4 ascending and over 2 descending; in the left hand, 3 crosses over 2 ascending, 2 over 3 descending. Diruta remarks disapprovingly that some players use, in the left hand, 3 over 4 descending and 2 over 1 ascending.

Other Italian authors (Adriano Banchieri in 1609, and later Lorenzo Penna and Bismantova) seem to have favored 1, 3, and 5 as the "good" fingers (3 being the most important). In this system, 3 still crosses over 2 and 4, but the beat/finger correlation is reversed: 3 falls on accented notes. Penna is more specific than Banchieri and Bismantova; he describes scales with 3 crossing over 2 (right hand descending, left hand ascending) and 3 crossing over 4 (right hand ascending, left hand descending).

The English left no theoretical accounts of fingering until the end of the seventeenth century, but Penna's system is the basis of much original fingering in the sources of virginal music and is the same as that espoused in the preface to Henry Purcell's *Choice Collection of Lessons* (1696). English sources often show 2 crossing over 1 instead of 3 over 2 in ascending left-hand scales; this was also an Italian practice, as Diruta mentions. The basis of the English/sometime Italian approach is seen in Example III-28, from an oft-quoted prelude by John Bull. It is apparently a teaching piece and therefore has its fingering indicated in full.[3]

The Prencourt manuscript, *Short, Easy and Plaine Rules* (ca. 1700) is unusual among English sources in advocating 2 and 4 on accented notes in the right hand (with the usual finger crossings) and left-hand patterns of 1–2–3–4–3–4 descending and 4–3–2–1–2–1 ascending.

EXAMPLE III-28.
John Bull, Praeludium, mm.1–6.

The premises of any fingering system are subject to considerable revision when applied to actual music. On-beat patterns, for instance, often begin with 2 in the right hand in virginal repertory. Sometimes, as also in late seventeenth-century German sources, the same finger is used on two notes in succession, especially if the first is relatively long; such choices and other variations are sometimes necessary for a comfortable fingering sequence over accidentals. Scalar passages in many sources throughout Europe rely heavily on 3 in the right hand and 2 or 3 in the left as "good" fingers, crossing them over adjacent fingers in upward or downward scales.

Spanish commentaries on keyboard fingering (ranging from 1555 to the early eighteenth century) show a variety of scalar fingerings, each used in different musical contexts. (Linear patterns are often the main topic in treatises on fingering.) The approach seems to be less highly systematized than in the many beginner's pieces in other sources and more in touch with the variety of actual musical situations. Thumb-under technique appears in right-hand descending scales such as 5–4–3–2–1–3–2–1 (Sancta María) and 4–3–2–1–3–2–1 (Correa de Arauxo, 1626) and in left-hand ascending scales such as 4–3–2–1–3–2–1 (Luis Venegas de Henestrosa, 1557). (Correa de Arauxo even recommends groups of 5–4–3–2–1 for fast scales.) Finger crossing as in virginal repertory is also prominent, but allocation of strong fingers to strong beats does not appear to be a feature of Spanish fingering of any period.[4] The correlation between strong fingers and strong beats seems to have died out generally during the seventeenth century, although vestiges of it survive in playing manuals. Fingering in actual music does not appear to be as systematic as treatises suggested it was around 1600.

The first book to discuss seventeenth-century German keyboard fingering was Daniel Speer's *Grundrichtiger, kurtz, leicht, und nöthiger Unterricht der musicalischen Kunst* (1687; expanded 1697). This author's brief account recommends the standard finger crossings of Penna, but with no clear correlation between fingers and accented notes. Contemporary with Speer's volume is Johann Speth's *Vermehrter Wegweiser* (1693), the second edition of an organ method first published in 1689 and kept in print until 1753.[5] The fingerings show crossings of 3 over 2 and 4 in the right hand, and 3 over 2 and 2 over 1 in the left. The text correlates 2 and 4 in the right hand and 2, 3, and 4 in the left with accented notes, but this relationship varies in the book's fingered passages using actual music, many of which show 3 on accented notes in the right hand and 2 and 3 on accented notes in the left. Example III-29 shows an excerpt in which the principal fingers seem to be 3 in the right hand and 2 in the left. The few fingerings found in the music of Heinrich Scheidemann and Samuel Scheidt, from earlier in the century, also show this approach.[6] In the example, note the separation of melodic groups by consecutive use of one digit so that each unit of the sequence receives the

EXAMPLE III-29.
Fingerings from the 1693 *Wegweiser*.

same fingering. This technique often occurs in other fingerings of English and Continental music.

Another German treatise of some importance is Johann Baptist Samber's *Manuductio ad Organum* (1704). This author's examples of scales and various passages strongly favor 2 and 4 on accented notes with various crossings of 3 over 2 and 4, and 2 over 1. Samber is notable for advising against playing long held notes with the same finger in succession (allowed by many sixteenth- and seventeenth-century authorities), although he often fingers faster values that way in order to permit a comfortable pattern of crossing.

Almost nothing is known of keyboard fingering in France in the early seventeenth century, although specimens from later in the century appear in the organ music of Guillaume Nivers (1665) and André Raison (1688). Raison's pieces are very sparsely fingered, to the extent that no system of patterns can be deduced with certainty. The fifth finger is marked with comparative frequency, as a way of showing the position of the hand. Repeated notes receive different fingers. Descending conjunct right-hand lines begin with either 4 or 5, suggesting (in common with earlier and later examples) that a note's rhythmic position does not necessarily dictate the choice of finger in the sense of "good" or "bad." Nivers apparently did not adhere to this principle either, as shown by the fingerings in Example III-30.

Saint Lambert (1702) commented that nothing was freer in harpsichord playing than fingering. He showed certain basic fingerings for chords and intervals, but for single lines the only examples he gave are those in Example

EXAMPLE III-30.
G. Nivers, fingered passages.

III-31. The rest, he says, is up to taste and convenience. In an appended comment at the end of his treatise, Saint Lambert adds that for "very fast" scales, as in diminutions, the fingering of 2 crossing over 1 (right hand descending, left hand ascending) is useful because "it is easier to withdraw the thumb from beneath the second [finger] than to withdraw the second from under the third, when one descends with the right hand by these last two."[7] Saint Lambert applies the same principal to the left hand.

EXAMPLE III-31.
Saint Lambert, fingered passages.

The numerous fingerings that François Couperin provided for his own works in his *L'Art de toucher le clavecin* (1717) should be studied by everyone who plays his music. The extracts quoted in Example III-32 show that, in common with his predecessors, he employed scalar finger crossings but with no consistency regarding beat stress. As mentioned earlier, Couperin was the first to indicate finger substitution.

EXAMPLE III-32.
F. Couperin, excerpts from *L'Art de toucher le clavecin*,
including "La Milordine," *Ordre* 1, mm.14-16.

Scale fingering receives the most attention in early accounts, if only because the diversity of musical texture defies the general rules that can be formulated in the limited space allotted to the subject in most treatises. The fingerings fundamental to basic intervals are often presented, although the degree to which they were followed in practice is questionable. Diruta, for instance, assigns 2 and 4 to thirds, 2 and 5 to fourths, 1 and 4 to fifths, and 1 and 5 to octaves. Saint Lambert gives more detailed advice, showing fingerings for both chords and intervals, with alternatives for small hands and for intervals with accidentals, avoiding the thumb for the latter. His right-hand fingerings appear in Example III-33.

EXAMPLE III-33.
Saint Lambert, fingering for chords and intervals in
the right hand.

Saint Lambert's treatise concludes with two dances in which the fingering is indicated thoroughly. The fingerings shown for various intervals in the left hand are not consistent with the basic interval fingerings given earlier, but depend, as one would expect, on the musical context.

Parallel intervals, as mentioned above, were often played with the same pair of fingers. Repeated notes frequently show changing fingers in all countries and periods.

If the fingering of J. S. Bach's Praeludium and Fughetta discussed above is representative of his own manner of fingering, it appears likely that Bach took equal advantage of thumb pivots and finger crossings with nearly all conceivable combinations of fingers. The only fingerings extant from the composer's own hand are a brief exercise and the Little Prelude in g. The famous *Applicatio* for W. F. Bach shows old-style finger crossings (see Example III-34a). The prelude is generally fingered according to the way its broken chords would lie under the hand if played together as units, an approach sometimes termed "harmonic fingering" (see Example III-34b). In several places, nonadjacent fingers play conjunct notes, perhaps to ease the hand into a change of position (Example III-34c). As in the Praeludium and Fughetta, the widest intervals are often played by 1 and 5, but the piece shows very few instances of one finger playing consecutive notes. In Example III-34b, mm.5-6, the right hand fingering is 5–2–1, whereas Vogler's style of fingering for the Praeludium would probably use 5–1–1. Note that 5 and 1 are used freely on accidentals.

Schools of fingering were in a state of transition through much of the eighteenth century, particularly around 1750. In some areas, finger crossing persisted, side by side with increased use of "modern" thumb-under technique, arising from the increasing use of keys with many accidentals. Michel Corrette's *Les amusemens du Parnasse* (1749) shows finger crossings in pairs

EXAMPLE III-34.
J. S. Bach: a. *Applicatio*, mm.1-4. b. Little Prelude in
g, mm.1-6. c. Ibid., mm.9-10.

(2 over 1 and 3 over 4 in both hands) for the C-major scale and fingerings
such as those in Example III-35 for more remote tonalities. Elsewhere, Corrette shows fingerings for *batteries* and repeated notes (Example III-36).

EXAMPLE III-35.
M. Corrette, fingering patterns.

EXAMPLE III-36.
M. Corrette, fingerings for *batteries* and repeated notes.

The standardization of today's usual approach first appears in the treatises of Hartong (1749), Marpurg (1750), C. P. E. Bach, and Kirnberger (1781), which present modern scale fingerings and advocate more or less equal use of all the fingers. Older styles, of course, did not die out all at once, and admixtures of finger crossing and thumb-under techniques were often cultivated. As Glyn Jenkins remarks,

> The paired fingerings that had prevailed almost universally in pre-1750 tutors posed a considerable problem to teachers of C. P. E. Bach's generation. The older method had become such an established part of keyboard performance that they were reluctant to discard it entirely. Daniel Gottlob Türk, writing in 1789 when the modern manner had almost entirely superseded the old, recalled that Friedemann Bach could play complex runs "roundly and with astonishing speed" merely by using his three middle fingers.[8]

Indeed, C. P. E. Bach commented on the frequent advantages of finger crossing in the keys with fewer accidentals:

> Crossing and turning, the principal means of changing the fingers, must be applied in such a manner that the tones involved in the change flow smoothly. In keys with few or no accidentals the crossing of the third finger over the fourth and the second over the thumb is in certain cases more practicable and better suited for the attainment of unbroken continuity than other crossings or the turn [of the thumb].[9]

The modern player must come to grips with early fingerings on several points: the essential differences between early and modern players, the differences among particular early systems, the musical effects of a given style of fingering, and the nature of any compromise in approach.

The players of earlier times were not called upon to render so many and such diverse musical styles as are today's performers. The range of musical and keyboard figurations encountered by any one player would have been far more limited and the player's response more automatic, technically and perhaps musically. Even the great figures—William Byrd, for instance— would hardly have had to deal with the divergent requirements of a sarabande by François Couperin and one of Domenico Scarlatti's sonatas that imitate guitar figurations. Also, some patterns of fingering that may seem clumsy or unnecessary to the modern player were the norm in an earlier time and school; much experience is needed to adopt some aspects of early fingering into one's automatic physical responses. (Beginners should perhaps be inculcated impartially with both finger crossing and thumb-under techniques.) The difficulty of thoroughly assimilating early fingerings is compounded if one attempts thoroughly to absorb opposing schools of fingering: following, say, Diruta's accentual use of 2 and 4 in early Italian music, and accentual 1, 3, and 5 in virginal repertory. Both systems cross 3 over 2 and 4, but the relation of fingers to stressed and unstressed notes is diametrically opposed. The approach that appears in virginal music (there are no extant keyboard treatises from Elizabethan or Jacobean England) is not as strict as Diruta's, and one wonders how much the latter's practice adhered to his theory. Perhaps it is significant that the Italians were divided in their preferences. As mentioned, most schools of playing did not follow any ironclad rules in the diversity of actual musical situations. Perhaps the main points to emulate in early fingering are use of varied finger crossings and diverse groupings of consecutive fingers to fit particular figurations, both for physical comfort and a feeling of correspondence between physical movements and musical phrasing. The Spanish school presents the most diverse and pragmatic range of examples.

❧ Fingering, Rhythm, and Articulation

The subject of early fingering has raised a great deal of interest in recent decades, sometimes with surprising results. Just as some players propound a level of detachment as the basis of touch in early periods, so too are there players and writers who deduce automatic rhythmic and articulatory effects from early fingerings. These rhythmic effects may be dismissed altogether, as the only ones that can definitely be associated with particular fingerings are those that are assisted, not dictated, by them. Various modern writers have in fact arrived at antithetical rhythmic results from identical musical instances.[10] No early source makes any sort of association of either a rhythmic or an articulatory nature with fingering; rather, the authors stress evenness, smoothness, and control as a basis of fine playing.[11] To say that early fingerings produce rhythmic inequality is to suppose, in effect, that the performance of early keyboard music depended on a constant and indeed reliable degree of non-control. This idea is absurd and hardly compatible with the tone of the treatises. Further, as Isolde Ahlgrimm points out,

> From all the examples in contemporary texts that list the exceptions to inequality, it necessarily follows that even, balanced playing was the objective. With what fingerings could these exceptions have been executed if early fingering did not permit even playing? If early fingering in fact compelled a particular rhythmic pattern, then, what is more, all explanations of the different forms of unequal notes would be meaningless, for we could not play what we wanted but would have to play what the fingering would produce.[12]

Controlled playing is not necessarily even at all times. The point is that rhythmic inequality is up to the player, not determined by the fingering. Some fingering can of course assist the enunciation of fine rhythmic detail, but such effects entirely depend on context and the individual hand, not on generalized systems of fingering.

The relationship of articulation and legato to early fingering is rather more complex. Certainly some fingerings can assist in articulatory effects and others definitely produce them. It seems simplistic, however, to make unqualified attributions of articulatory effect to basic techniques of fingering. The basis of the usual argument is that finger crossings produce slurrings and articulations that are appropriate to the music associated with that approach. In regard to slurring, there is no reason to presuppose that pairwise and other finger groupings always slur the notes that fall under the consecutive digits. Finger crossing is extremely useful in detached and structured legato as well as legato contexts and can, indeed, impart great uniformity of accent as well as diverse groupings. It is true that the typical crossings of 3 over 4 and 2 can help to produce pairwise groupings but that is not an inevitable result. Diruta, for example, comments derogatorily on performers whose clumsiness prevents them from holding notes for their full length.[13] As quoted above, C. P. E. Bach associated such crossings with smooth playing; and Quantz's remarks on finger withdrawal (see chapter 2) show that he regarded it as a means for smooth and easy negotiation of crossings. The curve of the fingers, the position and flexibility of the wrist, and the suppleness of the fingers enormously influence the articulatory effects of finger crossing. Skillfully withdrawn fingers will bridge the changeovers in crossing. If articulations are desired, the hand or fingers can be lifted slightly on each pair. With practice, crossings can be used in many ways, from producing smooth evenness to varied timings and articulations. For the player not fully accustomed to them, some finger crossings will produce involuntary articulations, at least at high speeds, but Türk's comments on W. F. Bach's playing suggest that this element, too, depends on experience. Certainly for passages within the normal range of speed, the relationship between finger crossing and articulation is absolutely dependent on the player's discretion. If articulations were indeed inevitable at finger crossings, it is curious that the sources make no mention of them. Some sources, including writers as different as Tomás de Sancta María and C. P. E. Bach, describe both finger crossing and thumb-under technique without differentiating in any way between their musical results. Indeed, C. P. E. Bach mentions crossing as a means of creating unbroken continuity. If certain linear articulations always resulted from certain fingerings, then keyboard instruments would have treated line in an altogether idiosyncratic way, related neither to the voice nor to any other instrument. Again, if this were the case at any time and place, it is striking that no contemporary writer commented on it. Instead, the keyboard player is often urged to model his sound on the voice.

The fingering patterns offered in early sources are often inconsistent, if their effects are necessarily articulatory. If an articulation were inevitable when 3 crosses over 4 in the right hand, with a slur probable on the 3–4 pairs of notes, then according to Diruta's system one always slurs into a good note; and according to the systems of Banchieri, the virginalists, and others, one never does. The crossings are the same but the presumed musical results are radically, and uniformly, opposed. In fact, Diruta's system is inherently self-contradictory, if viewed from the standpoint of automatic articulation. As Ahlgrimn shows, his fingerings would produce inconsistent groupings from one hand to the other (see Example III-37a), and if these musical results were inevitable, the system would be unusable. Ahlgrimm remarks:

> Diruta's answer to "Il Transilvano's" question—whether in the left hand one cannot play with the first and second fingers ascending, and with the third and fourth descending—involves only arguments of instrumental technique. He never mentions that this would produce a shift in the phrasing [see Example III-37b]. This compels us to conclude that Diruta attached no significance of phrasing to fingering.[14]

Spanish authors offer varied fingerings and make no reference to different resulting articulations. For instance, Luis Venegas de Henestrosa (1577)

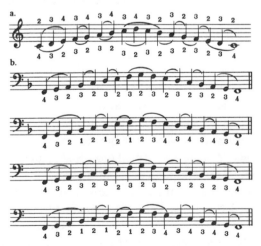

EXAMPLE III-37.
Isolde Ahlgrimm, realization of fingering patterns in
Diruta's *Il Transilvano*.[15]

offers different right-hand and left-hand scale fingerings (including right hand descending 3–2–1–3–2–1 or 3–2–3–2 and left hand ascending 4–3–2–1–3–2–1–3–2–1 or 4–3–2–1–2–1–2–1[16]). Hernando de Cabezon (1578) gives left-hand scale fingerings of 4–3–2–1–4–3–2–1 (ascending) and 1–2–3–4–3–4–3–4 descending.[17] As mentioned, the Spanish examples show appreciation of diverse linear contours. It is true that uniform application of crossing patterns to different scales will allow smooth negotiation in some instances and present awkwardnesses in others. The Spanish descriptions often take this fact into account; authorities from other nations (Diruta, for instance) sometimes outline only the basics, formulating rules that may or may not apply to a given instance. Hence the "departure" from rules in contemporary musical scores that show fingering. This may also explain why later examples of fingering, such as Nivers's and Saint Lambert's, formulate no thoroughgoing rules. The usual finger sequences have to be adapted to the particular line. Given this premise and the flexibility of the patterns, such presentations do in fact show what is essential, whose exact implementation depends, as Saint Lambert suggests, upon circumstance: a very economical system for the teacher!

Most of the treatises that describe fingering are intended for beginners and show only the fundamentals of technique, in regard to both fingering and other matters. It is hardly questionable that in earlier epochs, as now, fine artists would find their own subtleties of fingering along with all other aspects of artistic performance. Early fingerings can assist many effects, but to view them as rigid and specific in application and outcome is both illogical and unmusical. The musical effects of fingering lie not in rigid patterns and associated articulations, but in matching the articulation, timing, flow, and pauses of sensitive performance with the advantages and possibilities of the different fingers. Exceptions, due to instrument, individuality of hands, tempo, musical intent, and specific musical instances, can be found for every "rule" postulated for any fingering system, early or modern. Certainly the articulation or at least the subtle variations of weight distribution and/or the tactile feeling of a passage will require different fingerings for different hands, depending on the relative lengths, strengths, and flexibility of the fingers. Different fingerings will assist different interpretations and may vary from one performance to another. The music must guide the fingering, not the reverse. The main concern of any fingering, apart from general ease and grace in performance, should be to assist specific and precise rhythmic and/or articulatory effects. The finer aspects of good fingering will aid in the realization of such nuances (those that defy notation), as well as facility and, on the clavichord, good tone production.

Finger crossing sometimes appears in relation to legato, as in Example III-38; Michel Corrette put slurs over his examples of scales fingered with pairwise crossings. The technique can assist evenness and smoothness; thumb-under technique sometimes produces finger groupings at cross-purposes with the musical accent or contour, whereas groupings with finger crossings can correlate with the musical groupings more often than not. The relationship between physical motions and musical contour is an important advantage psychologically as well as technically and perhaps corresponds to some extent with the allotment of good fingers to good notes mentioned in the treatises. Of course, the hand must be trained to avoid inadvertent accents with both thumb and finger crossing and to permit accentuation through them only when desired. Sometimes a useful accent is produced by the thumb or a finger crossing onto a stressed note, but this must be subject to the player's control. Detached playing is of course facilitated by consecutive use of the same digit. Whether a definitive break or a minor articulation is desired, it is often best to finger so as to reinforce the effect, rather than to make it from what could be a legato basis. When Couperin wants pairwise slurring, he shows a fingering like that in Example III-39a; its 3–3 succession would not be necessary if 3–2–3–2 were assumed to produce the same effect. Virginal music is full of similar fingerings (Example III-39b).

EXAMPLE III-38.
F. Couperin, "L'Ausoniène," *Ordre* 8, mm.30-33.

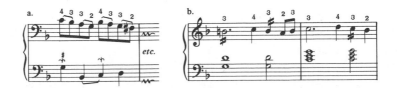

EXAMPLE III-39.
a. F. Couperin, "Les Sylvains," *Ordre* 1, m.9.
b. John Bull, *Dr. Bull's Ground*, mm.4-5.

Complexities of fingering that are actually unnecessary can nonetheless be useful for technical control or to extract the full flavor from a certain rhythm or texture. Their use depends entirely on the musical situation and the individual hand. Sometimes a passage in which the fingers willfully run away must be slowed down with a built-in awkwardness, which may also assist other musical inflections. This approach should not be used merely to compensate for an undisciplined technique and should not in any case be carried to extremes.

❀ Conclusion

Some students, even at an advanced level, are taught to work on a new piece according to the following sequence:

1. Write in the fingering.
2. Learn the notes.
3. Practice slowly.
4. Work up to tempo.
5. Work out the "interpretation."

This mode of attack is undoubtedly helpful for beginners and those building up a technique after a long period away from the keyboard. However, it seems to this writer that such an approach is of limited use and can eventually inhibit various learning processes. Given a certain level of technical and musical competence and experience, the following order might be preferred:

1. Rough out the interpretive ideas, based on previous experience with the style of the piece. (Is it a dance movement? What does it have in common with other dance movements the player has studied?)
2. Try the piece at performing tempo.
3. Work out the technical difficulties.
4. Write in fingerings as necessary for technical and expressive needs.
5. Refine.

Writing in fingering indiscriminately is sometimes a crutch and a waste of time. Certainly, writing it in thoroughly for a few pieces is a good learning device and an aid in cultivating good habits. One should do so whenever there is a specific technical difficulty or a musical situation requiring special fingering, or when one is learning a new fingering approach (a specific old system, any new technique). However, if the full fingering is written in for every piece it may inhibit the development of rapid playing reflexes and discourage flexibility in refingering for different musical effects.

The player is best off who has the widest possible range of fingerings and who has mastered the fingering of basic figurations (scales, broken chords, repeated notes, parallel intervals, etc.). With this kind of control, one can vary the niceties of fingering in accordance with interpretive ideas. One should not be bound by preconceived ideas of fingering whether early or modern; they should rather be made to work for the individual. Praetorius cautioned that:

> Many think [fingering] is a matter of great importance and despise such organists as do not use this or that particular fingering, but this in my opinion is not worth talking about; let a player run up and down the keyboard with his first, middle, or third fingers [i.e., our 2, 3, and 4] or even with his nose if that will help him, provided that everything is done clearly, correctly, and gracefully.[18]

Centuries later, but from a similar perspective, Clifford Curzon described Artur Schnabel's working methods:

> One of the great precepts of Schnabel's teaching was that there was a right movement and a right fingering for every sound and phrase [which would depend on the interpretation, as well as on the hand of the individual]. . . . Schnabel never automatically took the easiest fingering. . . . He always wanted to achieve a "second simplicity," that second naivety you arrive at after having gone through all the tests, and out the other side. And he would try to do this by looking for the most natural way to play every bar of music: he would go through everything, every phrase, to see how he could play it best *without* practice—which did not mean simply going over and over different patterns and different fingerings, but rather, as it were, throwing his hand on the piano and seeing which way made the phrase speak most beautifully; it might be even the most eccentric fingering, but it was the fingering which most naturally suited a particular phrase.[19]

This kind of experimentation and learning never comes to an end, but always allows fresh technical and musical insights.

4

Articulation and Legato

THE HARPSICHORD AND THE CLAVICHORD are equally sensitive to subtleties of articulation and legato, and many of the points covered in this chapter apply to both instruments. However, the dynamic flexibility of the clavichord remains its outstanding attribute; and since the harpsichord relies heavily on its means of connecting and separating notes to simulate dynamic flux, much of the discussion refers directly only to the harpsichord. As the harpsichord's volume levels are essentially fixed, the player's only touch control of dynamics and tone quality is through articulation, legato, and timing. A harpsichord that sounds hard and dry under one player may yield warmer and more varied sonorities for another, who may produce more complex sifting of textures by the way tones are held and released, often differing considerably from the notation of the music. This chapter will consider the treatment of articulation and legato in regard to phrasing, notation, and adjustment of sonority for color and dynamic suggestion.

Levels of Articulation and Legato

The harpsichordist must possess a wide range of articulations and levels of legato. An instrument's responsiveness derives largely from the variety it will afford in this respect, which is often more important than sheer loveliness of tone. Articulation and legato may be divided into four basic levels, the second and third rather closely related: staccato and detached playing; "structured legato"—the near connection of notes; clean, simple legato—the bare linking of notes; and overlegato, in which one or more notes are sustained into those that follow. The first and last levels are open to infinite shading. The second and third form a narrower, more neutral range in between.

In general, the word *legato* signifies unbroken connection between notes, as occurs when a stringed instrument sustains a note at full volume and smoothly joins it to the next. On keyboard instruments, the impression of legato often requires that the volume of each note match that at the end of the preceding note. These volumes match most evenly within certain rates of movement. On the dynamically rigid harpsichord, the nearest approximation to the true legato of other instruments is among notes that follow in rapid succession so that one note succeeds another before the first has decayed noticeably. Overlegato can suggest wind or string legato among a wider range of values by partially submerging successive attacks. The clavichord can of course match the dynamics of note terminations and succeeding attacks; and a violin-like connection of conjunct notes can often be suggested by legato or overlegato coupled with slight dynamic adjustments. Strongly cohesive timing on either instrument can further the illusion of legato even when tones have actually faded between successive attacks.

Since the impression of other instruments' ordinary legato often requires overlegato on keyboard instruments, the word *legato* in keyboard parlance often includes degrees of overlegato as well. This use of the word is typical of both early and modern times. In the course of this book, the word *legato*, unless otherwise qualified, refers only to the third level of barely connected notes. Ideally for purposes of discussion, the dividing point between articulation and overlegato would be a single level. In actual practice, however, this dividing level extends over a small range of actual and near-connection of notes: simple legato and what is often today termed "structured legato." The latter refers to tones that are separated by the slightest of articulations, as when a finger moves smoothly and swiftly from one key to its neighbor so that the notes are heard as essentially connected. Control of this type of note linking is useful in resonant acoustics, in playing highly resonant harpsichords, and in dealing with fretted clavichords. It is not to be confused with audibly articulate nonlegato. The minute separations of structured legato are needed in a resonant acoustic in the same way that an actor must enunciate with exaggerated clarity in order to project the impression of normal speech from the stage. Care in projection must not lead to overstepping the bounds of structured legato into a highly articulate, even artificial style. The boundary between structured legato and a detached effect is very delicate in some playing situations. Even when heard in a resonant room, pieces written in a tender, vocal, or violinistic manner suffer from highly detached playing. The effect of smoothness must not be lost. The need for structured legato often increases from the upper to the lower ranges of an instrument.

Structured legato has another function, which is less dependent on room acoustics than on the harpsichord itself. In some instruments, the release of the key is accompanied by a small noise: the click of the returning quill and sometimes a sound as the string is damped. These sounds are more pronounced on some harpsichords than on others, and are stronger when two or more registers and/or louder, heavier voicing are used. At the level of simple legato, when the scissorslike, simultaneous rise and fall of the fingers cause one note to begin at the moment the preceding one ends, the noise of the first note's release can minutely interfere with the attack of the new note. Structured legato avoids this problem and yields cleaner tone quality than does simple legato. Again, the difference is one of clarity, not of audible articulation. Structured legato may also be preferable on instruments with complex (not necessarily beautiful) tone quality and/or a powerful attack. Drier, cleaner sounding instruments may find equivalent clarity with simple legato.

❦ Historical Commentaries on Articulation and Legato

Every articulation has a particular use, and no one type can be defined as "basic" to the harpsichord or clavichord, unless the most neutral can be chosen as a point of departure. A neutral touch would be simple or structured legato, according to the individual instrument and performing site. The various early authorities who describe the "basic" touch of the harpsichord, clavichord, or organ seem to agree that legato or structured legato is the point of departure at the keyboard.

Most specific descriptions of touch come from the eighteenth century. There are fewer sixteenth and seventeenth-century accounts, and they often refer to articulation and legato only for specific usages, rather than for general playing style. For instance, Costanzo Antegnati (1608) and André Raison (1688) refer to legato playing on certain organ registrations.[1] Frescobaldi remarks on playing the *canti fermi* in his *Fiori musicali* (1635):

> In the *Canti fermi*, although the notes may be tied [*legati*; i.e. linked together, legato], in order not to impede the hands one can break them up for greater ease, after having used all the facility that one may command.[2]

The player may detach the notes if legato cannot be maintained while managing the other parts, but legato is to be preferred. Frescobaldi does not comment on touch in general.

Diruta (1593/1607) remarks that an easy touch connects notes on the organ, while striking the keys separates them, as if a singer takes a breath after every note. He disapproves of organists who lose half the value of the notes, playing ♪↟♪↟♪↟ instead of ♩♩♩.[3] Diruta attributes not only differ-

ent musical and playing styles to the organ and harpsichord, but also differences in attack on the keys (see chapter 2). However, his concern with giving
notes their full value on the organ apparently had its counterpart at the
harpsichord, for in common with other writers (Frescobaldi, Lebègue, and
Saint Lambert, among them) he mentions the necessity of reiterating the
evanescent tones of the harpsichord[4] (see chapter 6, pp.156-58). A full sound
seems generally to have been desired, whether in regard to single lines or to
the sustaining of chords and complex textures.

Surprisingly, Saint Lambert makes no comments on harpsichord touch
in his treatise of 1702. However, in his book on accompaniment (1707) he
mentions legato playing on the organ, and states that the organ "has no need
of all the devices [broken and reiterated chords] used on the harpsichord to
supplement the dryness of the instrument."[5] Again, a full, connected sound
seems to be desirable.

Several authors describe legato as a general point of departure. François Couperin (1717) remarks that "it is necessary to preserve a perfect legato [liaison parfaite] in all that one plays."[6] Rameau (1724) describes a
clinging touch to produce legato (see p.20) and a scissorslike movement of
the fingers:

> From the finger by which one begins, one passes to its neighbor, and
> thus from one [finger] to another; observing that that which has just pressed a
> key leaves it in the same instant that its neighbor presses another: for the
> lifting of one finger and the pressing with another must be executed at the
> same moment.[7]

This technique produces simple legato, which is also advocated by Nicolo
Pasquali (1758):

> The whole intent and purpose of the preceding rules is to enable us to
> keep the fingers pressing on the keys during the entire duration of the notes.[8]
>
> ... when the vibration of a string ceases, before the vibration of another
> one begins, not only does this cause an unsatisfactory tone to come from the
> instrument in some of the notes of a running passage, but the music will also
> not be played as it is written.[9]
>
> Legato is the touch which this essay seeks to teach, since this is the most
> important touch for almost all passages, and the one in which the vibration of
> the strings is most complete for each note.[10]

(Pasquali's descriptions of various touches appears in full in Appendix 2.)

Quantz (see p.6 above) refers to a touch that can "obviate as much as
possible the natural weakness of the instrument, which is that the tones cannot be joined to one another as upon other instruments."[11] He apparently
wished that the harpsichord could join notes continued at full volume, as

string and wind instruments can, but that is of course not possible because of the decaying tone. As mentioned above, keyboard instruments can only approximate full legato through relationships of time and dynamics. Continuity of line and sound was sought in accompaniment, and in a vein similar to Quantz's, Lorenzo Penna recommended legato for continuo playing (see chapter 7, p.189).

Other authors appear to describe structured legato as a point of departure. Tomás de Sancta María describes the basic touch of the clavichord as follows:

> There are two requirements for playing clearly and distinctly. . . . The first and principal one is that in either ascending or descending passages the finger that plays a key is always raised before the one that immediately follows it plays. One always proceeds this way; otherwise, one finger interferes with the other, covering it up, which is like playing seconds. The performance is then dirty and ragged, sounding neither clear nor distinct.[12]

Guillaume Nivers (1667) describes organ touch as follows:

> An important ornament and a sign of good breeding in your performance is a distinct demarcation of all the notes and a subtle slurring of some. This is learned best from singing. To play the notes in a distinct and marked fashion, lift your fingers quickly but not too high. That is, for example, in playing a run of consecutive notes, lift each note promptly as you play the following one, for if you do not lift one until after the next is played, you confuse rather than distinguish the notes.
>
> To connect the notes, it is still necessary to distinguish them, but the notes are not released so promptly. This manner is between confusion and distinction and partakes a little of each. It is generally practiced with the *ports de voix* and in certain passages. . . . For all these matters consult the method of singing, for the organ should imitate the voice in such things.[13]

Although the organ's sustaining power and acoustic situation are different from the harpsichord's, Nivers' remarks are of interest. That Nivers gives the voice as a model suggests that by "distinct demarcation" he means clarity rather than a specifically articulated, detached style. This meaning is also borne out by the direction to "lift each note promptly as you play [rather than before you play] the following one."

One of the most famous eighteenth-century descriptions of keyboard touch is C. P. E. Bach's:

> Tones which are neither detached, connected nor fully held are sounded for half their value, unless the abbreviation *Ten.* (hold) is written over them, in which case they must be held fully. Quarters and eighths in moderate and slow tempos are usually performed in this semidetached manner. They must not be played weakly, but with fire and a slight accentuation.[14]

Other remarks by the same author, some of which appear below, suggest that this description is far more extreme than he intended.

J. D. Türk (1789) suggests minute separation of notes for "ordinary movement" and considers that C. P. E. Bach's description would lead to "choppy" playing. In his notational approximations of "ordinary movement," ♩♩♩♩ is played as ♪♫ ♫ ♫ ♪ or ♪. ♫.♫.♫.♪. These rhythmic patterns are perhaps notational approximations of structured legato, which often requires such treatment, especially in resonant rooms and low registers.

C. P. E. Bach's contemporary Friedrich Wilhelm Marpurg divides touch into three categories: slurring, detachment, and "ordinary movement":

> In direct contrast to slurring is detachment, which consists of sustaining a note not for its [full, notated] value, but for only approximately half of it. This is indicated by dots placed over or under the notes. . . . One often uses a small, straight stroke for the same purpose. . . . Both slurring and detaching are contrary to ordinary progression, which consists of very swiftly raising the finger from the preceding key just shortly before touching the following note. This ordinary method of progressing is never indicated since it is always presumed.[15]

(Marpurg describes finger substitution on sounding notes and remarks on its advantages for connecting notes and ensuring a flowing performance.)

Structured legato as "ordinary movement" is quite possibly the thrust of all of these passages. C. P. E. Bach's description seems to be the least accurate; his intent appears more clearly in the context of other remarks, which show that he regarded ordinary movement as a sane median between excessive detachment on the one hand and muddy, constant legato or over-legato on the other:

> When notes are to be detached from each other strokes or dots are placed above them. . . . Notes are detached with relation to: 1) their notated length, that is, a half, quarter, or eighth of a bar; 2) the tempo, fast or slow; and 3) the volume, forte or piano. Such tones are always held for a little less than half of their notated length. In general, detached notes appear mostly in leaping passages and rapid tempos.[16]

> There are many who play stickily, as if they had glue between their fingers. Their touch is lethargic; they hold notes too long. Others, in an attempt to correct this, leave the keys too soon, as if they burned. Both are wrong. I speak in general, for every kind of touch has its use.[17]

What C. P. E. Bach rather inaccurately described for ordinary movement, and elsewhere suggested for marked, detached notes, fits Marpurg's account of the latter. Marpurg's description of ordinary movement seems to agree with those of Tomás, Nivers, and Türk; the approach appears to be structured legato. These accounts are not elaborate descriptions; the authors are usually more concerned with beginning players and the common beginner's fault of playing with a lazy hand and blurring the notes together: playing that is indeed, as Tomás says, "dirty and ragged, sounding neither clear nor distinct." It is possible to read some of these descriptions as showing the basis of playing to be a detached style. However, the authors' differentiation of ordinary movement from detached playing and their concern with clarity and vocal models suggest that the level of detachment was only what was necessary for clarity, rather than what the listener would perceive as articulation.

What Baroque authors often term "legato" or "slurring" perhaps often approaches overlegato and is most frequently employed with ornaments (especially appoggiaturas) and affective passages.

Obviously, different players had different styles of playing, in earlier periods as now. Remarks similar to Bach's (in the preceding quotation) appear in France in the 1690s, in comments by Mr. le Gallois on the "brilliant style" as opposed to the "legato style." Although the former has many virtues, he says, many of its practitioners add too many embellishments, or

> they strike the keys instead of flowing smoothly from one to another. . . . We see also that the most expert musicians, following a middle path in this, as one must in everything, only use this lightness of hand and rapidity of execution with great moderation, for fear, as I have said, of muddling and confusing what ought to be neat and distinct.
>
> But if the brilliant style has its defects, the legato style also has its own, which are easy to observe in those whom affectation causes to slur their playing in an agonizing manner. For they so contort their hands and fingers, they pass them over each other with such excess, knotting them in an extraordinary manner, that it becomes ugly and pitiable. Thus all one can say about it is that their playing is indeed so very legato that it sounds more like the playing of a hurdy-gurdy, in which because of the slurring the playing has no rhythm, than like true harpsichord playing.[18]

This remark recalls Diruta's complaints of organists who detach the notes excessively. Extremes of detached and legato playing were known to le Gallois, to Diruta, to C. P. E. Bach—and could doubtless be found in every school of playing.

Türk, late among eighteenth-century authorities, provides one of the few detailed descriptions of varied approaches to articulation and legato:

> For a *heavy* execution every tone must be played firmly (with emphasis) and held out until the very end of the prescribed duration of the note. *Light* execution is that in which every tone is played with less firmness (emphasis), and the finger lifted from the key somewhat sooner than the actual prescribed duration . . . the terms heavy and light in general refer more to the sustaining or detaching of a tone rather than to the softness or loudness of the same.[19]

Compositions which have a more serious purpose, such as fugues, well-composed sonatas, religious odes and songs, etc., call for a heavier execution than, for example, certain playful divertimentos, humorous songs, lively dances, and the like.[20]

Following these definitions, Türk advocates heavy style for movements that are serious or pathetic, lighter styles for movements that are brisker or joyous. Slower movements are generally heavier than rapid movements, as longer note values are usually heavier than shorter ones. (This principle would hardly apply to embellishments in short values although some rapid flourishes are advantageously reduced in volume by structured legato or even minute detachment.) Both heavy and light attacks are generally to be found in one movement; Türk comments that the type of attack depends entirely on relative note values, contrasts of mood, and so forth. (It is interesting to note that Türk mentions overdotting as being usual in pompous movements. He notes the heavy style as ♩♫♩ and the light rendition as ♩.♫♩.♫ .)

❧ Dynamics, Articulation, Legato, and Phrasing

The words *phrasing* and *articulation* are often confused. One may refer to two notes as "phrased together," or to phrasing in terms of various units of musical thought: two- and four-measure phrases, periods consisting of several phrases, and so on. It is up to the performer to clarify the relationships among the various compositional units; the players influence is often greatest on the local level.

Although a phrase is perceived as a unit, some notes within a phrase may be articulated one from another while others are connected. Articulation and legato can imply dynamic variation as well as delineate subphrases: the two functions are closely related. Dynamics, articulation, legato, and timing can accent or undermine tones as the phrase or phrasing requires. Musical textures often suggest dynamic variations that guide the performer in shaping the phrases by whatever means, dynamic or otherwise, are available. Articulation and legato are often most important for their role in emphasizing or de-emphasizing notes.

Among the many ways of inflecting a musical phrase, varying the dynamics is perhaps the most natural for both the player and the listener. Very slight dynamic inflections are often more important to phrasing than large-scale variations in volume. Minute changes can vary linear stresses enormously; the harpsichordist emulates these through articulation and legato.

Articulation, legato, timing, and dynamics are the basic elements open to manipulation by the performer. They are mutually influential, and their modes of interaction produce many more varieties of phrasing than the sums of their individual possibilities. The clavichord can utilize all of them; that is one reason for its unsurpassed expressivity. The harpsichordist faces an unusual instrument, whose clarity and tonal qualities allow many shadings of articulation and legato but which is incapable of graded dynamics, excepting those written into the musical texture. (To be sure, the harpsichord can make variations in timbre and abrupt dynamic changes by means of its registers. However, many of the finest harpsichords are quite limited in registrational possibilities, and the instrument's normal use is based in flat planes of tone. Variations in timbre and volume through registration changes are secondary means of expression at best; they are discussed in chapter 8. Some clavichords, too, are more responsive to a small range of inflection than to large-scale dynamic changes.) Thus, the harpsichordist cannot employ elements of timing, articulation, legato, and dynamics altogether independently. Although the first three are "dynamic" elements as well, the relative stresses that they and variations in musical texture provide are not usually independent of variations in volume. (See chapter 5, pp.107-108.) Instead, they often generate the dynamic element on the harpsichord. Articulation, legato, and timing imply dynamics; musical textures realize dynamics. Music whose textural density varies in opposition to marked dynamics (e.g., *piano* is marked as the texture thickens) is probably for the clavichord or the piano, not the harpsichord. Although the harpsichord is for the most part dynamically rigid, the player must continue to think in terms of the dynamic flux natural to music, which often in reality can only be implied. (One reason that C. P. E. Bach recommended cultivation of both the clavichord and the harpsichord was to keep the harpsichordist sensitive to dynamic nuance.) The suppleness and variation of texture in fine harpsichord writing is the surest guide in this realm, and the player's ear must be trained to respond to whatever the writing and instrument suggest. Dynamically effective changes in texture, however slight, should be brought out by any available means. (Some pieces do not suggest much small- or large-scale dynamic flexibility. In a constant, rhythmically active texture, for instance, the rhythmic drive and/or harmonic inflections and large-scale phrasings are often predominant over dynamic variations. Other pieces may require all the dynamic resources, real and implied, that an instrument can offer.)

Apart from variations in timing and dynamics, a note can be stressed by detaching it from the note preceding it and de-emphasized by slurring the previous note into it. The time consumed by the articulation is generally taken from the preceding note. Especially strong accents take the time from the start of the stressed note; this treatment, called *suspension* by the French, is discussed in chapter 5. When one begins to experiment with different articulations and with ways of blurring notes together with different degrees of legato, the harpsichord's seeming disadvantage of decaying tone duration is revealed as a highly advantageous complement to its flat dynamic level. One reason for the lack of articulatory sensitivity in many early twentieth-century harpsichords is that the builders often sought as an ideal a long, sustained tone of very gradual decay. That kind of sound quickly leads to muddy textures if much of the gentle legato blurring possible on classically based instruments is attempted. Certainly a sustained tone, of sorts, can have its advantages. Some instruments have a fairly rapid initial loss of volume, but continue to sound considerably longer at a softer level. This kind of decay rate can be very useful to the player. Different styles of instrument and different individual harpsichords have variations best suited to particular types of textures, generally representative of the period, school, and nationality of the particular harpsichord. In terms of relative balancing of overall volume, decay curve, and sharpness (even explosiveness) of the pluck itself (ictus), a given harpsichord will often tell its player what is best for a piece in the realms of articulation, legato, *rubato*, and tempo.

The harpsichord is by nature an articulate sounding instrument. Notes begin at a precise moment, in contrast to the vagueness possible on some stringed and wind instruments. The ictus of the pluck imparts a slight accent akin to the "chiff" on some organ stops; and this accent is reinforced by being minutely sharper in pitch than the sound produced when the string settles into vibration. The sharpness of the pluck on even mellow instruments gives the harpsichord great brilliance and rhythmic energy and ensures at least a certain degree of clarity in all but very heavy or low-range textures. For sharp, detached effects certain varieties of the instrument can hardly be bettered, but on dry instruments, very sharp staccatos must be avoided or approached with care, for the string may be damped before the pitch has had time to assert itself. (The clavichord is far more receptive than the harpsichord to short, heavy, accentual staccato.) Many resonant instruments, however, respond even to notes of the briefest duration, and a fine harpsichord has an immediacy of touch and tonal response that allows infinitely varied levels of detached playing. The range of legato blurring is often more limited and depends on the nature of tonal decay in the various ranges of the instrument. (Overlegato can be used more freely in the upper ranges than in the lower.) For *cantabile* playing it is often necessary to cover the attacks of notes to a greater or lesser extent; the niceties of playing then lie less in clarifying important notes than in obscuring others. The ictus itself, even covered, provides a degree of clarity. Articulatory emphasis of notes is less an intrinsic requirement of the instrument than an important end of a spectrum, from extreme overlegato blurring to sharp levels of detachment. Use of these factors depends on the nature of the musical texture, the instrument, and the musical ideas of the player. The player must be as ready to mold the interpretation or its realization to the possibilities of the particular harpsichord as to manipulate its range of nuances.

Some passages produce a full enough sonority that the individual ictus is more or less covered by the mass of ongoing sound; thin, unvaried textures often require the greatest subtleties of adjustment to be kept from sounding bare. (Delicacy of timing as well as ornamentation and embellishment can help in such cases.) Thin textures must often be treated in terms of overall sonority rather than as independent lines. Articulation for rhythmic or dynamic impetus can sometimes be made in one part rather than both even if both are open to strong articulation.

Regardless of texture, the bass should usually receive primary attention in determining articulations and legato for both the bass itself and the parts above it. The bass is a dominant factor because it provides the harmonic foundation; on the harpsichord, it produces the fullest sound of the texture, thereby requiring the most judicious articulation. The soloist must take cues from the bass for the upper parts, just as a continuo player decides on the textures of the realization partly in accordance with the implications of the bass.

❀ Articulation of Motives

The treatment of a motive throughout a movement should be consistent with the musical use of that motive, which may vary considerably and suggest different articulations or (usually) different shadings of one basic articulation. The nature or at least the intensity of a motive will of course vary throughout a movement and often requires comparable variation in performance. One must take careful account of the rhythmic and intervallic structure of each motive, generally and in respect of each iteration: Does it rise or fall (usually signifying an increase or decrease of energy respectively)? What are its most characteristic intervals? Does it contain or sometimes show significant chromatic inflections? How does it relate to other motives and to the harmonic rhythm? How is it altered in length, intervals, or rhythm?

Baroque music often shows pervasive use of one or several motives, ranging from two or three notes to a full melodic phrase, which may provide the material for an entire composition. A piece may be built from one or more motives that are endlessly recombined contrapuntally or that complement one another and produce distinctly contrasting phrases. A single line is often built of horizontal linkages of melodic cells, a procedure that is one aspect of the Baroque theory of figural composition.[21] (Musical analysis, mainly by German theorists of the seventeenth and early eighteenth centuries, drew on the terminology used to analyze rhetoric; the term *figure* can connote anything from a motive to a compositional technique or a structural division of a piece.) If a work contrasts strikingly different figures or puts one or more through various intervallic or rhythmic permutations, they often must be brought out individually, by various means according to context. However, indiscriminate delineation of each enunciation of a figure may overemphasize the local level of construction at the expense of larger units, the phrases built from many iterations of the melodic cell(s). Often the tinier motivic units are like individual stones in a mosaic, and the larger and more varied groupings may be of greater interest. If a phrase is built from many statements of a brief figure, indiscriminate articulation of each statement could submerge the sense of the phrase as a whole, to say nothing of interphrase relationships and rhythmic drive and cohesion. If clarification of a figural basis seems necessary, it is usually sufficient to make the point in the opening iterations of the figure(s) or at important moments in the course of the piece, rather than remain preoccupied with them throughout the work. Similarly, not every iteration of a fugue subject requires the strong profile that may be desirable in the exposition.

Not only the musical employment of a motive, but the different instrumental ranges in which it occurs and the dynamic contour of certain passages may require modifications in its treatment. Similarly, passages articulated to bring out rhythmic features often require different articulation from similar passages given a weaker rhythmic profile. With respect to texture, passages that are on the border between linear independence (counterpoint) and chordal homophony may be open to widely varying treatment. In intimate surroundings, for instance, one may wish to bring out linear features; in a large hall it may be more appropriate to articulate such writing in a way that stresses its homophonic aspects.

❧ Variety of Articulation and Sonority

Assuming the historical validity of a full range of detached and legato styles on the early keyboard instruments, the player must achieve dynamic inflections by the most diverse uses of the full spectrum of articulation and legato. Application of this range of effects will vary constantly with the needs of the music, the instrument, and the acoustic environment, which must be considered as the ultimate extension of the instrument. A dry acoustic will allow more overlegato than will a very resonant space. Factors such as registration, tempo, and fluctuations of tempo can complement or work against effects of articulation and legato. Complete cooperation among all these elements will allow the fullest expression of musical ideas. The harpsichordist must never fight the instrument or demand more than it can give, but must always demand that it suggest to the fullest what it cannot realize. With a proper balance maintained among expressive elements, this very reserve can be expressive.

A piece of music makes certain stresses naturally; others must be brought out. Both sorts range from stressing single notes to clarifying large formal structures. Some require the performer's elucidation; others are comparatively less open to personal approach and/or hardly require "interpretation." Indeed, the belaboring of obvious musical points can lead to caricature in some instance. A musical device that obtrudes itself is unsuccessful because it draws attention away from the natural flow of the music; the use of many obtrusive or misplaced devices is the definition, or one definition, of mannered playing. For example, some notes are naturally stressed by context. Articulation before such automatically accented notes often stands out as a mannerism, in that it is musically unnecessary.

Articulation and legato can influence the actual volume of a passage in the effect they have on the sonority: sustained notes build up sonority and volume; detached notes do not. In terms of dynamics, the contrast of articulatory silences with instrumental sound is one of the harpsichord's most valuable resources, as much for adjusting the volume of an overall texture (see Example IV-5) as for the enunciation of individual lines. Rests, too, should be considered in both roles. In many contexts, notated rests can be construed as articulating the ensuing note as much as terminating the preceding. Rests should, as well, be fully realized or extended in many cases as a means for lightening the sonority. Note durations can be abbreviated to lighten a texture (reducing the overall sonority) or to stress a note in retrospect (as with staccato), as well as for articulatory stress of the following note. Notes falling on the beat can often be stressed by being detached from the ensuing notes as well as by overholding. J. S. Bach sometimes indicates ♫♫♫ patterns for this purpose (see p.92 below). Early release of notes can lighten a texture in rhythmically active or quiescent contexts. Emphatic rhythms such as ♫ can be rendered ♪ ♪; as Türk suggests, ♫ can become ♫♫. Long inactive notes in a context of shorter ones can be abbreviated: for instance, ♫♩ can become ♫♪ 𝄾 or ♫♪. 𝄾 , ♫♩_♫ can become ♫♩ 𝄾♫ , etc. François Couperin similarly describes the aspiration (♩ = ♪ 𝄾) in terms of reducing the volume. (See chapter 5, pp.134-135).

A uniform level of detachment will increase the sonority without stressing particular notes; varying degrees of detachment will also decrease the sonority, but provide contrasting accentuations depending on the degree of articulation before individual notes. Thus the harpsichordist is often in a situation unusual for other instrumentalists: levels of detached playing are used to minimize volume rather than to stress tones, and the musically deemphasizing legato quality is used to build up sonority. These approaches to articulation and legato are relevant to large-scale adjustments of sound and must be differentiated from stress and de-emphasis of individual notes and beats. The difference is that between actual and implied dynamics; but the two techniques can be used together, articulation reducing the overall volume and being varied for particular effects, as desired. Juggling the different levels of legato and articulation always depends on the many variables of the music at hand.

The devices of uniform versus varied detachment are most useful with notes of medium duration. They are less effective with very long or very rapid notes: the sustaining power of the instrument is too limited in the former case, and the rush of new attacks in a rapid flourish is too overwhelming in the latter. Context is all important.

Tempo also affects these factors: fast tempos and rapid notes increase the density of textures and the apparent or even the actual volume. (Intensity of sound is a dynamic factor, whether it actually increases volume or not.) Tempo affects the degree to which notes within a median range of speed may be blurred together. For these reasons, choice of tempo is related to the kind of overall sound desired, articulated or connected.

The above points can be illustrated by Example IV-1. (The treatments suggested for it are intended only for purposes of illustration.) Such a passage is open to minute adjustment of volume by overall speed and by application of different levels of detachment or legato; uniform detachment of one or both parts will sound softer than an overlegato rendition, or even legato or structured legato. (Uniform detachment of the eighth notes would have to be slight and precise to reduce the volume; more than slight detachment at a rapid tempo could produce excessive clatter instead of dynamic reduction.) If the detachment is uneven, the notes of longer duration will stand out more, both by virtue of their length and by receiving greater articulation. (The same is true of notes given emphatic, special brevity. A note more markedly detached than its neighbors will often stand out, if only in retrospect.) In Example IV-1 dynamic tapering of each measure could be effected by progressively reducing the duration of each quarter note. This technique automatically stresses the first note of each measure by articulation and tapers the sonority of each measure. Further emphasis at each barline could be made by delaying the attack of each opening quarter note.

Slightly detached accompaniment of a melody is often useful in balancing sonorities when the middle and low ranges of a poor instrument (harpsichord or clavichord) tend to overwhelm the treble. Subtle articulations, not necessarily heard as such, can reduce the volume of the lower parts. The upper part(s) can achieve greater sonority when played from a legato basis. The range of articulations or their point of departure must sometimes be selected with a care for textural clarity, particularly in dense contrapuntal

EXAMPLE IV-1.
J. S. Bach, *Italian Concerto,* Presto, mm.155-57.

textures and/or passages in the lower ranges of the keyboard. Such writing is often clearest if based on levels of slight articulation or structured legato.

Varied articulation is extremely useful for delineating different beat strengths, especially among uniform note values. The most important beats receive the greatest preceding articulation and are usually held longer than the preceding note. However, successively greater articulations will often produce or imply an effect of *diminuendo* because of built-in beat stresses and/or time inflections made by the player.

Articulatory stressing of beats is open to infinite gradation on a sensitive harpsichord or clavichord, and on the latter it can of course be reinforced by variations in dynamics. If the factors of timing, registration, and musical texture are kept constant, dynamic effects on the harpsichord can be graded on a continuum from strong articulations before accented notes (*forte*) to weaker ones (*mezzo forte*) and so on to various degrees of structured legato, legato, and overlegato (*pianissimo*). This scheme applies mainly to moving note values (quarters, eighths, and sixteenths); long notes have little articulatory influence, and very short ones are open to less variation. Improvisation of embellishments can provide more dynamic variety to inflexible passages, both for the dynamic function of the increased rhythmic movement and for the varied articulations available with some shorter notes. Articulation of beats is further influenced by varied texture, range (lower notes being more sonorous than higher), and the factors of sonority and dynamics already discussed.

Changes in harmonic tension and rhythmic activity also influence dynamic effects and the player's articulatory response. Foreign notes in a diatonic context often sound louder than those belonging to the tonality, whether they are made louder by the player or not. Thus, an appoggiatura generally sounds louder than its resolution; the effect is enhanced by slurring the two notes together and often by articulating before the appoggiatura itself. A change to a slower surface rhythm or any decline of activity often has a softening effect, and, other factors being equal, articulation should not interfere with it. Given a constant texture, a gradual change from articulation to overlegato in the course of a phrase can suggest a slight *diminuendo,* helping to create a rounder, "softer" cadence. An increase in rhythmic activity, rising lines, or a faster harmonic rhythm all generally create an effect of *crescendo* that can be paralleled by a *crescendo* of increasing detachment, or a progression from levels of legato to levels of detachment. In most such cases, the intensity of sound created by progressively greater articulation more than makes up for the loss of sonority: the implied volume is usually more effective than the lost actual volume. In many textures, a *crescendo* from detached notes to a resonant buildup of sustained harmonic tones is also effective; and similarly, a *diminuendo* in sustained contexts can be achieved by releasing all but the harmonically essential tones. In every context, the relative effects of dynamic implication through articulation and legato and actual dynamic variation through sustained or detached textural elements must be weighed carefully.

A useful exercise in varied articulation of an absolutely constant texture and tempo is the reiteration of a single note or a heavy chord with varying accents, such as . The accents must be achieved through articulations (and perhaps minute adjustments of timing); there is no variation of texture to assist the player. Similarly, volume (sound mass) can be significantly varied with close or articulated reiteration of accompanimental chords such as often occur in J. S. Bach's transcriptions of Italian orchestral concerti.

Different degrees of sustain can vary the stress or even the apparent dynamic of a note followed by a rest, particularly in the bass; a longer note is more emphatic. When notes and rests alternate regularly, dynamic variety can be increased by holding the notes from minutely beyond their written length to somewhat short of it. Such dynamic tapering is especially effective when followed by a textural accent (Example IV-2a). The bass line in Example IV-2b can yield varied accents by slight prolongation or foreshortening of the single notes.

EXAMPLE IV-2.
J. S. Bach: a. Praeludium in E♭, mm.13-14.
b. Prelude in D, *WTC* I, mm.6-8.

When a loud or fierce quality is desired, the greater sonority that results from more or less sustained playing will often be more than compensated for by the strong accents, the edge to the sound, and the vitality that result from a more articulate or even choppy approach; this treatment is effective in the left-hand part of Example IV-3. Such playing is often useful in accompanying a large group of instruments and/or voices, when the harpsichord's rhythmic accent and support are its main virtues. Generally, brisk harpsichord writing, as occurs in orchestral-style movements or in music arranged from orchestral scores, often benefits from a basically detached style.

EXAMPLE IV-3.
Antoine Forqueray, *La Marella*, mm.1-5.

The sustained notes and chords that make up the accompanying parts in much Renaissance and early Baroque dance music are often merely rhythmic punctuation. They frequently benefit from a strongly detached rendition, even close to staccato at times, despite the long written values (see the left hand part in Example IV-4). Fast runs often gain brilliance and clarity from a slightly detached rendition.

EXAMPLE IV-4.
Giovanni Picchi, Passemezzo, mm.27-28.

A slightly detached or structured legato rendition is often successful in movements in which actual legato cannot be uniformly maintained. A representative case is the thick voicing of the harpsichord part in the first movement of J. S. Bach's Sonata in E for violin and harpsichord.

The variation in dynamics available through graded articulation in a constant texture is often useful for phrasing: the sonorous buildup and release helps to group notes. The accompaniment texture in Example IV-5a allows much manipulation, and the phrases are receptive to varied treatment. Note the buildup and thinning out in the last two measures, accompanied by a comparable increase and tapering of rhythmic energy in the top line. This variation can be reinforced by holding notes together from one beat to the next in heavy textures and by playing in a more detached fashion in the thin areas. Example IV-5b is even more open to this kind of treatment because the accompaniment is written with considerable dynamic shading. Careful shading from sustained to detached articulation can produce an extremely varied dynamic range. In most cases such accompanimental chords should not be relegated to a softer manual unless the instrument's balance absolutely requires it. A greater range of volume between closely reiterated and articulated chords is available if the sound is based in a full tone.

EXAMPLE IV-5.
D. Scarlatti: a. Sonata in E♭, K. 193, mm.58-65.
b. Sonata in D, K. 282, mm.15-22.

In accompanimental figures on the clavichord, reiterated chords and intervals, such as abound in eighteenth-century keyboard writing, are obviously open to considerable dynamic nuance. Such shading coupled with the instrument's sensitivity to articulation makes a wide palette of effects available. A soft cantilena can be accompanied by detached or even somewhat staccato chords or intervals, played *pianissimo*. This effect can be ravishingly delicate, but care must be taken with this kind of treatment. It can degenerate into a pointillistic quality rather than maintain an overall sustained texture.

❧ Overlegato

Overlegato is one of the most important means of extracting the full depth of sonority and singing tone from the harpsichord; in some ways it is analogous to the sustaining pedal of the piano. Its use on conjunct notes is most flexible in the higher ranges of the hapsichord, where the sustaining power decreases. Parallel passages appearing in different parts of the compass may require different treatment because of this factor. Overlegato on chord tones can be used more freely throughout the range. Saint Lambert discusses this technique, which is sometimes notated by slurs (*liaisons*); when the tones covered by a slur all belong to one chord:

> One plays all the notes that the slur covers and this is the effect of the slur: one holds all of these notes after playing them, although their value is expired, and one releases them only when it is time to release the last.[22]

Other comments and examples by Saint Lambert make clear that only harmonic tones, not passing tones, are held under a slur. Marpurg describes the same thing, and such slurs appear from time to time in the later literature. They are rarely indicated in earlier repertory, although slurs are one of the essentials in the notation of the unmeasured prelude.

Held chord tones and overlegato in general are important to resonance and variety of expression, and the fact that neither is frequently notated should not inhibit the player who is new to the harpsichord literature. Parts are often notated only in terms of part-writing, not sheer instrumental sound. The notation often requires filling out, not only with ornamentation and embellishment, but with instrumental subtleties not suited to notation because their precise application must vary between instruments and in different circumstances. Nonetheless, some eighteenth-century repertory is notated with a fair degree of completeness; the detailed notation of a composer such as François Couperin can be unusually revealing of instrumental technique.

EXAMPLE IV-6.
J.-P. Rameau, Allemande in e. a. m.1. b. mm.17-18.

Jean-Philippe Rameau, among others, occasionally indicates normal tone holding, either with note values or with a slur (see Example IV-6). A more famous example, and one which implies a normal practice of tone holding, is J. S. Bach's notation of François Couperin's "Les Bergeries." Example IV-7 compares the opening of the piece in the original notation and as Bach copied it. Couperin's carefully marked sustained tones were taken for granted by Bach, who apparently did not feel it necessary to mark them in such detail. Bach's approach is the most usual.

EXAMPLE IV-7.
F. Couperin, "Les Bergeries," *Ordre* 6, mm.1-3.
a. Original notation. b. As notated by J. S. Bach.

EXAMPLE IV-8.
a. J. S. Bach, Prelude in G, *WTC* II, mm.1-3.
b. D. Scarlatti, Sonata in F, K. 541, mm.21-23.
c. D. Scarlatti, Sonata in c, K. 526, mm.35-36, 86-88.

Bach's own writing is full of single lines that suggest two parts (Example IV-8a). The two "parts" can often be sustained against each other for maximum sonority; when they resolve into one the effect can be one of dynamic tapering. Similarly, the sonority of Example IV-8b can be considerably influenced by the degree to which the effective bass is held; treatment of the bass G is open to much variation. Scarlatti sometimes writes in tone holding in the first statement of a passage but leaves its realization to the player in subsequent occurrences (Example IV-8c). The longer that chord tones can be held over without compromising linear independence the more a texture is open to dynamic variation, depending on which tones and how many are sustained, and how long they are sustained.

The dividing line between sustaining chordal members and complete overlegato blurring can be a fine one. On many instruments, the high range in Example IV-9 will allow one to hold all the right-hand sixteenth notes. Particularly in a large room or hall, this seemingly extreme measure will not create confusion but merely cause a heightened ringing of the instrument. Some harpsichords will require a more selective sustaining: perhaps held chord tones, with the passing tones blurred into them but not held over, as Saint Lambert describes. Obviously, many adjustments are possible. In any case, the lower the range and the greater the sustaining capacity of the harpsichord, the greater will be the care required to prevent the resonant effect from degenerating into a mere morass of sound.

EXAMPLE IV-9.
L. Couperin, Allemande grave in F, mm.9-10.

EXAMPLE IV-10.
J. S. Bach, Fugue in c♯, *WTC* I, mm.77-79.

Rapid notes are often best de-emphasized by overlegato. Many ornaments and embellishment figures can sound explosive because of their rhythmic activity and succession of rapid attacks. Similarly, it is often effective to cover the notes preceding a leap with overlegato, especially for contrast if the leap is articulated, as in ⟨notation⟩. Selective use of overlegato ranges from softening the attacks of individual notes to submerging one part in favor of another more clearly rendered. Since sustaining the legato part may build up enough sonority to submerge the articulated line, some textures are not especially successful with this treatment.

Overlegato can often be used as the basic touch in *cantabile* music. One may begin from a general level of slight overlegato, sufficient to submerge the succession of plucks; even a uniform touch of this kind is successful in many contexts. (For instance, a uniform or varied overlegato could be used in Example IV-10. With the low range of the bass, a certain level of covering beyond a simple legato is desirable on some instruments for a *cantabile* quality.) Small groups of notes can be phrased by varying degrees of overlegato and legato, such as ♫♫ . (The bracketed slurs represent overlegato.) In an overlegato context, even small articulations are often enough to expose the attacks of the most emphatic notes; those least emphasized receive the greatest degree of overlegato.

Again, the exposing and covering of notes is a realization, in terms of harpsichord sound, of the varied dynamic levels heard in the player's imagination. The touch must be as varied as the music itself. The ironic point about playing in this manner is that, however delicate the nuances generally achieved or suggested, and however successful the control of submerged attacks and dynamic implication, the first note of a piece, or of a phrase following a pause, cannot be covered: it emerges at full volume, so to speak. The player is powerless to control this phenomenon in the realm of touch. Careful control of rhythmic flow and direction, however, can do much to ameliorate such situations. Control of rhythm can also make up for moments in which the movement of the music entirely overrides the sustaining power of the instrument and hence obviates the resources of overlegato.

Overlegato on the clavichord can lend an extra sheen to the sound. Since the attack of sustained tones can be varied dynamically, the clavichord's use of overlegato is even freer than the harpsichord's. Its function need not be limited to building up sonority and obscuring notes; it can also be used purely as a color device.

❧ Chords

The harpsichord, unlike the clavichord or piano, cannot voice chords by dynamic emphasis of one note over another. The only approach to such adjustment is by early release of one or another member of the chord. Chordal textures are nonetheless open to considerable variation in sonority. Releasing some members of a chord ahead of others can effect a *diminuendo* or a quickly dissipating accent. Notes added to chords beyond those indicated in the score (whether harmonic or nonharmonic; see also chapter 6) and released at once or gradually can also create accents and various dynamic effects. This area of playing is often beyond the limits of musical notation. Such extra, sonority-based notes depend so much on the circumstances of instrument, acoustic, and interpretation that they could hardly be specified in many scores. (A player's readiness and ability to vary texture develops naturally from experience in continuo playing.) A small additional accent, for instance, can sometimes be made by adding, briefly or for a sustained period, the fifth above the root of a chord notated in the bass. On climactic chords one might fill in several extra chordal tones, sounding them in a rapid arpeggio and perhaps releasing them almost immediately but in rapid succession. The latter effect can create a heavy, fast-diminishing gust of sound reminiscent of a full chord played on a bass gamba. Example IV-11 shows a written-in chord that suggests such treatment. (Indeed, the piece was originally written for the gamba.) The chord's heavy texture creates an accent, but the sound is too heavy and crude on many instruments if all members of the chord are sustained for their written duration.

EXAMPLE IV-11.
A. Forqueray, *La Boisson*, mm.25-26.

EXAMPLE IV-12.
J. S. Bach: a. Prelude in f, *WTC* II, mm.1-4.
b. Prelude in b♭, *WTC* I, m.22.

Nonsimultaneous releases can avoid abruptness in quiet passages. For instance, staggered release of the notes of the successive thirds in Example IV-12a prevents too sudden a cessation of sound and minimizes the slight click of the returning quills. Such releases are sometimes easily effected by rolling the hand off the keys. Chords can be released in the same manner, usually from bass to treble. Sometimes a violin-like holdover of the top note, just beyond the release of the other chord tones, is effective in creating a sudden *diminuendo*. Such a release of the diminished-seventh chord in Example IV-12b can sound rather wistful, and it also prevents the excessive noise and suddenness associated with the release of very full chords. Arpeggiation of a chord from bottom to top, with the releases following in the same order, soon or even immediately thereafter, can be highly accentual, either at chordal climaxes (Example IV-13a) or in accompanimental chords. In the latter case, holding the melody or even the melody and subsidiary right-hand parts against more detached chords in the left hand can be very effective. Variations of stress are possible by longer holding or a slightly more gradual break of the chords on accented beats. They are effective whether the melody or the right-hand part is to be legato and sustained, slightly detached, or, as is most frequent, a mixture of both. A texture open to a variety of such treatments is shown in Example IV-13b. (Arpeggiation is discussed in relation to timing in chapter 5 and to figuration in chapter 6.)

EXAMPLE IV-13.
a. J. S. Bach, Prelude in D, *WTC* I, mm.34-35.
b. G. Frescobaldi, *Five Gagliardas*, Gagliarda II,
mm.1-6.

🌻 Texture

Variety in legato and in releases is also very useful in balancing varied sonorities across the range of one registrational setting. The voicer can leave the bass range of a sonorous harpsichord to resound at its fullest if the player has learned to balance the different strengths and qualities of bass, mid-range, and treble by minute adjustments of legato or articulation. Again, one must begin by considering the overall sonority rather than relative linear emphases, although their most successful musical integration must be sought. In this case the instrument is truly instructing the player.

Some examples of the finest harpsichord writing, in terms of flexible texture that suggests variations in dynamics, are found in the music of Frescobaldi, Froberger, French composers of the seventeenth and eighteenth centuries, and the sonatas of Scarlatti. Such music is most suited to a beginning study of nuance on the instrument, as it is most easily manipulated. Scarlatti's music is particularly felicitous in this regard, and his style is often more accessible to the newcomer than those of the other composers mentioned. The player will readily grasp the dynamic and coloristic significance of Scarlatti's changes of range; surface rhythmic activity; imitations of guitar, drum, and voice; and gradual or sudden thinning and thickening of textures. Indeed, so skillful is the composer that many passages hardly require further manipulation by the player; but the effect is greater when such inherently flexible writing is performed on a sensitive harpsichord by a player whose touch and timing can extract the most from every textural nuance.

Other music is open to fine adjustments but offers fewer direct openings to the player. Many pieces require that one take advantage of the slightest variations in a constant texture to allow some breathing in the density of the writing. The player must always be on the alert for significant changes in texture, however minute.

EXAMPLE IV-14.
J. S. Bach, French Suite in c, Allemande, mm.5-7.

Example IV-14 illustrates such small textural nuances. A modulation to E♭ concludes in m.5. The music next turns to the dominant of G major, to cadence in that key at the double bar. At the juncture where the music begins its move to G major the bass rests for an eighth-note value (marked in the example by an *x*) and momentarily only one note is heard, the soprano E♭. This temporary thinness is significant as a changing point in tonal direction and a letup in the rather uniform texture. The low bass E♭ must not be prolonged into the ensuing rest; a minute retardation at this point, dwelling on the area of the rests, will make the most of this comparatively *piano* moment.

🌸 Slurs

Slurs are rarely indicated in most early keyboard literature, and it is sometimes difficult to judge whether a given slur marks an exception to usual practice or occurs despite the fact that it typifies usual procedures. Slurs may indicate note functions, suggest string bowings, delineate short motives, or show legato groupings; in some such cases they cannot be taken literally in their modern meaning. This is a large subject and cannot be dealt with extensively here; a few comments are offered below.

Slurs are most often shown in conjunction with ornaments and embellishing figures. This practice is typical from the seventeenth through the eighteenth century and recalls Nivers's and C. P. E. Bach's suggestions for legato on ornaments. The purpose of such slurs is perhaps less to specify legato than to clarify the function of embellishing notes. D'Anglebert, for instance, often slurs escape tones to the note preceding them: ♫ . Similarly, many slurs seem to signify a *diminuendo* on the notes they include rather than specific articulation of the group from surrounding notes. Context is the determining factor. Of course, many slurs are specifically articulatory, but the modern tendency to regard most slurs as articulatory is largely derived from the nineteenth-century habit of marking phrases by slurs. Interpreting early slurs in this manner is often anachronistic.

Slurs are a prominent feature of unmeasured preludes, in which they serve two main purposes: sometimes they show ornamental/embellishmental figures, which the unmeasured notation often makes necessary; but generally they serve as *liaisons*, described above. Occasionally in measured literature it is not clear whether a slur is intended as a *liaison*, sustaining the notes beyond their written values, or as a sign for legato. Often either interpretation is musically valid.

The study of early violin bowings and flute tonguings is helpful in understanding early approaches to articulation. However, it must be borne in mind that the harpsichord is naturally articulate in sound and sometimes needs to cover its attacks, whereas the flute and violin, with their naturally sustained tones, must sometimes work from the opposite end of the spectrum and devise means of ensuring clarity. Slurs reminiscent of violin bowings often appear in Baroque and classical keyboard music; a literal interpretation is not necessarily the intention behind the slurring, in the sense of creating an audible break around slurred groups. In many instances it seems more likely that the articulation realized on the keyboard should be equivalent to the effect of the violin bowing, which is often less specifically articulate than the literal meaning of the slur in keyboard terms. Donald Francis Tovey comments:

> Some things that violins can do are impossible on the pianoforte, and some things have quite a different meaning on different instruments. Thus in the first movement of [Beethoven's] *Eroica* Symphony the rhythm of [Example IV-15a] would lose all energy if the violinists bowed it as [shown in Example IV-15b].

EXAMPLE IV-15.
L. van Beethoven, *Eroica* Symphony, first movement, mm. 65-66. a. Original bowing. b. Variant bowing.

But on the pianoforte the latter form of slur is the only possible one. An attempt to separate the semiquavers from the following quavers would lead to a worse loss of energy than that which Beethoven's violin-bowing avoids. Yet Liszt, in his pianoforte arrangement of the *Eroica* Symphony, reproduces Beethoven's bowing on the assumption that no pianist will misunderstand it.[23]

Similarly, the frequently encountered slurring ♫♩ does not necessarily mean a sharp articulation at the bar line. Such slurs often suggest de-emphasis of the successive notes under the slur rather than specific articulation of the notes following it. Violinistic slurs were employed in keyboard music at least through the early nineteenth century. The source of this type of slurring should be recognized, so that too literal an interpretation does not defeat the intent of the notation.

Some slurs suggest the continuity available on the violin through the bowings they indicate. Mozart's Alberti bass figures, for instance, often slurred by the measure, seem to call for a sustained rendition rather than the choppiness of a literal realization in one-measure units. Similarly, in Example IV-16, the slurs recall string bowings and do not require articulation of quarter values. If any stress on them were necessary, it could be accomplished more gracefully with slight agogic accent.

EXAMPLE IV-16.
Johann Mattheson, Suite in A, Tocatine, mm.13-14.

EXAMPLE IV-17.
S. Scheidt, Passamezzo, Var. 8, "Imitatio violistica,"
mm.1-2.

Keyboard realization of some string-style slurs may involve time stresses at the beginning of the slur and/or overlegato on some or all of the ensuing notes under the slur, as much as actual articulation. Samuel Scheidt (1624) indicates the string origin of the slurs in Example IV-17 by labeling the passage "Imitatio violistica." Changing bow direction every four notes can produce dynamic accents rather than articulations *per se*, and the keyboard will make a poor imitation by markedly articulating between all slurred groups.

J. S. Bach sometimes uses similar slurring. Example IV-18 is representative and probably requires execution similar to the Scheidt example. The slurrings in Examples IV-19 and IV-20 also recall string bowings. Sometimes notes are emphasized by staccato, as in Example IV-19. These passages seem to imply slurring into the staccato notes across the bar line (cf. Tovey, above).

EXAMPLE IV-18.
J. S. Bach, Trio Sonata in e, first movement, mm.5-7.

EXAMPLE IV-19.
J. S. Bach, *Italian Concerto.* a. Presto, mm.59-64.
b. [Allegro], mm.14-16.

EXAMPLE IV-20.
J. S. Bach, Partita in b, Gigue, mm.33-34.

Bach rarely shows slurs in his keyboard music, in comparison to his other scores. Descending pairs are sometimes slurred (Example IV-21), and he occasionally uses the French *liaison* (Example IV-22).

EXAMPLE IV-21.
J. S. Bach, *Goldberg Variations,* Var. 15, m.1.

EXAMPLE IV-22.
J. S. Bach, Partita in e, Toccata, mm.21-23.

Bach occasionally employs slurs in a way that draws attention more to musical function than to specific articulations, just as d'Anglebert indicates ornamental function by a slur. Peter Williams has pointed out that in Bach's Passacaglia and Fugue in c for organ, the purpose of one of the few slurs is to mark the first variation whose motive begins on the beat rather than before it.[24] The slur is not really necessary, except to show that the rhythmic pattern is different in Variation 15 (see Example IV-23).

EXAMPLE IV-23.
J. S. Bach, Passacaglia and Fugue in c, motives from
Vars. 4, 5, and 15.

EXAMPLE IV-24.
J. S. Bach, Duet in a, mm.37-38.

Motives are sometimes slurred regardless of the bar line (Example IV-24). Slurring over the bar line into a strong beat is often ineffective and can be confusing given nonaccentual rhythms or chord changes; however, original slurs often cross the bar line into a beat or measure that is not particularly stressed.

François Couperin often slurs over the bar line, with both ornaments (Example IV-25a) and large intervals (Example IV-25b). That he did not regard these notated slurs as the only exceptions to a general "rule" of bar line articulation seems apparent from his frequent use of the sign ' at bar lines. This sign is introduced in Book III of his harpsichord pieces to mark phrase endings and breaths; it is often used to indicate phrases that span the bar line as well as those that concur with it. If one never slurred over a bar line, there would be no point in marking articulations there (Example IV-26). Example IV-27 shows similar slurrings of motives and ornaments in Couperin's keyboard works.

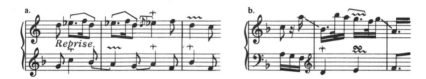

EXAMPLE IV-25.
F. Couperin: a. "Les Abeilles," *Ordre* 1, mm.9-11.
b. "Galliard-Boiteux," *Ordre* 18, mm.58-60.

EXAMPLE IV-26.
F. Couperin, "Les Vestales," *Ordre* 16, mm.65-66.

Slurs occasionally suggest *glissandi*, an interpretation that is further reinforced in Example IV-28 by the *Allegro* tempo and the *bravura* style.

Another kind of smooth cadence occurs in Johann Jakob Froberger's *Lamento* for Ferdinando IV, a piece in the delicate, rather free style that characterizes the composer's most personal compositions. Slurrings from the composer's autograph are shown in Example IV-29. Most of them are typical of standard usage: ornamental figures and flourishes receive slurs to show their function and legato treatment (Examples IV-29a, b). The conclusion is unusual, however. The final measure (Example IV-29c) abandons the C meter and any real rhythm; it is slurred in a way that suggests, along with the note stemming, that the hands alternate by groups of four notes. The hand alternation, the dissolving meter, the lack of consistency between pitch

EXAMPLE IV-27.
F. Couperin: a. "Le Rossignol en amour," *Ordre* 14,
mm.14-16. b. "L'Amphibie," *Ordre* 24, mm.17-19.
c. "Les Brinborins," *Ordre* 24, mm.1-2, 5-6.
d. "Rigaudon," *Ordre* 2, mm.1-2.
e. "La Nanète," *Ordre* 1, mm.24-26.

EXAMPLE IV-28.
D. Scarlatti, Sonata in C, K. 487, mm.159-65.

EXAMPLE IV-29.
J. J. Froberger, *Lamento*. a. m.1. b. mm.10-11. c. m.25.

pattern and slur pattern, and the offbeat pattern of slurs (♪♫♫♫ ...) all strongly suggest that a linking of each unit of four, rather than of articulated groups, is the intent of the slurs. They indicate legato groupings within each hand, and the alternation of hands assures a smooth ascent. Certainly, if articulations were desired, the use of alternating hands would be a clumsy way to achieve them, especially in so delicate a passage. For the player, the slurs also reinforce the forward drive (however leisurely the pace) of the final ascending scale, whose beaming is displaced by one sixteenth note from the preceding meter of the piece.

   C. P. E. Bach's employment of slurs is not unusual for his time, but his use of the word *tenuto* (abbreviated *ten.*) on notes to be held for their full length is not often encountered. *Tenuto* is specified in several situations. Most frequently it is found on notes whose weak metric placement would otherwise suggest early release to lighten the sound (Example IV-30a, b). This evening out of metric stress also occurs in passages like Example IV-31, in which all beats seem to receive equal emphasis and a sustained sound in the right hand opposes the detached left-hand notes. This kind of metric evenness recalls Beethoven's use of *sforzando* markings for the same purpose.

EXAMPLE IV-30.
C. P. E. Bach: a. Rondo in a, mm.1-3. b. Rondo in c, m.46.

EXAMPLE IV-31.
C. P. E. Bach, Rondo in F, mm.217-20.

   Sometimes notes in a strong metric position receive special emphasis through *tenuto*. In Example IV-32a, the marking is somewhat redundant, but it is necessary in Example IV-32b, where it is unlikely that the second beat would receive durational (and perhaps dynamic) stress without it.

EXAMPLE IV-32.
C. P. E. Bach: a. Rondo in B♭, mm.25-29.
b. Rondo in E♭, mm.60-62.

❧ Articulation and Ensemble Playing

When the harpsichord is played by itself, articulatory stresses and legato blurring can give a compelling illusion of dynamic stresses, especially when allied with subtle time inflections (the subject of chapter 5). These delicate dynamic suggestions are easily overbalanced, however, when the harpsichord's effects of implication are heard in contrast with instruments (or voices) capable of actual dynamic shading. The use of much articulatory stress is likely only to render the harpsichord less audible. Since the instrument is frequently softer than the other parts of the ensemble, many articulatory stresses (and consequent reduction in sonority) may further reduce its overall dynamic level and prevent the notes themselves from being heard clearly. (Of course, this does not matter when the harpsichord's only purpose is to provide rhythmic support for a large ensemble with full chords on strong beats.) When playing with other instruments, the obbligato harpsichord is often heard to best advantage if its stresses are made through time, in coordination with the other players. The continuo player can best achieve variations in volume by changes in fullness of texture. Such treatment is preferable to a constant texture using implied dynamics, which are of course useful, but rarely make their point in the overall ensemble. (Articulatory stresses can, of course, be advantageously employed with respect to varied textures.) *Piano* will benefit from thin textures and legato or near-legato; *forte* will use heavy textures (up to as many parts as can be managed by the two hands, as shown by sources from various nations and periods) and a wider range of articulation and legato.

The player realizing a figured bass has an advantage over the player of an obbligato part, in that a continuo part realized on the spot can be adapted to particular performance circumstances. Nonetheless, discreet textural adjustments can be made in obbligato parts, just as in solos.

5

Timing

TIME IS THE QUANTITATIVE ASPECT OF
music, whereas articulation and dynamics are qualitative elements. Distribution of musical materials in time contains inherent points of stress and
repose: the listener automatically assigns more or less importance to notes
according to length and context. For instance, a long note will stand out in
an otherwise uniform context of short notes. Inherent time stresses also
depend on patterns emerging among notes of varied length. Patterns co-
here on many simultaneous levels: the surface rhythmic groups, the metric
pulse of beats below the surface rhythm, and larger units of beats in
phrases, sentences, and paragraphs. Without exploring beyond this metric/
rhythmic frame in any work, cross-currents of rhythm and meter may be
found when patterns of these elements admit of more than one grouping.
Stresses inherent in harmonic patterns and melodic contours may eliminate some metric or rhythmic grouping possibilities and/or admit others.
The qualitative elements of articulation and dynamics can provide further
reinforcement to musically inherent groupings or create new cross-
currents.

In dealing with this many-layered web, the player must decide which
groupings are unequivocal in the music and which are open to varied interpretation, as well as which must be brought out by the player and which
make their points automatically. Each element contains its own hierarchies.
Those in the music (harmony, melody, meter, rhythm, notated performance
directions) as well as those at the player's discretion (choices of tempo,
rhythmic variation, agogics, articulation, legato, dynamics, and instrument)
will modify and influence one another in endless permutations. The relative
importance of adjustments of timing, articulation, and actual or implied dynamics fluctuates constantly. In some performance circumstances, expression may rely more on delicate timing than on articulatory finesse; another
situation may reverse their importance in the same composition. More fre-

quently, these elements work together but influence different areas: delineation of different beat strengths may depend entirely on articulation rather than on any time adjustment, while the latter is reserved to bring out larger aspects of phrasing. Articulation, timing, and dynamics may also mitigate one another's effect, the player allowing them to work at cross-purposes to create a rich palette of effects.

❧ Tempo

The tempo chosen for any movement will vary with different interpretations, different performance sites, and the nature and resonance of the instrument used. The tempo that is precisely "right" for a piece is that which is best suited to other factors of a particular interpretation. A successful tempo allows fullest expression of all the relationships that the performer wishes to bring out in the music. It is the time frame allowing events to unfold at the pace that puts their proportions in clearest relief; and it permits the most effective realization of dynamics implied by textural variations or time inflections. Judicious selection of tempo also allows the particular instrument its fullest range of articulation and legato, depending on the textures and rhythms of the music, the decay rate of the instrument's sonority, and the resonance of the room. One should experiment with the fastest and slowest rates that allow realization of a given conception. Apart from its relationship to tone and articulation, a fast tempo as opposed to a slow one may allocate vastly different distributions of weight to certain passages, particularly to reiterated phrases and sequences. At a fast speed, an entire set of phrase iterations or sequential statements may emerge as one unit, standing in relief against other large units. At a slower tempo, each separate statement of the phrase or sequence will tend to acquire its own weight and be open to more individually varied treatment. For instance, the tempo for many Scarlatti sonatas depends on whether the player intends reiterated phases to emerge as one block or separately.

The selection of a tempo can also affect the precise degree of rhythmic acuity or assimilation in some passages. "Fast" tempi usually accommodate assimilation more gracefully than do slower ones, but the choice must be made consciously: technical difficulties are often eased by slight rhythmic assimilation that may be musically out of place. (This is one reason the fast speeds are often nominally "easier" than slower tempi.) Certain kinds of rhythmic shaping, whether involving sharpened or assimilated rhythms, are best managed at relatively faster or slower tempi depending on the individual situation.

❀ Instrument, Acoustic, and Articulation

In earlier centuries, keyboard instruments, and music generally, were heard in a far more resonant environment than is usual today. The room in which an instrument is heard strongly affects its sonority; and for the clavichord's low volume and the harpsichord's natural dryness, a resonant room has considerable advantage. It heightens the available range of nonlegato playing and only slightly inhibits extremes of overlegato. Obviously, a dry room will tolerate faster tempi better than will a highly reverberant space. In setting a tempo for a resonant acoustic, however, the danger of blurring a few passages at a high speed is less important than selecting the tempo that allows the greatest variation of relative sonorities. Sensitivity to textural nuance can counteract the effect of what may at first appear to be too slow or fast a speed. If a brilliant effect is sought in a live room, an even, well-maintained tempo will appear faster than one that, although in fact more rapid, is treated to much time adjustment, or whose rapid notes blur into larger impulses altogether. For languishing pieces in a resonant hall, there is a temptation to select too slow a tempo; the *affect* should be communicated through means other than an excessively slow speed, which will not allow sufficient buildup of sonority for real legato or overlegato. On the other hand, the use of overlegato simply to allow an effect of uniform smoothness rather than selective blurring will sometimes necessitate a tempo slower than might otherwise be selected. The resonance of particular (usually low) notes or ranges may suggest lingering on certain passages more on some instruments than on others. Variations in resonance across the range of an instrument can suggest differing treatment of the same passage when it is reiterated at a different pitch level. Interaction among the variables of desired effect, tempo, time inflection, instrumental attack, sustain, and acoustic must be weighed constantly by the player. Depending on variations among these factors, vastly different solutions must sometimes be found to produce the same musical effect.

❀ Tempo and Meter

The relationship of tempo to meter is of course important to music generally. The perception of beats in music places certain bounds on the range of tempo applicable to a given music: if the time signature indicates quarter-note beats, speeds below a certain rate will tend to suggest eighth notes as the beat level, rather than quarters; faster speeds may imply halves. Perception of the grouping of notes into beat units can also be affected by small rhythmic inflections or by articulation: the grouping ♩♩ stresses quarter notes, while ♫♫ stresses halves. Perception of beats in a particular tempo also varies with the individual listener. Some hear a given value as the pulse within a wider latitude of tempo than do others.

It appears that in Renaissance music, a fundamental tempo was represented by the *tactus*, a basic pulse rate. Various permutations of the mensural system of rhythmic notation could derive different speeds from their varied proportional relationship to this standard tempo. Although the degree to which this theory extended into practice is questionable, remnants of the system survived into the seventeenth and eighteenth centuries. Certain time signatures inherited from Renaissance notation and the prevalence of particular rhythmic values continued to imply tempo, at least to the extent of suggesting a certain range of speed. For instance, Girolamo Frescobaldi (1624) equates time signatures and note values with tempo—the larger the denominator of the signature, the faster the pace:

> in the groups of three or six, if they are long values one should bring them out slowly; if in smaller values, a little faster; if of three semiminims, faster; if of six against four, one may give their rhythm by playing in a lively measure.[1]

The music referred to by this commentary shows time signatures with corresponding measure contents as follows, presented here in apparent order of tempo from slowest to fastest: o$\frac{3}{2}$ with ○○○; ₵3 with ♩♩♩; 3 with ♩♩♩; and $\frac{6}{8}$ with ♩♩♩♩♩♩, apparently accented in two ♩. beats. Depending on context, these signatures may offer approximate ranges of tempo or, in relation to one another, exact proportions.[2]

The relationship between tempo and time signature was not an exact one during the Baroque. The subject crops up in many composers' prefaces and performance manuals throughout the seventeenth and eighteenth centuries. These suggest that time signatures often constitute only a rough guide to tempo. The authors are usually more concerned with the feeling of pulse that a signature and its range of tempo must convey than with fixed rates of speed. One of the lengthiest and clearest accounts of Baroque ideas on tempo, pulse, and meter is included in Johann Philipp Kirnberger's *Die Kunst des reinen Satzes in der Musik*. Although Kirnberger, a pupil of J. S. Bach, wrote during the 1770s, some of his remarks show him to stand in conscious reaction against many late-century tendencies. His aesthetic point of reference and the practices he describes are of the high Baroque.

Like Frescobaldi, Kirnberger regards time signatures as signifying tempo:

> Regarding meter, those having larger values, like alla breve, 3/2, and 6/4 meter, have a heavier and slower tempo than those of smaller values, like 2/4,

3/4, and 6/8 meter, and these in turn are less lively than 3/8 or 6/16 meter. Thus, for example, a loure in 3/2 meter has a slower tempo than a minuet in 3/4 meter, and the latter is in turn slower than a passepied in 3/8 meter. Regarding note values, dance pieces involving sixteenth and thirty-second notes have a slower tempo than those that tolerate only eighth and at most sixteenth notes as the fastest note values in the same meter. Thus, for example, a sarabande in 3/4 meter has a slower tempo than a minuet, even though both are written in the same meter.

Thus the *tempo giusto* is determined by the meter and by the longer and shorter note values of a composition. Once the young composer has a feeling for this, he will soon understand to what degree the adjectives largo, adagio, andante, allegro, presto, and their modifications larghetto, andantino, allegretto, and prestissimo add to or take away from the fast or slow motion of the natural tempo. He will soon be able not only to write in every type of tempo, but also in such a way that this tempo is captured quickly and correctly by the performers.[3]

These general characters [of meters] are defined even more specifically by the particular note value that prevails and by rules that determine progression by larger or smaller intervals. The character of 3/4 meter is entirely different when quarter notes are used almost exclusively throughout than when many eighths and even smaller values occur, and when it progresses mostly by small intervals than when leaps occur more often.[4]

The prevalent note values thus influence both the mood (weighty or light) and the precise tempo assigned to a particular instance of a given meter. This principle was apparently so well understood that use of words to specify tempo was not always necessary. On the other hand, Saint Lambert comments

The signs [time signatures] then show the tempo of the pieces only very imperfectly; and musicians being aware of this fault often add to [i.e., supplement] the sign in pieces they have composed, one of these words, LENTEMENT, GRAVEMENT, LEGEREMENT, GAYEMENT, VÎTE, FORT VÎTE, and similar ones, thus to supplement the powerlessness of the signs, to express their intentions.[5]

For Saint Lambert and doubtless many others, general usage of time signatures was not as clear as Kirnberger felt it was or ought to be. In any case, time words were used in two ways, to reinforce the general pace and mood supposedly set by the time signature alone and/or to modify the meaning of the signature, as when the word *andante* changes the primary and secondary pulses of 4/4 from quarter and half notes to eighths and quarters. Even for Kirnberger, the exact tempo that might be assigned to a time signature was apparently less important than the proper rhythmic accent and feeling the pulse on the proper values.

Kirnberger describes the characteristic tempo and accentual feeling of many time signatures. For example, he regards 3/4 as the most variable sign with respect to tempo:

> Its natural tempo is that of a minuet, and in this tempo it does not tolerate many sixteenth notes, even less thirty-second notes, in succession. However, since it assumes all degrees of tempo from the adjectives adagio, allegro, etc., all note values that fit this tempo can be used, depending on the rate of speed.[6]

The meter 4/4 (C) is open to less variation. Kirnberger differentiates between two varieties, distinguished by their fastest note values:

> Large 4/4 time is of extremely weighty tempo and execution and, because of its emphatic nature, is suited primarily to church pieces, choruses, and fugues. Eighth and a few sixteenth notes in succession are its fastest note values. To distinguish it from small 4/4 time, it should be designated by 4/4 instead of C. The two meters have nothing in common except for their signatures.
> Small 4/4 time has a more lively tempo and a far lighter execution. It tolerates all note values up to sixteenth notes and is used very often in all styles.[7]

He comments that "fast meters" (those with large denominators) were already out of fashion at the time he wrote, and laments that fact at the end of his description of 6/16:

> [6/16] differs greatly from 6/8 meter in the hurried nature of its tempo and the lightness of its execution. J. S. Bach and Couperin have written some of their pieces in 6/16 meter, not without good reason. Who does not know the Bach fugue at (a) . . . ? [See Example V-1.] If this theme is rewritten as at (b), the tempo is no longer the same, the gait is much more ponderous, and the notes, particularly the passing notes, are emphasized too much; in short, the expression of the piece as a whole suffers and is no longer the one given to it by Bach. If this fugue is to be performed correctly on the keyboard, the notes must be played lightly and without the least pressure in a fast tempo; this is what 6/16 meter requires. On the violin, pieces in this and other similarly light meters are to be played just with the point of the bow; however, weightier meters require a longer stroke and more bow pressure. The fact that these

EXAMPLE V-1.
J. S. Bach, Fugue in F, *WTC* II, mm.1-4. a. Original.
b. Rewritten in 6/8.

and several other meters ... are considered superfluous and obsolete today indicates either that good and correct execution has been lost or that an aspect of expression which is easy to obtain only in these meters is entirely unknown to us.[8]

🌸 Dance

For an understanding of tempo and particularly rhythmic accentuation, it is important that the player be familiar with Renaissance and Baroque dances—at least acquainted with their typical time signatures and rhythmic patterns. The influence of the dance goes far beyond music intended for dancing and stylized pieces bearing dance titles. Many musical contexts include patterns typical of certain dances; this usage extends from the Renaissance well into the classical period. Recognition of dances and sensitivity to the phrasing of the individual types (and their subdivisions) can be achieved by playing and comparing many examples of each variety. The study of extant choreographies and their execution is of immense help, especially regarding ranges of tempo and rhythmic accentuation.[9] The performance of instrumental dances is often more influenced by dance accent than by tempo *per se*. Many of the stylized dances in art music are not intended for actual dancing, and sometimes the musical complexity requires a slower tempo than might be suitable for dancing. Kirnberger's comments on the interrelationship of tempo and prevalent note values (pp.101-102) bear out the danger of overgeneralizing as to tempo. Certainly a keyboard sarabande with many elaborate embellishments should not necessarily be heard at a tempo appropriate for one that is danced. The latter, if presented in a choreography with its own music, usually shows a simple tune in perhaps quarter- and eighth-note values. However, the two sarabandes can be accentuated in the same way. (Choreographies and their music sometimes differ in accentual points; for instance, a hemiola suggested by dance steps may not be mirrored in the music.)

The relationship of tempo to dance steps depends to some extent on the individual dance and its choreography. Baroque choreographies often varied; Renaissance dances showed more stability. In the latter, each dance (pavane, galliard, branle, etc.) had its own fundamental steps and step sequence, whose usual variations were only elaborations superimposed upon the basic pattern. In Baroque court dance, on the other hand, all the dances were constructed from a common repertory of single and complex steps. The steps themselves are not a constant and invariable guide to tempo, for the same ones appear in various permutations and combinations in different dances of varying accent and tempo. The appropriate tempo for executing a given step also depends on the size of step taken.

Baroque dances appeared in many different choreographies; those for any one dance type would have general characteristics in common but could differ in many details. Thus, tempo and accent patterns were more standardized in Renaissance dance than in the Baroque. The interrelation of musical and dance accent exhibited more constancy in Renaissance dance than in Baroque dance, where these factors could often work at variance. (This aspect is apparent from choreographies whose music survives with them.)

Each Baroque dance is open to variations of mood, although a given type usually fits within a general range of character: French sarabandes and courantes are noble, rigaudons and bourrées are light and even frivolous, etc. According to Johann Mattheson, each type contains subdivisions according to usage. For instance, he divides the sarabande into categories for dancing, singing, and instrumental performance:

> This species expresses no passion other than *ambition* [*Ehrsucht*]. There are, however, the following differences between the kinds listed above: the danced *sarabande* must be even more narrow [-minded?] and bombastic [*enger und hochtrabender*] than the others. There must be no passages of runs, since *grandezza* despises them and insists on seriousness.[10]

Several Baroque and *galant* sources contain catalogues of dances, describing general categories of tempo and mood. Whether the typical dance patterns appeared specifically as dances or as, say, a fugue, the rhythmic variety and characteristics were to be brought out and contrasted to the maximum. Mattheson describes the courante tune "Hope" (Example V-2), calling attention to contrasts between phrases and varieties of mood:

> Up to the first half of the third measure, marked by a cross, there is something courageous in the melody. From there to the first half of the eighth measure, marked by a similar cross, yearning is expressed, especially in the last three and one half of these measures and by means of the repeated cadence to the fifth below. Finally toward the end, i.e. in the ninth measure, there is some joy.[11]

EXAMPLE V-2.
Anonymous, Courante "Hope."

Mattheson's description is highly subjective, but his intent to characterize the different turns of the melody is clear. Quantz makes the same point in more general terms:

Since in the majority of pieces one passion constantly alternates with another, the performer must know how to judge the nature of the passion that each idea contains and constantly make his execution conform to it.[12]

Kirnberger echoes Mattheson, calling attention to the diversity of type within each dance category:

In order to acquire the necessary qualities for a good performance, the musician can do nothing better than diligently play all sorts of characteristic dances. Each of these dance types has its own rhythm, its phrases of equal length, its accents at the same places in each motif . . . finally one easily recognizes in a long piece the various and intermingling rhythms, phrases, and accents.

. . . it is impossible to compose or to perform a fugue well if one does not know every type of rhythm; and therefore, because this study is neglected today, music has sunk from its former dignity, and one can no longer endure fugues, because through miserable performance which defines neither phrase nor accents, they have become a mere chaos of sounds.

Though we have said above that each dance melody has its own distinctive character, still one must not assume that the same kind of dance has the same nuance in all countries. Moreover, a trained ear will easily distinguish a Viennese minuet from one of Prague or Dresden. The Dresden minuets are the best, as the French are the worst.

Often a dance has even an entirely different character according to the nations that have adopted it: the courante, which in Germany and France has a serious, firm character, is in Italy gay and light.[13]

🌻 Tempo Modifications

Perhaps more important than the selection of absolute tempo is the subtle adjustment of the basic speed in the interests of phrasing and dynamic suggestion, although one tempo may be more suited than another to relative structuring of agogic accents. Time stresses are often the most effective way of delineating phrases and subphrases. Early authorities often discuss bringing out phrase contour in terms of agogic accent; the elements of strong and weak, rhythmic inequality and rubato generally, and innumerable other small variations in timing (see below) are all for the purpose of bringing out the hierarchies of subphrase, phrase, and larger units. Kirnberger describes good performance as that which clarifies such structural elements:

A musical composition, like a speech, consists of several periods (or sections). And as in a speech these periods are constructed of sentences, these in turn of words, which are made up of longer and shorter syllables, so the musical period likewise consists of phrases, these of motifs (or phrase members), which are made up of longer and shorter notes that either are only passing in effect or have their own characteristic stronger and weaker accents.

If a speech is to achieve its proper effect, it must be delivered well; and likewise, a musical composition attains its beauty only through a correct and good performance.[14]

Adjustments of timing can contribute to phrasing by modifications that affect tempo, meter, or rhythm, or imply dynamic changes, or both. Very minute, hardly perceptible inflections can create small accents and/or dynamic implications. This is often crucial on the dynamically rigid harpsicord, but the player must be aware in any context of the point at which rhythmic inflections become striking enough to be perceived as such, and how the continuum from subtle to overt rhythmic adjustment relates to other expressive elements. Rhythmic distortion results if one exceeds a certain limit of dynamic implication through agogic accent. Some very strong rhythmic inflections require real dynamic variation, or they will sound forced in the actually flat dynamic level. Extremes of timing often work most successfully with varied musical textures that supply contrast in real dynamic terms.

Modifications of tempo should work in conjunction with actual or implied dynamics and effects of articulation and legato. The relative importance of these elements is in continual flux. On the whole, the larger the performance space or the more a passage depends on holding notes together for a full sonority, the greater is the importance of time stresses in proportion to articulation and legato.

Even when the instrument is not capable of dynamic variation, it is important that the player think in dynamic terms and be able to imply dynamic nuances by other means. Subphrases, phrases, and larger units are shaped by changing harmonies, melodic contour, metric/rhythmic activity, changing textures, and ornamentation. These are active, fluctuating elements both in themselves and in their relationships. A dramatic change in harmony or harmonic rhythm, a rising or falling line, a change in rhythmic energy—all are "dynamic" in the larger sense, and their expression through contrasts and gradations in volume is often a natural musical response to such elements. The player should cultivate sensitivity to these "structural dynamics" and to their instrumental realization in terms of the aggregate of agogic and articulatory stresses, legato groupings, and rhythmic variation, as well as dynamic changes, even on instruments that, like the clavichord, allow dynamic flexibility. On the harpsichord, a rhythmically unyielding performance will hardly bring out the full possibilities of the instrument, but time stresses must be carefully integrated into the musical structure and in relation to other expressive means. Unlike the clavichord, the harpsichord cannot compensate dynamically for errors made in time stresses; indiscriminate use of "expressive" effects without a clear conception of their use is one of its chief dangers. Even when a mistake is made in allocating emphasis, the player must be ready to follow through on the implications of that error. Otherwise there will be no logical continuity of phrase.

Timing must work together with articulation and legato as means of phrasing and expression. Individual players and even instruments may lean toward one or the other as primary expressive means. Such preferences depend on personal disposition and musical and acoustic circumstance. A division of elements has been necessary between this and the preceding chapter for purposes of discussion, but these factors, whatever their balance, remain in continual fluctuation in actual practice, together forming innumerable permutations. These interlocking dependencies depend entirely on individual musical circumstances. Timing, articulation and legato, and actual dynamic stresses can all reinforce one another, but there is an obvious danger of excess when two or three such stress devices are used simultaneously. One or another, or all, must usually be moderated; and in the ranges of stress that each element receives there are, again, many possible permutations. For instance, will legato help or hinder careful timing for rhythmic drive in a given passage? One element can also undermine another, to provide further expressive shadings. An example is treatment of timing (straightforward or even hurrying) to modify articulatory or dynamic stressing. Again, it is the clavichord's extreme receptivity to all such permutations that makes it perhaps the supremely expressive keyboard instrument. The possible variations among agogic accent, articulation, legato, built-in textural variations, and registration constitute the harpsichord's dynamic range, from *sforzandi* (employing several stress elements) to the most neutral playing. Unlike a true dynamic range, this continuum shifts with musical circumstance.

Whether or not timing is the dominant factor in a given context, all adjustments of time depend on careful preparation and a steady basis. This is true whether the adjustment is a single agogic accent or a large-scale alteration in tempo. Slight bending of the time in advance of the larger emphasis on the stressed point avoids confusion for the listener. Time may be bent, but should rarely be broken. Such preparation is necessary for perhaps all but the slightest of agogic inflections and' should be in proportion to the strength of the accent. An agogically stressed downbeat or a massive change of tempo is prepared through the subdivisions of the preceding upbeat or group of beats. Time variations depend on adjustment of offbeat notes; whether the preparation requires the time of a single beat or group, subsidiary beats are more flexible and active than main beats, and subdivisions of beats are the most flexible of all. Treatment of offbeats and subsidiary beat divisions determines the placement of downbeats and the degree of accent they receive.

However far-reaching, time inflections lose their meaning if not made in reference to a governing tempo. The overall proportion of agogics depends on maintaining a sense of one fundamental pace, however frequently the tempo may depart from it. Time inflections should also be proportioned to one another; a small-level inflection must not be made so broadly as to be confused with a major stress of greater structural significance. Just as dynamic expression involves small-scale inflection and large-scale contrast, so timing operates on many levels. Playing that ignores the larger levels in favor of individual beat stresses can often sound mannered, losing continuity and sense of phrase; for instance, time stress placed on all statements of a brief figure or characteristic rhythm can lose focus on the larger arrangements of that figure. Too uniform a stress eventually loses even its small-level significance. On the level of the measure, also, uniformly styled inflection of strong-weak patterns can easily become sing-songy and meaningless. (This is especially the case with motoric pieces with entirely uniform surface rhythm.) Concentration on the large levels exclusively can make the music sound rushed and lacking in focus, in that too few musical points of arrival are dwelt upon sufficiently.

Just as the written page presents a frame of general tempo, meter, rhythm, and inherent harmonic and melodic stresses, so must the player set up a well-balanced scheme of relative performance stresses for the aural presentation of the written framework. Although time stresses all are relative, excessively free playing can cause time adjustments to lose much of their meaning. The more adjustments made, the more they must conform to overall proportions. The freer one's playing, the more necessary are a sure grasp of the salient arrival points and phrasing of a composition and the ability to organize them into a cohesive whole. It is a useful exercise to play a work (whether the piece is new or well known to the player) with completely uninflected, neutral timing, so that the music may suggest the places to flex the time. Economy in time stress allows more significance to the time emphases that are allowed; one rarely needs to adjust constantly.

Obviously, these remarks apply mainly to movements or sections that are founded on a single basic tempo. Again, the best foundation tempo is that which most readily allows one to bring out the musical groupings and articulations that the player perceives. (One and the same speed may seem too slow, too fast, or appropriate depending on the player's manipulation of phrasing through modifications of time, articulation, and so forth.) Even free, rhapsodic works of episodic construction (many toccatas, for example, or unmeasured preludes) require some kind of time frame, but it may operate mainly on the level of phrase and phrase group. Music whose overall structure is loose can often assimilate freer treatment than can highly organized works. (Obvious examples for contrast are a Frescobaldi toccata, with its typical "patchwork" construction, and a Bach fugue, with all of its impulses deriving from a few motivic fragments.) Episodic pieces rarely show a large-level hierarchy of impulses, so each phrase or phrase group can absorb large time adjustments, which make them entities in themselves to some degree. In tightly hierarchical structures, the impulse of each phrase and all larger groupings must relate to the whole.

EXAMPLE V-3.
C. P. E. Bach, Variations on the Folia. a. Var. 8,
mm.1-3. b. Var. 11, mm.1-7.

Careful proportioning of stress and maintenance of a fundamental pace allow broader and more effective agogic accent than is successful with looser time organization; and larger phrase groups can be related through a single impulse. Such sensitive timing often provides effective dynamic suggestion. In terms of overall timing, a phrase begun slightly early will have a louder effect, especially if, as in Example V-3a, the phrases have been clearly delineated and make up a rhythmic sequence. The *fortissimo* indication for m.3 is reinforced by a minutely early attack on the chord; such treatment must be proportioned to the time distribution made in the preceding phrases. The sudden dynamic changes in Example V-3b can probably be effected more by timing than by actual variations in volume, even on a dynamically flexible instrument. Some of them are reminiscent of Türk's illustration of irregular stresses conveyed by dynamic marks (Example V-7), and their realization in purely dynamic terms can easily sound mannered. (In a related way, many of Beethoven's *sforzando* indications merely signify equality of beat stress in contrast to normal metric accents.) Adjustment of timing for delicate dynamic stresses is probably what C. P. E. Bach had in mind in the following well-known passage:

If the Lessons are played on a harpsichord with two manuals, only one manual should be used to play detailed changes of *forte* and *piano*. It is only when entire passages are differentiated by contrasting shades that a transfer may be made. This problem does not exist on the clavichord, for on it all varieties of loud and soft can be expressed with an almost unrivalled clarity and purity.[15]

Time adjustments are of two main sorts: variation in the timing of one or more lines against an unyielding metric/rhythmic background (true *rubato*); and variation of timing in all parts, e.g., *accelerando* and *ritardando*. Both categories are of course open to adjustments ranging from the obvious and deliberate to those so subtle that they escape the listener's notice. The essence of devices such as the latter form of timing and certain effects of legato and articulation is to produce their effects unobtrusively. However "artificially" the player achieves his musical ends, the means must sound natural to the listener. Again, a device that draws much attention to itself detracts from expression. The player must be aware of what the instrument and music do naturally without underlining in performance, what expressive devices can be made to appear natural, and at what point the player's manipulation of material intrudes itself unfavorably on the listener.

🌸 Strong and Weak

Most music depends largely on alternations of strong and weak in terms of metric and rhythmic values, harmonic stress, melodic movement, phrasing, and, often, ornaments and textural variation. In Renaissance and Baroque keyboard music these elements often work congruently. Baroque theorists describe strong and weak time elements in terms of beats and their relative stresses within measures of different meters. For instance, 4/4 contains one primary, one secondary, and two weak beats per measure; the first beat is the strongest and the fourth the weakest. These descriptions tally essentially with current teaching on the nature of different meters. The early treatises discuss rhythm, meter, and time signatures only from a general perspective and it is a mistake to apply their elementary accounts of, for instance, beat stress in time signatures, in a wholesale manner to actual music. Important dissonances, for example, often fall on weak beats, which may then require more weight than a textbook description would suggest. Often enough, though, the music seems to be composed with a particular regard for the bar line, and on this basis many pieces show subtle rhythmic puns and regroupings.

Various kinds of accent are dealt with by early writers, but when speaking of meter and rhythm they are likely to describe stress in nonspecific terms or in reference to dynamics or time. Time stress seems most frequently to be described or implied, but whether all references to lengthening beats actually refer to time accent is questionable. With some authors, calling beats "long" and "short" may be equating them with long and short syllables in poetry, which are not necessarily lengthened in time but can be stressed by other means as well. In music, the degree and manner of stress should be varied as much as in good spoken delivery, an analogy often made by early writers. Quantz's instructions for bringing out "good" beats unequivocally describes time stress:

> Here I must make a necessary observation concerning the length of time each note must be held. You must know how to make a distinction in execution between the *principal notes*, ordinarily called *accented* or in the Italian manner, *good* notes, and those that pass, which some foreigners call *bad* notes. Where it is possible, the principal notes always must be emphasized more than the passing. In consequence of this rule, the quickest notes in every piece of *moderate tempo*, or even in the *Adagio*, though they seem to have the same value, must be played a little unequally, so that the stressed notes of each figure, namely the first, third, fifth, and seventh, are held slightly longer than the passing, namely the second, fourth, sixth, and eighth, although this lengthening must not be as much as if the notes were dotted.[16]

Quantz then describes the circumstances and exceptions to this practice, which is that of French inequality, discussed below.

Other authors' accounts may refer to "lengthening" in terms of poetic syllables, but at first glance they often appear to be speaking in terms of actual time stress. Thus, Perrine (1680) remarks that in "all sorts" of lute pieces, the first beats or the first beat divisions of the measure must be made longer than the others.[17] Etienne Loulié (1696) states that in duple meter, "the first and third quarters of each measure are longer than the second and fourth, although they are marked equally, in whatever meter it may be."[18] Kirnberger refers to pressure (*Druck*) on notes to be stressed and to lack of pressure on unstressed notes, as in 18/16 meter. (In the latter, no note is stressed; Kirnberger cites "Goldberg" Variation 26 as an example.) Johann Gottfried Walther (1732) comments on fine distinction of note values according to beat:

> Quantitas Notarum extrinseca & intrinseca (lat.), the extrinsic and intrinsic values of notes; in execution, each note of the same value is distinguished according to its nature, namely, by dissimilar lengths: the uneven beats are long and the even beats are short.[19]

Walther's principle applies most readily to duple meters (1 2 3 4), although it ties in with Saint Lambert's statement that "beats 1 and 3 of triple meter are heavy."[20] This is often the case with French courantes. On the other hand, sarabandes and chaconnes often seem to accent the first and/or second beats, passing lightly over the third beat except in cases of hemiola; and

3/8 is often described as having an accent on the first eighth note of every measure or of every other measure. Again, the treatises can only provide a starting point for analysis. Notes receive emphasis not only according to beat position but also because of harmonic stress (as in the case of *appoggiaturas*), approach by leap, or irregular rhythmic factors. Johann Daniel Türk, writing of the *galant* style, speaks of dynamic accent and illustrates passages with both regular and irregular accents. (Example V-4 shows Türk's illustrations of normal degrees of stress, their relative strengths indicated by plus signs; and Example V-5 shows special and irregular accents, marked by ∧.)

EXAMPLE V-4.
J. D. Türk, illustrations of regular accents (+).[21]

EXAMPLE V-5.
J. D. Türk, illustrations of irregular accents (∧).[22]

Türk also speaks of time accent, perhaps more conservatively than did his predecessors quoted above:

> Another means of accent, which is to be used much less often and with great care, is lingering on certain tones. The orator not only lays more emphasis on important syllables and the like, but he also lingers upon them a little. But this kind of lingering, when it occurs in music, cannot, of course, always be of the same duration, for it appears to me to depend primarily upon 1) the greater or lesser importance of the note, 2) its length and relationship to other notes, and 3) the harmony which is basic to them.
> Because it is recognized by everyone, I do not have to provide evidence for the possibility of lingering somewhat longer on a very important note than on one less important. . . . As far as how long a note should be held is concerned, I would like to establish the rule that it should at the most not be lengthened more than half of its value. Usually the holding of a note should be only scarcely perceptible, for example, when a note becoming important enough to receive an accidental is already marked by the height of its pitch, or by an unexpected change of harmony, etc. That the following note loses as

much of its value as has been given to the accentuated note goes without saying.

Holding a note for a longer or shorter time depends also on the length of the note and its relationship to the others, for it should be easy enough to understand that one can linger longer on a quarter note than on a sixteenth. If shorter note values follow an accented note then a hold may be dispensed with, because in this case the longer note accents itself without assistance.[23]

Very few sources describe strong and weak in terms of units larger than beats, although extension of the concept to the level of the measure is mentioned by Roger North (late seventeenth century), Wolfgang Printz (1696), and Leopold Mozart (1756)[24] and is described most fully by Kirnberger:

> In duple as well as in triple meter, there are melodies in which it is obvious that whole measures are alternately strong and weak, so that a whole measure is heard as only one beat. If the melody is of such a nature that the entire measure is felt as only one beat, two measures must be grouped together to form just one, whose first part is accented and the other unaccented. If this contraction were not to occur, the result would be a melody consisting only of accented beats, because of the necessary weight of the downbeat. This would be as unpleasant as a sentence in speech consisting entirely of one-syllable words, each of which had an accent.
>
> This resulted in compound meters, namely, compound 4/4 from two combined measures of 2/4, compound 6/8 from two combined measures of 3/8, etc.
>
> This combining [of measures] actually occurs only so that the player can arrive at the proper performance and play the second half of such a measure more lightly than the first. These meters—for example, the compound 4/4 and the simple common 4/4—can easily be distinguished, since, in the former, the cadences fall naturally on the second part of the measure and last only half a measure. . . . Otherwise, compound meters are no different from the simple ones with regard to weighty and light performance and tempo.[25]

(Kirnberger goes on to explain that the combined meters are barred the same as their simple forms. In fact, his explanation seems to stem largely from a need to account theoretically for the occurrence of cadences of the half-measure, of which more below.)

What Kirnberger describes in terms of strong and weak measures is natural to musical phrasing in general. His discussion shows the Baroque period's orientation to the bar line in calculating stresses in a composition—a dance-related characteristic, largely lost with the more free-wheeling agogic accent of the nineteenth century. (Anthony Newman, who has drawn attention to the matter of strong and weak in several publications,[26] quotes a letter from Liszt, in which the latter inveighs against the "old style" of regular, metrically based accent.) Kirnberger's is the only lengthy Baroque description of strong and weak on a level above that of the beat. North, for instance, refers to loud (stressed) and soft (unstressed) measures but does not elaborate on the subject. Leopold Mozart's string tutor places down-bows on alternate measures in 3/8, thus yielding strong–weak measure alternations, typical of the passepied, for instance, and forming Kirnberger's compound 6/8. Wolfgang Printz, referring to strong–weak–strong–weak patterns, says, like Walther, that the first and third measures are intrinsically "longer" than the second and fourth. All these brief references suggest what Kirnberger describes.

Strong measures begin a new phrase; begin or sometimes complete a sequence; are harmonically, texturally, or dynamically accented; contain cadences, large leaps, or other distinguishing features; or begin a movement on a downbeat. Weak measures continue a phrase, pattern, or harmony; are undistinguished harmonically or texturally; or begin with a rest or a tied note. They alter nothing initiated in a preceding strong measure. Often they are softer, although a measure whose softness (whether marked or textural) is arresting, can often be termed strong. (With a slower tempo, a slower beat rate, and/or an increased surface rhythmic activity, differentiation of strong from weak at the level of the measure diminishes.) Some measures are in between or ambiguous. Newman suggests the labels S, W, and (S) (semi-strong) and illustrates typical passages of measures in SWSW, SSW, and S(S)W patterns.[27]

Both strong beats and strong measures are to be accented, weak beats and weak measures passed over more lightly. How are they to be projected in performance? Some music makes its own stresses almost inherently with such impact as to need little reinforcement by the player; it is only up to the performer not to distort the built-in accents. As discussed before, stresses by dynamics as well as by articulation and time are available to the clavichordist; the harpsichordist, while still thinking in dynamic terms, is restricted in the main to articulation and timing. As mentioned by early authors, strong beats and strong measures are often stressed through time. Agogic accent on the opening beat of a strong measure or entire phrase sometimes generates more rhythmic energy than issues from a strong beat that does not belong to an overall pattern (such as an isolated but important dissonance). The "extra" time of the stress must be absorbed by the timing of the phrase and its preparation. The musical circumstances of strong beats, especially those that mark a strong measure, are usually conducive to absorption of the time used in the stress, for their harmonic strength, texture and ornaments suggest the agogic accent in the first place. A thick chord or even a single low, resonant note may require time for clarity and/or for the sound to resonate fully. Such resonance often helps to generate the rhythmic thrust of a measure or phrase, and the time stress is its natural ally. Ornaments sometimes suggest strong beats or measures; whether written or added by the player, they can

be rendered so as to consume the time of the accent. Arpeggios and suspended notes, discussed below, also assist the graceful management of
agogic stresses. Time accent is also available through contrast, by deliberately undermining some rhythmic values so as to stress others.

Articulation and legato can also differentiate strong from weak, articulating small accents and contrasting larger units through variations in sonority (see chapter 4). In Example V-6, contrasts in overall sonority by means of
held (strong) or detached (weak) notes can differentiate strong from weak on
the level of the measure.

EXAMPLE V-6.
A. Forqueray, *La Marella*, mm.39-43.

In the *galant* period, dynamics are often specified to counteract the
usual stresses. As mentioned above (p.110), time stress is sometimes preferable to dynamic realization of these passages. Türk illustrates normal as opposed to specially indicated stresses (Example V-7). Similarly, some slurs
seem to counteract small differentiation of beats and even measures (Example V-8).

EXAMPLE V-7.
J. D. Türk, illustrations of abnormal and normal beat
stresses.

Phrasing and other stresses of early keyboard music are usually organized in accordance with the written meter. Time "freedom" that reinforces
the metric/rhythmic stresses, rather than that which ignores them, is most
often appropriate for the literature. However, dynamic markings, slurs, or
the music itself can suggest shifts of emphasis. Whether metric or
countermetric stresses seem necessary, the notation itself is rarely suggestive.
A few notational habits imply *rubato* notation (see below) but they occur
infrequently. One should be aware of early notation's limits for expressing
time adjustments. If a strongly nonliteral interpretation seems musically ap-

EXAMPLE V-8.
D. Scarlatti, Sonata in G, K. 454, mm.19-21.

propriate but questionable because it is not expressed in the notation, the player should consider the notational options that were open to the composer. Could the passage have been expressed another way? Could it be notated as the player imagines it with the conventions of its period? Relatively few fine rhythmic nuances appear in early notation; stresses from harmonic, melodic, and other elements are many and varied; and the player must flex the notated rhythm in accordance with the many fluctuations of the other musical elements.

✿ Cross Rhythms and Bar Lines

Although Baroque composition is often oriented to the bar line, unheeding adherence to the indicated meter may work at variance with the actual musical content. The bars sometimes signify only pulse, not stress. Variety of phrasing often includes not only different quantities of measures but different groupings of half measures and other beat units. Unlike the freer phrase construction of much Romantic music, the earlier repertory frequently depends for its effect on variation from a preestablished pattern. A few instances from the inexhaustible store in the repertory will suggest lines for further analysis by the reader.

Built-in bar line stresses are sometimes obviated by the composer by writing phrases around the bars. The constant W–S–W–S beat structure seems intended to ensure a more even flow for the composition than normal orientation to the bar line would suggest. Thus, a smoothly flowing 6/8 will sometimes appear as ♫♫♫ |♫♫♫ rather than ♫♫♫.♫♫♫|. J. S. Bach's Fugue in F (quoted in Example V-1) uses the flowing 6/16 meter, and the nonaccentual character of the piece is further reinforced by bar line displacement. Kirnberger found it necessary to evolve his theory of set-together measures in order to account for cadences at the half measure ("feminine endings"), such as often occur in Bach's allemandes. According to Kirnberger,

The concluding note must always fall on the downbeat of the measure. If this does not happen, it indicates that somewhere in the melody there is an extra or missing half measure. The concluding note in music is always accented.[28]

Occasionally pieces are written against the bar line, as if to conform to Kirnberger's rule. The refrain of Couperin's "Les Calotins" is written thus (Example V-9); the commas indicate the phrase divisions and act as effectual bar lines. This kind of writing involves irregular phrase lengths at some point (the half measure mentioned by Kirnberger) and is of fairly frequent occurrence in the Baroque—particularly in gavottes, which always begin on the half measure. Bach's works contain many sophisticated instances of phrasing that groups variously across and between bar lines. The Scherzo of his Partita in a is full of punning counterstresses of bar line, texture, and harmonic change (Example V-10).

EXAMPLE V-9.
F. Couperin, "Les Calotins," *Ordre* 19, mm.1-4.

EXAMPLE V-10.
J. S. Bach, Partita in a, Scherzo, mm.1-4.

Virtuoso figurations often show regrouping of the rhythmic stresses against the bar line, which come out congruently with the bar line at the end of the phrase (Example V-11).

Hemiola is a standard feature in the repertory, particularly at cadences. One may differentiate between those that require stress on each of the duple subdivisions and those that need it on only one or two of them. Sometimes surface rhythm and harmonic and/or textural groupings are counteractive (Example V-12).

Contrapuntal parts occasionally proceed in a polymetric fashion. Example V-13 is a particularly clear instance, but the metric and rhythmic congruence of different parts is often ambiguous. Harmonic and/or linear

EXAMPLE V-11.
J. S. Bach, *Chromatic Fantasy,* mm.64-67.

EXAMPLE V-12.
L. Couperin, Courante in d, m.10.

EXAMPLE V-13.
J. S Bach, *Goldberg Variations,* Var. 8, mm.1-2.

groupings are sometimes vague in relation to the notated meter. Nonaccentual rhythms combined with a weak profile of harmonic change can allow various metric interpretations.

The interrelation of musical lines creates many types and shades of stress between linear cohesiveness and independence. Passages that make a clear differentiation between melody and accompaniment form one end of a spectrum; at the other end is counterpoint among equally important, autonomous parts. In simple homophony, the accompaniment adjusts itself to the needs of the melody when necessary; delicate timings in the solo line may or may not require inflection in the accompaniment. Independent attention received by the accompaniment is likely to involve adjustments of its sound mass through timing and articulation, and even they are often made in relation to the melody. In true polyphony, parts sometimes yield to one another in importance, but on the whole adjustments of time should be made in consideration of all voices. If the rhythm of one part presses forward, it should not be weakened by another that might suggest delay. Independent *rubato* treatment is often appropriate. Apart from homophony and true polyphony, keyboard music abounds in textures that vacillate between real linear independence and interdependence, between true counterpoint and pseudocounterpoint. Even many fugues show this discrepancy; a piece nominally in three parts may consist in many passages of two real parts and a third, subsidiary "filler." *Style brisé* (the term originates in the twentieth century) produces many of the keyboard's most beautiful and flexible textures. However, the player must often change focus from one kind of counterpoint to another. Coordinated, interdependent parts require careful balancing of the overall rhythmic flow as opposed to stresses made in independent lines. The many shadings from near-independent polyphony to near-homophony that characterize *style brisé* are more additive in nature than real polyphony and require consideration less of individual lines than of the large rhythmic motion to which single "parts" only contribute. Careful inflection of a single additive "part" will often enunciate too clearly the line's rhythmic stops, starts, and jerks, which are meant only to complement another "part" in a graceful rhythmic flow. Example V-14 illustrates such a texture. With any kind of counterpoint, the player should ask the following questions: Is the rhythm of this passage the result of the rhythmic profiles of strongly independent lines or does it derive from the relationship of only partially independent lines? Has it elements of both? If the first, are the independent lines more important than the overall motion? Where does real polyphony end and pseudopolyphony begin, from one passage to another or in the course of one phrase? Are diverse interpretations possible?

EXAMPLE V-14.
J. S. Bach, Fugue in g, *WTC* II, mm.51-54.

Reiterated pedal tones can sometimes emphasize cross-rhythms or phrase groupings. On the harpsichord, if no further rhythmic impulse is desired, the tones are often best left to die away; the ear will supply what is actually missing. On the clavichord, tones can sometimes be reiterated softly without the rhythmic impetus usually suggested by the harpsichord. Sensitive rhythmic control in general will allow even notes that have died away to maintain their function and suggest the sustaining of all parts of the musical fabric. As C. P. E. Bach puts it:

> Tones will sing on the harpsichord as well as on the clavichord if they are not detached from each other, although one instrument may be better constructed for this purpose than another.... Even when the tempo is too slow or the instrument not good enough to sustain tones properly, it is better to sacrifice a little of the clear flow of a legato passage than to disrupt it with trills [to sustain], for a correct performance will be ample compensation for the lack of sonority. There are many things in music which, not fully heard, must be imagined.[29]

🌸 Rubato and Inequality

The word *rubato* is commonly applied, now and in the past, to several adjustments of musical time. It refers to time adjustments made in one part or beat and restored elsewhere, or to extra time taken without being made up subsequently. These are the most ordinary forms. The former is typified by rhythmic adjustments made in a solo line above an unvarying accompaniment, the latter by common yielding of several parts together. A third type is most common in piano music by Chopin, in which disproportionate note quantities such as eleven against six are played independently against one another. This usage is mentioned by C. P. E. Bach; in Baroque and *galant* music it is most common in highly embellished passages. The last-named type of *rubato* is clear when it occurs; use of the former two is up to the player.

The first two varieties of *rubato* are all that concern us here. Like other forms of time modification, they resist actual notation because their time values are irrational. Most *rubato* may be defined as differentiation in time between essential and nonessential notes. Many embellishments require such treatment (see chapter 6). It involves time stress on accented notes and/or deemphasis in time of unimportant notes by pulling them slightly askew from strict subdivision of the pulse.

In keyboard literature of the seventeenth and eighteenth centuries, *rubato* is occasionally suggested by certain rhythmic details of notation. In the music of Froberger, for instance, occasional thickets of small rhythmic subdivisions suggest *rubato*-like assimilation (i.e., reduction) of the written rhythmic variety rather than exaggeration or literal realization of the differ-

EXAMPLE V-15.
J. J. Froberger, *Tombeau de Mr. Blancrocher,*
mm.24-25.

ent values. Indeed, the piece from which Example V-15 comes bears the
composer's direction to play "sans observer aucune mesure" (without ob-
serving precise measure).

Another kind of approximate rhythmic notation appears in Example
V-16. In common with some Italian and English composers, Froberger
suggests an accelerating trill by notation whose meaning is fairly obvious
but whose appearance is clumsy. Most writing like this, in which small
details of rhythmic subdivision contrast against the broad sweep of a passage, implies rhythmic assimilation. Music that is not written with the almost neurotic notational care shown by Froberger is open to similar
agogic treatment; the contexts in which Froberger shows such detail
should be examined carefully and can be used as a guide to similar
passages in other music of the period.

EXAMPLE V-16.
J. J. Froberger, Toccata in D, mm.1-3.

It is hardly possible to categorize types of nuanced notation. Of most
general use is the dotting of notes to suggest stress. Just as Quantz differentiates strong from weak rhythmic subdivisions by time stress (see p.112),
so Froberger often suggests a strong beginning to a beat or measure by
dotting the first note of a passage (Example V-17). A literal rendition is
hardly appropriate to the thrust of the passage; the dot probably means
that the opening of the figure is stressed in time, perhaps even that the
overall run should accelerate. (Frescobaldi, Froberger's teacher, advocates
crowding runs into the last portion of available time, in order to make a
brilliant effect.)

EXAMPLE V-17.
J. J. Froberger, Toccata in G, mm.5-6.

Similar, apparently nonliteral stress dots appear in other contexts, as shown in Example V-18. Like the dotted note in the run, they all seem to indicate *rubato*-like lingering rather than a precise rendition that focuses on small divisions of rhythm. The overall smooth motion hardly suggests a strongly dotted or even literal performance. Perhaps the notation reflects the way subdivisions of beats were sometimes stressed by contemporary performers. The literature abounds in passages that do not use such dotted figures but are otherwise entirely similar. This is significant for the performance of both types, suggesting an approach to rubato for undotted passages and nonliteral rendition for those with dots. (Note that this use of dots has nothing to do with passages subject to the French style of over-dotting, an issue open to much debate.[30])

EXAMPLE V-18.
J. J. Froberger: a. *Tombeau*, m.9. b. Allemande in D, m.15. c. Allemande in g, m.11.

Froberger's type of *rubato* dot occasionally appears in later music. J. S. Bach's Praeludium in b for organ contains some dotted passages that recall Froberger. No dot appears in the opening statement of the piece (Example V-19a), but one turns up in the dominant restatement (Example V-19b). Its absence in the first instance suggests only a *rubato* treatment in the second, which may also be the meaning of the dot in the cadential figure (Example

EXAMPLE V-19.
J. S. Bach, Praeludium in b. a. m.1. b. m.27.
c. mm.16-17.

EXAMPLE V-20.
J. S. Bach, Toccata in d, m.24.

V-19c). Bach occasionally uses the *rubato* dot elsewhere, as in Example V-20, a passage strongly reminiscent of Froberger's toccatas.

The convention of rhythmic inequality appearing in some countries and periods, particularly the French *notes inégales*, can perhaps be regarded as stylized, almost systematized, *rubato* in the sense of slight rhythmic fluctuation against more or less unyielding meter. The practice involves rendering equally written notes unequally. French inequality applies normally to conjunct notes of the value prevalent in a composition, usually half the beat value. In C and ₵, sixteenth notes are eligible for inequality, as they are often the prevalent value. Some sources suggest inequality for all values below the eighth note in C. Usually the on-beat notes are lengthened, a style termed "long–short" in modern literature on the subject.[31] In any context, the overall metric/rhythmic focus depends on several rhythmic levels, particularly the relationship between main and subsidiary pulse values (e.g., stressed and unstressed quarter notes in 3/4 time) and of first and second subdivisions of the pulse (eighths and sixteenths in C and 3/4, for instance). This fact is crucial for time inflections generally, for rubato particularly, and is probably one of the foundations of conventionalized inequality.

From 1665 until well past the mid-eighteenth century, a great many French sources (and a few Francophile English, Dutch, and German authors, such as Quantz, quoted previously) describe or write out the long–short variety of inequality. Short–long inequality is generally ignored, except for mention by Loulié, actual notation by Gigault (organ book of 1685), and directions for short–long treatment of slurred, descending pairs in François Couperin's ornament table of 1713 and Pierre-Claude Fouquet's of 1751.

Short–long inequality is mentioned by Tomás de Sancta María (1565), and it presumably applies to much sixteenth- and seventeenth-century Spanish music. It is also the usual form of Italian inequality (mentioned by Caccini and Frescobaldi for vocal and keyboard music respectively), although vocal examples show both long–short and short–long types. Frescobaldi, in his sole reference to the practice, remarks that sixteenth notes played against eighths in the other hand are to be "somewhat dotted" in the short–long style.[32]

Written-out inequality appears in many English and some French sources of the late seventeenth century; a common form is ♩♫♩. (Occasionally a piece appears with equal notes in one source and dotted rhythms in another.) In 1668, Benigne de Bacilly commented that inequality cannot be written successfully with dotted figures because that would lead to jerkiness in the execution. Thus it is likely that examples with written out inequality require some degree of rhythmic assimilation. (Such cases must be distinguished from those whose rhythms require literal or even exaggeratedly jerky interpretation. Other aspects of the music can guide rhythmic decisions, as can performance directions. "Tendrement" can imply assimilation, "vivement" exaggeration.) Guillaume Nivers, in his *Livre d'orgue* (1665), describes inequality as employing "semi-dots" after the stressed notes; he uses the suggestive notation ♫♩♩ for long–short inequality: literally a 3:2 ratio. French inequality usually applies to gracious rather than agitated movements, and Nivers's approach makes a good point of departure.

Although inequality is occasionally suggested in notation, it can only be approximated; this is the case with *rubato* notation generally. Inequality seems to have ranged from very slight to quite pronounced alterations of rhythm. It was always to be applied with discretion, apparently now more and now less, from phrase to phrase or even from beat to beat, depending on the continually changing nuances of the music. Perhaps the jerkier forms of the practice were less varied than its subtler applications.

Rhythmic alterations of whatever style must be made in reference to their effect on the phrase or phrase groups. Generally speaking, assimilated or regular rhythms and rhythmic inflections draw the listener to the overall musical line, whereas acute enunciation and irregularities of rhythm or its inflection tend to stress the local level—depending of course on the variety in other, nonrhythmic elements. Uniform inequality, uniform overdotting, and other steadiness of surface rhythm are "weak" in the sense of being neutral; in their relationship to strong time inflections, they are effective in grouping larger impulses. Carefully graded inequality, or any rhythmic adjustments, can vary the degree of local versus overall emphasis and thus help to bring out the contour of a phrase.

❧ Rhythmic Variety

As we have seen, convincing adjustments of musical time depend on sensitivity to its different, simultaneously functioning levels: surface rhythm, metric pulse, and larger, often overlapping beat units grouped by rhythmic and melodic impulses and harmonic rhythm. Overall tempo, time modifications, articulation, legato, and dynamics should originate in these factors and their relationships.

Meter, harmonic rhythm, melodic impulse, and large and small units of surface rhythm work in constantly changing coordination. Often they work congruently, but one or more elements can fall into groupings that may or may not undermine the other hierarchies. A common example is hemiola, when chord patterns imply a duple regrouping across the notated triple meter. Another case is that of surface rhythmic cohesion that variously complements or contrasts with meter and harmonic rhythm. This relationship is given to many subtle counterpoints of stress; and the degree to which the rhythmic forces undermine the metric/harmonic underlay is often equivocal. Often the musical interest stems from unresolved contrast, as with tension between syncopations and meter: if either gives in to the other, the effect is lost.

Metric and harmonic factors tend to work in large values, rhythmic factors in units of all sizes. The player must recognize when rhythmic subdivisions provide a continuous thrust based on larger underlying values and when they reflect a breakdown of the latter. Articulation should conform to the requirements of these different situations. Separate articulation of each member of a group of rhythmic iterations is often appropriate when it mirrors similar disruption in other elements, but no performing inflections should distort cohesion between rhythm and other elements. If articulatory enlivenment is desirable, some degree of general detachment is often more effective than articulatory isolation of each unit. If legato is for some reason imperative, then manipulation of rhythmic inflection must make up for the loss of forward drive caused by the smoother sound. In some contexts, legato has the advantage of grouping notes into large units, reflecting their larger rhythmic thrust, even if the tonal quality inhibits momentum.

The rhythmic surface is inherently the most plastic of all levels of musical time, and it reflects and colors the larger motions of line, meter, and harmony. Phrasing is largely a matter of clarifying these movements. There are many valid ways of looking at a piece's arrangement of these factors, although the core of a work's musical construction is usually less open to different views than the interrelation of levels nearer the surface. Different performances offer varying emphasis on the many levels of these relationships. Whatever the focus, many proportions are relatively fixed, while others are open to varied treatment.

The player's main access to conveying large- and small-scale features is through choice of tempo and the inflection of surface rhythm in accordance with the impulses set up by the music's metric and rhythmic layers, melodic and harmonic groupings, and so forth. Basic tempo has much to do with the focus on large units: as mentioned, reiterated phrases, for example, tend to emerge as an entity or as individual statements depending on whether a tempo or various inflections crowd them into a single unit or allow them more individual space. Articulation, legato, dynamics, and rhythmic inflection can relate and project surface rhythms from the smallest local features to their largest import of fundamental activity.

Strong harmonic changes, striking intervals, and so on not only encourage the player's reinforcement for their own sake, but often assist preparation for local or more far-reaching time stress. Dissonant *appoggiaturas*, for instance, are often helpful in initiating a *ritardando*. Rhythmic subdivisions of larger values are the key to adjusting time, both for local agogic accent and for large-scale changes of tempo. In this sense, there are many notes, beats, and beat divisions that are important for the performer, not in the sense of the metrically "strong" or "good" beats mentioned in early treatises, but regarding those that allow preparation for the musically stressed notes. (See "Strong and Weak," above.) A note can be stressed more or less in proportion to the preparation it receives. Phrasing is often a matter of well-proportioned impulses, rhythmically inherent in the music and related to larger rhythmic, metric, and harmonic movements. The impulses are made manifest by the player's manipulation and reinforcement of the surface rhythm, supplemented or even largely replaced by dynamic and articulatory variation. Weak units, whether weak beats, measures, or even phrases are upbeats to strong ones. In turn, a strong inflection at the beginning of a phrase can generate rhythmic impetus throughout the phrase or ensuing group of phrases. Rhythmic impulses, like dynamic impulses and curves, must be carried through to the end of a phrase or phrase group, unless a deliberate interruption is desired or is built into the music.

In a sense, rhythmic drive and cessation form a primary factor in music, diversified in its expression on the keyboard among rhythmic adjustment, dynamics, articulation, and legato. Rhythm itself, in large- and small-scale aspects, is often a reflection of harmonic weight and grouping, although rhythm may often occupy the foreground. The player's handling of rhythm depends partly on perception of the relative dominance of rhythmic and harmonic factors. Are the pitches secondary, forming only a neutral medium for the expression of rhythmic activity? Or are rhythmic divisions delicate reflections of harmonic weight and its vertical and horizontal aspects? All degrees of relativity occur between these two extremes.

Although the forward thrust of rhythmic energy is strongly subject to melodic and harmonic influences, progression from fast values to slower ones is usually more striking, and more often typical of phrase junctures, than movement from slow to fast notes. It also allows readier time inflection; that is why a strong beat in an unyielding context can often be more strikingly delineated when rhythmic subdivisions (embellishments) are improvised just in advance of it.

The factors of rhythmic drive and the many forces that beget and modify them assume greater influence on phrasing in seamless, ongoing compositions of uniform surface rhythm than in pieces given to general pauses, strong dynamic and textural contrasts, marked variations and disruptions in surface rhythm, and the like. In the former case, the paucity of textural and rhythmic contrasts makes the player's expression dependent on minute variations of rhythm. As rhetorical pauses and other dramatic surface details provide inherently obvious proportion and division of phrases, the player's need of agogic accents becomes increasingly confined to local rhythmic details. Almost paradoxically, the treatment of agogics in seamlessly rhythmic pieces can often accept less flamboyant treatment than can more rhetorical works. A greater uniformity of surface rhythm generally reflects broader underlying units than occur in pieces whose surface articulation is rhythmically more varied.

Long notes suggest repose, however much they may be pregnant with activity due to faster notes in their immediate environment. (See the contrasting values delineating many phrases in Frescobaldi's music, as in Example V-21. The composer's directions require exaggeration of such contrasts.) Their enunciation must not imply subdivision, even if rapid counterpoints sound against them. Long notes must generally absorb the energy of preceding rapid notes and dominate them in retrospect. The grouping of faster notes (inherently and as the performer manipulates them) suggests longer values to various degrees and in an infinitude of ways. Generally, longer underlying values produce stronger impulses of short notes.

The breadth of the values underlying the surface rhythm and the strength of impulse that they afford it also affect the inflection of surface rhythmic

EXAMPLE V-21.
G. Frescobaldi, Canzona in F, mm.50-55.

values. Most often their exaggeration is called for, but assimilation is often necessary. For instance, the assimilation appropriate to Froberger's *rubato* dots, discussed above, is largely suggested by the values in whole and half notes that govern the flourishes in sixteenths, as in Example V-17. A precisely literal rendition of the ♪♫♫♫ flourishes can direct excessive attention to the small values, detracting from the sweep of the larger ones. Inflection of strong beats by time stress often involves sharpening the rhythm as well and is most effective with lines of varied rhythm. In cases of repetitive rhythm, forward drive can be effectively undermined by regular exaggeration of a reiterated pattern if the intensity of local iterations is more important than larger groupings. In many cases, the overriding constancy of a small-level figure mitigates the development of larger drive. This accounts for the pompous, static quality of many overdotted passages in French overtures.

Either rhythmic assimilation or exaggeration can assist the proportioning and projection of a musical phrase, sentence, or paragraph. In any case, the most effective approach is to find the point in a phrase that is its activating point: its crux, so to speak. This is the area of a phrase that generates its rhythmic impetus: often but not always the opening beat of a strong measure. Well-proportioned agogic emphasis of such a moment is the surest way to unite a strongly inflected rendering with a sense of the overall phrase.

Rhythmic inflection must often be accommodated in accordance with changes in surface and/or harmonic rhythm. Both are in flux in Example V-22. The generally sixteenth-note surface rhythm is governed by the bass and concomitant changes of harmony by quarter notes. This pattern changes at the double bar to quarters and eighths on the surface and a harmonic rhythm of one chord per measure. Time stress on the first beat of each mea-

EXAMPLE V-22.
D. Scarlatti, Sonata in a, K. 217, mm.42-46.

sure after the double bar can clarify the new, larger progress of the harmonic rhythm. The expressive, static quality of the quarter notes would be undermined if it were counted in terms of the previous sixteenths.

Variety of rhythmic activity is often comparable to variation in volume. Especially on the harpsichord's flat dynamic plane, changes in rhythmic motion are often highly suggestive of dynamic fluctuation; the greater note density of a rhythmically active passage implies and to some extent realizes an increase in volume, and *vice versa*. Contrasts in range or other factors can undermine these effects; for instance, phrases of greater rhythmic activity relegated to the treble will often sound thinner in opposition to phrases set in the sonorous bass, even if the latter are less active rhythmically. Frequently, though, dynamics can be suggested by following up the implications made by some rhythmic changes and reinforcing them with small timing adjustments. This treatment is similar to the dynamic qualities of textural change discussed in chapter 4, and the two factors often complement one another.

Occasionally, the proper tempo will allow strongly differentiated characterization of each note value in a piece. For instance, in J. S. Bach's Fugue in C♯, *WTC* II, the eighth notes, eighths followed by eighth rests, and quarter notes can be heard as rather emphatic; the sixteenths show considerably more forward drive; and the thirty-seconds (which run across the different voice parts in the concluding flourishes) are very brilliant in effect: each smaller rhythmic level shows a distinct increase in energy. Too rapid a tempo would decrease the heaviness of the slower values, and too slow a speed would compromise the brilliance of the flourishes and perhaps the drive of the sixteenths.

❀ Accelerando and Ritardando

Accelerando and *ritardando* refer to tempo changes of any dimension, whether the hurrying or delaying of a single beat's subdivision or of large units. They most frequently refer to adjustments of groups of beats. Although their application is largely covered in previous sections, a few specific comments are included here.

Ritardandos to end sections, movements, and even phrases are described by many early authors. Michael Praetorius, for instance, mentions very broad final cadences:

> Further, it is not attractive or worthy of applause when singers, organists, and other instrumental players habitually hasten from the penultimate note of a composition directly into the final note without any retardation. I believe therefore I should admonish players ... to remain some time on the

penultimate note, whatever it may be, lingering four, five, or six beats, and then at last moving to the final note.[33]

Frescobaldi describes general use of *ritardandos*: "In the cadences, even though written in notes of small values, one must sustain them. As the performer approaches the end of a passage, he must slow the tempo."[34] Praetorius limits his description of *ritardando* to the penultimate note; one wonders how much preparation may have preceded it. Frescobaldi suggests slowing at phrase endings. Plentiful use of this device is appropriate to his toccata style, especially to make the contrast between opposed phrases more violent. It is often less successful with the terse movements that constitute much early keyboard literature. The grand broadening of the final beats described by Praetorius is rarely necessary in keyboard works, although adjustment at the penultimate chord, as he mentions, is often all that is required; broad, long-range *ritardandos* often seem out of place in the repertory. Strong retardation is usually most successful when cadential harmonies are clear but less suitable in climaxes that depend on rhythmic energy or involve unusual harmonies whose tonal direction is ambiguous. Occasionally *ritardandos* are written into the music: perhaps a slowing of the surface rhythm when a last burst of energy occurs in a flourish and slower notes conclude (Example V-23). Slightly retarding the pulse is enough to reinforce the effect of the surface rhythm. Dances and other brief movements rarely require much *ritardando* to conclude; and in short, triple-meter pieces, emphasis on the usual cadential hemiola often slows the momentum sufficiently for an effective conclusion, as it breaks the accent pattern. Reiteration of the final chord (Example V-24) similarly obviates much need of *ritardando*.

EXAMPLE V-23.
J. J. Froberger, Toccata in G, mm.39-42.

EXAMPLE V-24.
Francis Tregian, arranged by Peter Philips, *Pavana Dolorosa*, mm.8-10.

Some pieces carry their full energy into the final beat, and any slackening of pace destroys the effect. In such cases, a slight breath before the last beat is sometimes sufficient to draw attention to the close; or a chord may be reiterated and arpeggiated to absorb the cumulative energy at the last phrase(s). A broken chord whose timing is out of step with the preceding pulse and pulse divisions is particularly effective in absorbing and dissipating cumulative rhythmic energy.

Acceleration is often useful for delineating phrases. Small phrases of one or two measures can often be brought out entirely by rhythmic impulse, beginning or ending with a slight pause and accelerating the pulse elsewhere, through the weak beats. The amount of acceleration necessary depends of course on context, but should be barely if at all perceptible to the listener. Similar acceleration often clarifies a weak measure or a succession of them. It can also suggest a *piano* effect on the harpsichord, but again should not be heard as an adjustment of tempo. Sometimes an effect of acceleration is produced by the inherent lack of stress characteristic of weak measures; then one may have to hold back the tempo if an effect of straightforward, uninflected motion is desired, in order to counteract the tendencies built into the neutral measures.

Overt acceleration is often successful with long phrases, especially in free-style works. Toccatas by Frescobaldi often seem to require acceleration to clarify the course of longer phrases and phrase groups: for instance, from the beginning of the development of one motive until a long concluding chord. Such acceleration should not undermine but grow naturally into accelerating the rhythmic subdivisions that are actually written in. Example V-25 shows a typical, acceleration-prone passage from Frescobaldi that includes a change in surface rhythm from sixteenth to thirty-second notes. Such passages often describe an arch in their timing, accelerating until the last notes, where a *ritardando* may be suitable, as the composer mentions in the quotation given above.

EXAMPLE V-25.
G. Frescobaldi, Toccata 8, Book 1, mm.8-9.

Although accelerations in rhythmic values can suggest tempo accelerations in rhapsodic pieces, a change in surface rhythm, such as from eighth notes to sixteenths in stricter pieces, can be undermined rather than enhanced by a concurrent change in tempo. A sudden change in values should be underlined by care in rhythmic enunciation rather than by adjustments of the overall tempo.

Ritardando and *accelerando* should be used with such regard to the basic tempo as is characteristic of true *tempo rubato*. In both kinds of adjustment, the underlying pulse is retained, either in actual fact (*rubato*) or as a point of reference. A sense of relativity in time inflections must never be lost.

❧ Suspension and Arpeggiation

The moment of attack in harpsichord tone is extremely precise. This definition endows the instrument with particular rhythmic authority, but it is not always an advantage. The harpsichord lacks the ability of a bowed instrument to spread its attack minutely in time. A violin bow can create a soft, suspended opening to a note or make a sharp attack: a range of attack in marked contrast to the unvarying precision of the harpsichord's plucking mechanism. The harpsichord is essentially powerless to modify the quality of a single pluck, but nonsimultaneous sounding of two or more notes written together ranks with articulation and legato as one of the most versatile and useful means of extracting variegated color and stress from the keyboard. This "spreading" of textures is a dynamic element on the harpsichord. It can color and accent the sound and provide a graceful way of using up the extra time of a strong time inflection, particularly when the surface rhythm is too static to bend with the accent. The technique is equally suited to the harpsichord and clavichord, but is far less frequently required on the latter; it is useful for reinforcing certain effects that the clavichord can essentially express in terms of purely dynamic contrast. Nonsimultaneity can add further weight to stresses made *fortissimo* or *sforzando*.

Fringing or *suspension* refers to the slightly nonsimultaneous rendition of two notes. (This use of the word *suspension* is derived from eighteenth-century French authors and is not to be confused with harmonic suspension.) The upper part usually sounds after the lower; this treatment is simply the arpeggiation of thin textures. A single note can also be fringed with respect to simultaneously sounded accompanying parts. The delay on the second note is extremely minute; it may range from barely perceptible to noticeable separations of attack. In most cases, suspension should not strike the listener as anything more than a softening of attack, which also stresses it in most contexts. Different instruments, different ranges, and different sizes of interval respond individually to this technique. One may experiment to determine how much departure from actual simultaneity will still be perceived by the ear as simultaneity, how much perceptible fringing is acceptable without sounding exaggerated, and what differences in tonal, accentual, or dynamic quality these variations provide. Stronger accents demand greater degrees of separation, which will actually be perceived as such.

In the seventeenth century, the French unmeasured prelude shows frequent suspension as well as arpeggiation; vertical alignment of parts occurs very rarely. Many cases of nonvertical alignment of what seems to be a basically simultaneous sounding of parts, but fringed, appear in unmeasured notation. Example V-26 shows several instances.

EXAMPLE V-26.
L. Couperin: a. Prelude in c, excerpt. b. Prelude in a, excerpt.

Although suspension is generally useful in keyboard technique, it received special comment and notation from French composers of the eighteenth century. Particularly emphatic use of suspension was notated with a sign that appeared in several ornament tables, including those of Rameau and Couperin. A note modified by the sign ⌃ was delayed minutely; the tables usually realize the delay as 𝆒 = 𝅘𝅥 , but no notation could account for the slight and variable degree of suspension possible in practice. Example V-27 shows a few cases of notated suspension; clearly, a fringed time stress rather than a rhythmically precise 𝅘𝅥 is called for.

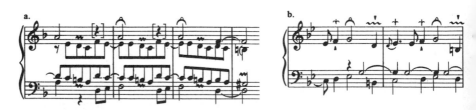

EXAMPLE V-27.
a. J.-P. Rameau, *L'Entretien des Muses*, mm.33-36.
b. F. Couperin, "Les Laurentines," *Ordre 3*, mm.19-20.

Several composers described use of the suspension. François Couperin comments:

> The sounds of the harpsichord are fixed, each one specifically, and consequently cannot be swelled or diminished. It has appeared until now almost impossible that one could give any soul to this instrument.... The sound

quality that I mean owes its effect to the cessation and suspension of the tones, properly placed according to the character required by the melodies of the preludes and pieces. These two ornaments [*aspiration* and *suspension*] by their contrast leave the ear in suspense, so that in cases where bowed instruments swell their sounds, their suspension on the harpsichord seems (by different means) to produce the desired effect on the ear.

I have already explained the *aspiration* and *suspension* by note values and silences in the table of ornaments which is at the end of my first Book. . . . These two names will no doubt have seemed new; but even if someone should boast of having made use of one or the other, I do not think that anyone will be annoyed with me, in general, for having broken the ice, in appropriating for these two kinds of ornaments names that convey their effects. . . .

Regarding the expressive effect of the *aspiration*, the note over which it [the sign] is placed must be detached less abruptly in passages that are tender, and slow, than in those that are light and rapid.

As for the *suspension*, it is hardly employed except in pieces that are tender and slow. The silence preceding the note over which it is marked must be regulated by the taste of the player.[35]

Couperin's account is of interest, for his is the most detailed description of the suspension. He describes it in terms of dynamic illusion and contrasts its effect of dynamic swell or accent with the diminishing quality of a note released early. Especially important is his comment on the variable length of the preceding rest, which depends on the player's taste. Couperin's ornament table illustrates the suspension and aspiration as in Example V-28. The delay of an eighth value is unusual; Rameau's and Forqueray's tables show the ♪ realization. Certainly so marked a delay as Couperin's realization implies is strongly accentual, whereas very slight fringing produces a gentler tone quality than does simultaneity, and one suited, as Couperin and others remark, for tender pieces. A wide range of effects is possible.

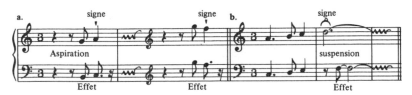

EXAMPLE V-28.
F. Couperin, ornament table (1713). a. Aspiration.
b. Suspension.

The effect of dynamic swell that Couperin attributes to a strong suspension is caused partly by expectation of the upper note and its delayed fulfillment and partly by the fact that the upper note, which is mentally heard with the bass entry, is produced at full volume only after it is expected. Couperin's ♪ notation of a strong suspension suggests that a similar dynamic effect may be intended by the French school's textural *cliché* of delayed bass notes, as in Example V-29. Although other intervals occur, the octave is by far the most frequent, and its delayed entrance suggests an increased depth and resonance. If a similar effect of swell is intended by this texture, the standard value of the eighth rest may well be a notational formality akin to Couperin's suspension realization and one open to adjustment calculated to produce an illusion of minute *crescendo*. Whether the effect is heightened in a particular instance by extending or shortening the rest is determined by the instrument, range, and context.

EXAMPLE V-29.
L. Couperin, Allemande in D, m.1.

Couperin identifies the suspension mainly with slow movements. Louis-Claude Daquin, writing in 1735, describes it in terms of playing an ornament:

> But I must observe that to play a *port de voix* well it is indispensable, when the small note is slurred, to play the bass note a little before the small note of the melody and to hold the small note a little longer before playing the mordent. [See Example V-30].[36]

EXAMPLE V-30.
L. C. Daquin, illustration of suspension.

Pierre-Claude Fouquet (1751) advocates liberal use of the suspension, again limited to slow movements. He also relates the suspension to arpeggiation:

> In all pieces whose execution is gracious or tender, one must play the bass note before that of the upper part, without altering the beat; this produces a suspension on each note of the upper part. If one encounters several notes in the bass [i.e., left-hand chords], they must be arpeggiated, that is to say, beginning with the lowest and so on, observing that the upper part sounds the

highest note last; this renders the touch soft, gracious, and [is] indispensable for pieces of sentiment.[37]

Fouquet's description seems to imply more general use of the suspension than does Couperin's account. Possibly a more flamboyant style of fringing became fashionable in France between the time that Couperin wrote (1717) and the time of later evidence on the suspension. Fouquet does not notate suspensions in accordance with the style he advocates, but by 1738 there appeared notation such as that in Example V-31. Possibly suspension was employed in a stylized manner (as reflected in the example) and as well as more circumspectly.

EXAMPLE V-31.
Charles-Alexandre Jollage, *La Marais*, mm.41-45.

A third variety of suspension notation, similar to that of the unmeasured prelude, is found in three gamba pieces by Antoine Forqueray ("La d'Eaubonne," "La Léon," and "La Sylvia"), arranged for harpsichord by the composer's son. The hands are often written out of alignment, with the left sometimes ahead of and sometimes behind the right. Presumably a very rapid downward break is intended when the right hand part precedes the left. This style of breaking is generally less useful than that in which the bass sounds first. Since the sign ∧ and the authors quoted previously refer only to the bass preceding the treble, it is possible that Forqueray's unusual notation was necessary to show an unusual practice; however, unmeasured notation also occasionally seems to show the left hand following the right. As with the sign for suspension, general use of Forqueray's notation would be clumsy; and the breaking of parts in these pieces (see Example V-32) is perhaps more extreme and/or frequent than is necessary or desirable in more

EXAMPLE V-32.
A. Forqueray, *La Léon*, mm.18-20.

usual repertory. The younger Forqueray says of the sarabande "La Léon": "To play this piece in the way I should wish it played, it is necessary to pay attention to the way it is written, the upper part almost never being together with the bass."[38]

As the French authors remark, the suspension is best suited to slow or moderately paced passages. Its employment with rapid notes is necessarily curtailed, although it can occasionally be useful. The effect is easily distorted through exaggeration or overuse; indeed, of all the keyboard player's devices, it is the most likely to become a playing mannerism, and discretion is necessary. Arpeggiation allows manipulation of many chordal members, but the exposed texture of two-part passages is much more susceptible to distortion.

The breaking of chords, ranging from barely perceptible spreading to elaborate patterns, both free and rhythmic, is important for tone quality, for stress and timing, and as an embellishment to playing. (The latter aspect is discussed in chapter 6.) As with other aspects of playing, the performer should strive for variety, cultivating an infinitely nuanced palette of arpeggio patterns and timings.

The tone of many harpsichords is such that four or more chordal members played with absolute simultaneity can sound harsh and dry. Occasionally a strident quality is desireable, as in some of the more aggressive sonatas of Scarlatti. While some particularly resonant harpsichords can tolerate completely simultaneous attack on full chords, still achieving a rich sonority, many instruments require minute spreading of them. Such essentially imperceptible breaking is analogous to the staggering of plucks in the harpsichord's action and fulfills much the same function: both aim to produce a warm quality of sound. Minute arpeggiation of loud chords is often necessary on the clavichord as well: a heavy, completely simultaneous attack on a full chord can sometimes produce an untoward proportion of percussive sound in relation to the musical tone.

Even more than with the suspension, tone quality can be varied by degrees of minute arpeggiation. Many shadings of what is perceived as an essentially simultaneous attack are available on a sensitive harpsichord or clavichord and can produce dramatic variations in the tonal quality and even in the clarity of a chord. As with the suspension, one should experiment with the various shades of near-simultaneity and minute, perceptible separation, noting their effects in different ranges and with different chord voicings. Closely written chords are most susceptible to variation; a combination of two 8′ stops usually allows the most flexible sound quality on the harpsichord.

The player's sensitivity to the broad spectrum of broken-chord effects, from the slightest to the grandest gesture, is important not only for the range of tone quality but for many aspects of timing as well. Any point of stress along the time line of a musical composition must be well prepared, particularly in pieces of regular pulse, although regulation of the relative stresses in free, perhaps recitative-like compositions is also of great importance. Perhaps works with an even pulse are more readily open to distortion through timing. In neither case should variation occur in time stress, arpeggiation timing, articulation, legato, and so forth unless it is rooted in the requirements of the music. The extra time consumed in stressing a metrical beat must not distort the metric and rhythmic shapes perceived by the listener; it must only accentuate them. As mentioned, slight retardation to prepare the time accents allows the line to flex rather than break; at the stressed points themselves, arpeggiation and fringing are of great assistance because they gracefully consume the time of the stressed beats. The extra time could otherwise distort the flow of the pulse.

Whether breaking a chord slightly or broadly, evenly or with an acceleration in the upward or downward sweep, the sounding of the different chord members must never be uneven. The clumsy sound of a jumbled chord, some members almost evenly spaced, others bunched together, is both tonally and for timing one of the keyboard's most unattractive effects. Breaking should follow either a straight line or a geometric curve, never a jagged line.

The relationship of the two outermost parts to the beat is variable. Perception of the beat falling on the bass or soprano part of a broken chord or fringed interval often depends on the context, but it can also be affected by the timing of the break. In fringing two notes, the bass often sounds as though it precedes the beat, however it is placed. The player can do little to change the effect because in most cases the ear hears the upper part as receiving the accent. In arpeggios it is often best that the bass be heard on the beat. Deliberate pausing on the bass, context permitting, will often assure that it is heard as falling on the beat, with the remaining parts coming after. Other ways of placing the bass of a rapid chordal roll depend on context and may be found by experiment and careful listening. Often, however, the beat will be unavoidably heard in the soprano, as in fringing. Occasionally, when the arpeggio adds stress to a strong point, the time consumed by the accent could be construed as placing the beat "across" the entire time of the break, and care must be taken with the surrounding beats to create this effect. Such cases are rare, however. In some contexts, playing the bass and soprano together (or slightly fringed) and following with the remaining chordal members ensures the beat placement and distributes the chord as well. There is nothing intrinsically wrong with arpeggiating ahead of the beat, but it can make some bass entries awkward and in ensemble playing, it can confuse the other parts.

Arpeggios ahead of the beat are perhaps most apt in situations where the bass is of no contrapuntal importance, for example, when reiterating a harmony on an unstressed beat. Some written-out arpeggios show breaking ahead of the beat (Example V-33). Sometimes when a thick texture suggests a broken chord, the rhythm of the ongoing lines does not permit on-beat arpeggiation. Whether on or ahead of the beat, broken chords must be placed decisively and with a firm understanding of their rhythmic significance. This is especially important when accompanying other instruments, whose parts mark the beat clearly. Uncontrolled arpeggiation by the harpsichordist is annoying to the listener and harmful to the ensemble.

EXAMPLE V-33.
a. Della Cjaia, Sonata V, Toccata, mm.4-5.
b. Matthias Weckmann, Toccata in a, mm.1-3.

EXAMPLE V-34.
Bury le Fils, Loure, mm.4-6.

There is an infinite range of relative time stresses and corresponding arpeggiations. Other factors allowing, the stronger the beat stress, the broader and slower the arpeggio. Arpeggios create a dynamic effect as well as a time stress, although the dynamic quality of the same treatment will vary with different musical contexts. A break that lends a *forte* quality to one passage may soften the acerbity of another; and the dynamic effect is mostly dependent on the concomitant time stress. The player may feel an initial impulse to distribute the tones in order to soften a passage, but a simultaneous sounding of them is frequently less obtrusive in quality. Strumming a succession of accompanimental chords makes all the beats heavy and renders the chords more prominent rather than subduing them. This is sometimes desirable, as the unusual notation of successive broken chords in Example V-34 suggests; and broad and persistent breaking is often useful for sonority and the imitation of guitar strumming, as in many Scarlatti sonatas. However, in most cases only important chords require breaking. Broken and unbroken chords require sensitive rhythmic placement, and the relativity of beat strength must be reflected in varied simultaneous, near-simultaneous, and arpeggiated treatment of chords.

❧ Conclusion

The concepts and details discussed in this chapter can of course form only a rough paradigm for the performer's expression of phrasing and other structural elements. The relationships of various aspects of timing among themselves and with other expressive means are in constant flux in any piece of music and in any set of performance circumstances; they must be continually weighed and reevaluated by the player. Such relationships are highlighted by the contrast between the harpsichord and the clavichord, for whereas time stresses contribute to the harpsichord's range of implied dynamics, they reinforce the dynamic variation of the clavichord. Perhaps for this reason above all, parallel cultivation of both instruments is instructive. However, in any musical or instrumental situation a sense of the relativity of time stresses within a composition is of primary importance. Often the most compelling playing is that which is so well controlled that the slightest adjustments make their point clearly. Extreme freedom can be equally successful, but any degree of time variation must be proportioned to the whole.

6

Ornamentation and Embellishments

ORNAMENTATION AND EMBELLISHMENT
receive extensive coverage in both early treatises and modern commentaries
on performance practice. This emphasis is altogether in proportion to their
musical importance in general and certainly to their roles in keyboard styles.
The idioms of early keyboard writing and even the tonal qualities of the
harpsichord and clavichord are closely tied to the expressive shadings and
brilliance available through ornaments and embellishments. They are considered below in regard to their musical functions, especially dynamic and
accentual implications. The realization and improvisation of notated ornamentation and embellishment must be coordinated with other musical elements. This chapter presents some general observations on ornamentation
and embellishment and a few particulars on specific national styles. A complete musicological presentation of the ornamentation and embellishment of
different schools and periods is clearly beyond the scope of this book. The
present discussion is mainly concerned with the integration of ornaments
and embellishments into musical utterance as a whole, so that they may best
serve expressivity. (Some aspects of the technical negotiation of ornaments
are treated in chapter 3 and Appendix 1.)

Both ornamentation and embellishment refer to the "extra" notes that
supplement and modify the skeletal, structural tones of a composition. Ornaments intensify single notes; they are more or less standardized figurations (trills, mordents, etc.), often represented by sign, and usually center on
and accent one note. Embellishments are less stereotyped and include all
kinds of written-out or improvised notes that connect or envelop structural
notes. (To be sure, such a definition of embellishment can be interpreted
even to include subsidiary notes of structural motives. The degree to which a
note or note group is structural or embellishmental is of course variable.)
This distinction between ornamentation and embellishment is not ironclad;
ornaments can have connective functions and embellishmental figures can

intensify the notes they surround or lead to. Frederick Neumann[1] differentiates two aspects of the subject: the connective and intensifying functions just described and functions of primarily melodic or harmonic importance. Harmonic graces generally fall on the beat rather than before it; melodic graces, like connective and intensifying functions, vary in their beat relationships. Both ornaments and embellishments usually embody the smallest units of surface rhythm. As with texture, the varying density of rhythmic movement can be heard as a dynamic function, and this factor must be evaluated in the realization of written graces and the addition of new ones.

Ornamentation

The symbols used for ornaments are merely a stenographic convenience, a shorthand for standard formulas. They probably represent a codification of playing formulas that were originally improvised and sometimes written out. (See Andrea Gabrieli's frequent use of the written-out ornamental formula ⌠⌠⌠⌠⌠ .) Whether ornaments appear as written formulas or are represented by signs, the flexibility of their improvisational origins should not be lost in performance. (It may be this kind of flexibility that prompts composers occasionally to write out ornaments for which signs normally suffice. J. S. Bach employs the usual symbol for a mordent, ✦, but in his Fantasia in c [BWV 906], for instance, many mordents are realized, on the beat, as ⌐.) Indeed, signs may have developed in part to preserve the flexibility of realization, which may be lost in writing out the figurations. In no way do the signs suggest mechanical or unvarying relations, even when the same quantities and patterns of notes are used from one realization to another. A particular ornament or pattern can require diverse treatment depending on musical context and expression. Whether connective or emphatic in nature, ornaments must be made an integral part of the line. What an ornament (or embellishment) does to a line can often be discovered by playing the passage without it. This experiment can frequently explain the ornament's presence.

APPOGGIATURAS

The *appoggiatura* (which has received more comment than any other ornament except possibly the trill) is perhaps the most directly expressive ornament. Movement from the ornament to its resolution provides a decrease in energy and a decline in harmonic tension; for this reason, the sources are unanimous in stating that the *appoggiatura* (or any dissonance) is louder, or otherwise more stressed, than its resolution. (An exception occurs in Toinon's table of ornaments from 1699, which prescribes a *crescendo* from the *appoggiatura* to its resolution.[2] Toinon's comments pertain to woodwind instruments. The effect of *crescendo*, in the sense of an increasing tone on the *appoggiatura* alone, is impossible on keyboard instruments, although the resolution can sound louder through attenuation of volume on the *appoggiatura* itself.) The two notes are always slurred; Rameau's realizations of the *port de voix* and *coulé* in his ornament table of 1724 shows overlegato (Example VI-1).

EXAMPLE VI-1.
J.-P. Rameau, table of ornaments (1724), *port de voix*
and *coulés.*

It is important to differentiate the true *appoggiatura*, a dissonance moving to its resolution, from other similarly notated passing notes. (The treatises do not always make this distinction.) The French *coulé* is essentially melodic rather than harmonic, often proceeding from a weak note (the ornament) to a stronger one—the reverse of the strong-to-weak *appoggiatura*. Notation does not always distinguish harmonic from melodic functions. Interpretations can vary, but many *coulés* can be played ahead of or across the beat. (See the slurred notes in Example VI-2. In Example VI-1, Rameau shows *coulés* on the beat.) Baroque composers, the French in particular, frequently softened disjunct movement to dissonances or chromatically altered notes by ornamenting them with *appoggiaturas* and *coulés*. (See Example VI-3.) This softening effect is often useful, but the dramatic effect of some notes can be inhibited by added ornaments of any kind.

EXAMPLE VI-2.
Nicholas Gigault, Benedictus (1685), *ports-de-voix* and
coulés written out by the composer.

EXAMPLE VI-3.
Toinon, from table of ornaments (1699).[3]

Rameau, in his *Code de musique pratique*, mentions the need for variety in the execution of ornaments to prevent their becoming "insipid"; this variety was mentioned as one reason for notating ornaments with symbols. No one solution, whatever rules may be adduced, need be regarded as the only "right" one, and the notation assures such variety. Each new musical situation requires a slightly different timing or dynamic stress; the irrational time values necessary for the realization would be hampered by normal rhythmic notation. (There is a danger of precluding such flexibility when graces are written out.) Sometimes *appoggiaturas* were fully written out. C. P. E. Bach and Türk even proposed standardizing the notation for *appoggiaturas* of various lengths. These suggestions did not gain general acceptance, probably because of the inherent requirement of flexibility. Bach and Türk did retain the small-note representation of *appoggiaturas,* reinforcing the practice of not writing them out in full. The use of small notes or symbols prevents one from mistaking the nature of the ornament or adding yet another ornament to the written one. However minute, the stress inherent in the *appoggiatura* probably led Mozart, for instance, to write the opening of his *Rondo alla Turca* as he did (Example VI-4a) rather than with full note values (Example VI-4b). The original notation calls attention to the ornamental function of the *appoggiaturas* and thereby suggests a slight time or dynamic stress on the first note of each group, as it swings the upbeat toward the bar line. The "realized" notation of Example VI-4b suggests a more uniform or neutral treatment.

EXAMPLE VI-4.
W. A. Mozart, *Rondo alla Turca,* mm.1-2. a. Original notation. b. "Realized."

The dynamic effect of the *appoggiatura* and its variable timing can often be effective in initiating adjustments of time; the ornament's stress is particularly helpful in preparing *ritardandos.* The realization of written *appoggiaturas* or their addition to the music often depends on this usage. Because of its harmonic strength, the *appoggiatura* is especially useful in time adjustments, but many ornaments, embellishments, and small values in general can serve this purpose.

TRILLS

Trills can perform many functions, from accenting a note to softening its effect, or from gently prolonging it to creating a brilliant clatter. Fine pianists pride themselves on their varied trills (Artur Schnabel commanded at least a dozen distinct types), and although the harpsichord has no dynamic variation, it can produce a wide range of trilled effects. The clavichord lacks the glitter of some of the harpsichord's ornaments, but it can of course shade them dynamically. Harpsichordists in particular should guard against uniform and inexpressive rendering of ornaments, and especially against what artists so diverse as Wanda Landowska and Ralph Kirkpatrick each referred to as "doorbell trills."

All trills have a beginning, middle, and end, regardless of length or speed. Consciously or intuitively, the player must adjust the speed and number of repercussions to the time available, the desired effect, the course of the musical phrase, the acoustic, and perhaps the limitations of the hand or instrument. One should grasp firmly the kind of timing that each trill requires. Clumsy trilling often results from poor judgment of the available time in proportion to variations made in the course of the trill: its destination is unclear. A basis in perfect evenness is necessary before pursuing the finer shadings, although the latter are often technically easier; C. P. E. Bach warns that one must never trill faster than one can trill evenly.[4] François Couperin remarks that a trill accelerates almost imperceptibly.[5] This is a useful and natural approach, especially for longer trills, and is often approximated in the note values of written-out trills (see Example V-16). The rate of acceleration is determined by the length of the first note; the longer it is held, the more rapid is the overall acceleration. Conversely, the delay of the first note depends on the time available for the trill to achieve full speed and accomplish its termination. (More often than not, trills begin with the upper, auxiliary tone; pausing on it accentuates the note's *appoggiatura* aspect. J. S. Bach and d'Anglebert, among others, use the sign ⌣⌣ for trills with a strongly delayed auxiliary; other permutations appear in many written-out trills.) However varied the course of a trill, its timing should follow a smooth course of acceleration.

Control and clean proportions in a trill are generally more important than its speed. Especially for short trills in heavily ornamented music, a few repercussions will often more than suffice. Saint Lambert comments that short trills should always be rapid,[6] but there are degrees of rapidity. Short trills with few repercussions can concentrate them in the opening of the note value or distribute them somewhat more slowly and evenly. The degree of rhythmic absorption into the line depends on the accentual quality of the trill. In most contexts, and in line with Saint Lambert's observation, the repercussions should not be individually apparent, or the trill loses its meaning as an entity and can distort the rhythm of its own line or disturb the clarity of other parts.

Trills are of such varied musical function that one must ask if a given trill is intended to sustain a note (whether gently or with brilliance), to introduce or soften a dissonance (the auxiliary note perhaps becoming an "active *appoggiatura*"), to accent a particular note, to link notes, or to make a final subdivision of rhythmic activity. The last function is characteristic of many cadential trills.

Long trills may be necessary for rhythmic intensity, to link one note to another, or simply to sustain a note. Sustained tones are frequently marked with trills, or the addition of trills by the performer may be desirable. The execution of long trills depends on whether a purely lyrical or a brilliant quality is intended. In any case, the beating of a trill must always be faster than the values in other parts, or confusion results. Frescobaldi warns:

> If there is a trill for the right or left hand, and the other plays a passage simultaneously, the [written-out] trill must not be played note for note but rapidly, the accompanying passage being played less rapidly and expressively; otherwise there will be confusion.[7]

Long, brilliant trills can rarely be sustained at full speed by even the freest hand. However, the effect of sustained high speed in brilliant trills can be made by beginning and ending a long trill rapidly and allowing a slight relaxation in mid-course. Finger change is helpful in sustaining long trills (see chapter 3). Varied speed and intensity in a long trill can suggest dynamic nuance and can even help to adjust the focus of a phrase. (Skillful modulation in trilling can suggest a singer's flexibility, and the value of vocal models for trills, as for musical expression generally, cannot be overestimated.) Saint Lambert says that "it is more beautiful to begin it [a trill] slowly at first and increase the speed only toward the end."[8] A swell can be implied by beginning a trill slowly (just recognizably as a trill) and steadily increasing the speed, the rate of increase coinciding with the implied *crescendo*. The trill in Example VI-5 is open to such treatment; it must achieve enough speed by the entry of the left-hand eighth notes to avoid rhythmic confusion. The opening of a trill is its most sensitive area for suggesting a swell. A snapped ending to long trills can provide an accent and suggest a dynamic peak. A dynamic taper is sometimes successfully implied by slowing down at the end of a trill, but this effect is difficult to manage convincingly and depends strongly on context.

EXAMPLE VI-5.
J.-P. Rameau, *L'Entretien des Muses*, mm.25-30.

Trills occasionally appear with long bass notes, to sustain them and/or intensify them. Sometimes the sonority of the low range can compromise dynamic balance or the clarity of another part. If a softer upper-manual stop is unavailable or tonally incompatible with the other parts, clarity can often be improved by beginning with the main note and possibly delaying the start of the trill itself. Example VI-6 could be played in this way, which would be difficult to notate but is perhaps a valid interpretation of the existing notation. Expressive variations in time are sometimes less effective with low-register trills, and a rapid execution obtrudes less on the other parts with respect to rhythmic and textural clarity.

EXAMPLE VI-6.
J. S. Bach, Prelude in g, *WTC* I, mm.11-12.

EXAMPLE VI-7.
F. Couperin, "Le Rossignol en amour," *Ordre* 14,
mm.19-20.

The sound quality of a trill may be varied by articulation (harpsichord, clavichord) or by dynamics (clavichord), as well as by speed. A slightly detached touch can accentuate an aggressive trill; similarly, a highly slurred trill has a gentler effect. François Couperin's "Le Rossignol en amour" concludes with a written-out trill slurred in offbeat pairs (Example VI-7), a haunting effect that is difficult to render. The bracketed slurs may signify overlegato on the paired notes in an otherwise legato context, rather than articulation between each pair. Note that the approximate rhythms showing disjoint acceleration are modified by the verbal direction for gradual acceleration.

The clavichord can succeed much better than the harpsichord in coloring trills, not only by overall dynamic variation but by dynamic stressing of either the main or the auxiliary note. (To a more limited extent, the harpsichord can favor one note or the other by timing.) On some clavichords, slight fluctuations in pitch can also color a trill.

EXAMPLE VI-8.
Anonymous, *Can Shee*, mm.1-3.

Trill endings can be abrupt or aggressive, with or without an afterbeat. Often a short, rapid trill can accentuate the value of a melodic long note, as on the high F in m.2 of Example VI-8. Trills that lead into another note usually require a turned afterbeat, as at cadences. Emphatic terminations are occasionally suggested in the notation by a preceding rest (Example VI-9), a style that is perhaps applicable in many instances although rarely notated. Dynamic tapering at a trill's conclusion can be suggested by overlegato holding of the auxiliary note into the final note, or of the last note of the afterbeat into the note following the trill.

EXAMPLE VI-9.
J. S. Bach, Partita in b, Overture, mm.8-9.

Trills that accent a note are usually heard on the beat. A trill made ahead of the beat can also be emphatic in that it has the character of an upbeat and stresses its arrival point; but on-beat trills usually bestow the greatest emphasis. (A long trill terminating into the ensuing note stresses both its own main note and its arrival point and is therefore often the most urgent in effect.) Rhythmic evenness and/or minute detachment of the notes of a trill can lend additional emphasis. Although trills preceded by the note a step above the main note can link the former to the auxiliary (Example VI-10a), d'Anglebert's notation for detached preceding notes (Example VI-10b) shows that the step relationship does not preclude an emphatic trill. Trills that begin with a turn (shown by J. S. Bach and d'Anglebert as ⸜⸍ and ⸜⸍) can lend additional emphasis.

Many short trills and other ornaments require execution before the beat. Occasionally this treatment is used to avoid parallel fifths or octaves; sometimes it is necessary for technical negotiation or because of the orna-

EXAMPLE VI-10.
a. F. Couperin, ornament table (1713), tremblement lié
sans être appuyé. b. J. H. d'Anglebert, ornament table
(1689), detaché avant un tremblement.

ment's relationship to other parts. The rapid tempo indicated for Example
VI-11 can hardly accommodate trills on the beat; and execution before the
beat is often more graceful for trills that link two notes rather than emphasize one. Trills on metrically unstressed notes (as in 6/8 ♫♫) are often
linking rather than accentual in nature. Many trills are open to varied stress.
The short trills in Example VI-12 can be passed over smoothly (the trills
before, ahead of, or straddling the beat) or given accentual stress (rhythmic
realization on the beat). Different approaches can be taken in the repetition
(if any) of a section or phrase.

EXAMPLE VI-11.
F. Couperin, Les Folies Françaises, "La Frénésie,"
Ordre 11, mm.1-3.

EXAMPLE VI-12.
J. S. Bach, Prelude in c, WTC II, m.14.

The rhythmic realization of trills may focus on the main note or the
auxiliary regardless of which begins the trill or whether the trill begins on or
before the beat. Early treatises, ornament tables, and written-out trills show
that composers often differed in their preferences. Combinations of *appoggiaturas* and trills, for instance, sometimes suggest rendition with the first
note or the entire trill falling on or before the beat, or of the main note or

auxiliary note receiving rhythmic/metric focus. Neumann discusses such differences at length, comparing, for example, the "model" realizations of trills in ornament tables and music by composers of different approaches and nationalities.[9] Many French trills whose initial note sounds ahead of the beat are notated as beginning with a *coulé*; in many cases this may be the means of differentiating trills starting ahead of the beat from those beginning on it.

Trills are often compounded with other ornaments—*appoggiaturas*, turns, and other graces—and can be indicated by sign, written notes, or a combination. Many of these figurations are best played as a single gesture; both musical impulse and technical execution benefit by combining the notes into one motion. Example VI-13 is illustrative.

EXAMPLE VI-13.
J. J. Froberger, Suite in c, Gigue, mm.31-33.

Written-out trills with prefixes or terminations occur in some pieces, as in Example VI-14. Not all composers used specific signs for the various modifications of trills and other ornaments, and some figures are probably written out to show their shape rather than to specify the number of notes. (Louis Couperin, for instance, used only the signs ⁕ and ⁖. What he wrote as ⁕⁖⁖⁖⁖ in Example VI-14 could have been written by d'Anglebert as ⁖⁖.) Thus, written-out trills with prefixes or terminations frequently appear side-by-side with simple trill signs.

EXAMPLE VI-14.
L. Couperin, Prelude in C, excerpt.

Double trills (almost always for two hands) can be performed in a variety of ways. They are nearly always brilliant in effect, but the complexity and gorgeousness of their clatter can often be increased by ending, and occasionally beginning, one before the other. This device can also be used to taper the sound. (The more sound and energy generated, the more tapering can be accomplished by contrast.) Different lines with coincidental trills should often be treated individually, without running the trills together for mere brilliance. Occasionally, parallel trills appear for an effect of sheer noise, and it would appear to be against the composer's intention to try to ameliorate the sound, for instance, that of the parallel sevenths produced by the trills in Example VI-15.

EXAMPLE VI-15.
F. Couperin: a. "La Raphaéle," *Ordre* 8, m.2.
b. Passacaille, *Ordre* 8, mm.97-99.

MORDENTS

Many of the considerations that apply to the trill apply to the mordent as well. This ornament takes several forms; it is typically heard as 𝄽, which can be executed rapidly as an accent or more slowly as a melodic element. The number of repercussions and their position regarding the beat are also variable; like the execution of the ornament, these are determined by its musical function in a given context.

The mordent is extremely useful in its accentual capacity, for the accent can be varied both by speed and by the number of repercussions. C. P. E. Bach recommends the addition of mordents as a way of stressing bass notes, a capacity in which trills might be too active or time-consuming; such use of mordents also avoids the complex, *appoggiatura* function of the trill's auxiliary note. Snapped mordents can take the form of rapid execution and/or staccato on the final note of the figure: for instance, J. S. Bach's corrected copy of the *Goldberg Variations* marks staccato in the passages containing written-out mordents (Example VI-16).

EXAMPLE VI-16.
J. S. Bach, *Goldberg Variations,* Var. 14, mm.11-12.

Snapped mordents can also be rendered by simultaneous sounding of the notes with the lower tone released immediately (described by C. P. E. Bach and others) or in the way mentioned by Tomás de Sancta María, with the normal form modified by holding over the first note:

> The finger that plays the first key is not raised, but rather remains on the key. The finger that plays the second key is then pulled away from the key, sliding across it with a scratching motion. Moreover, the finger that plays the first key should press down a little on it, sinking it down. Notice that the finger that plays the first note in these two *quiebros* [i.e., regular and inverted mordents; Tomás prefers the former] is the same one that ends the ornament.[10]

(The inverted mordent known to Tomás [𝄎] is also mentioned by C. P. E. Bach and by Ammerbach, but does not seem to have been used as generally as mordents using the lower auxiliary.)

The mordent can sound more connective than accentual when played ahead of the beat (𝄎 or with several repercussions straddling the beat). This style is possible in Example VI-17 and is encouraged by the close proximity of two ornaments (the mordents and ensuing trills) at a fast tempo. At brisk speeds or in crowded contexts, mordents and trills are frequently clearer if they are played ahead of the beat (cf. Example VI-16), a rendering that is often more graceful rhythmically and sometimes allows the main note to be more easily distinguished.

EXAMPLE VI-17
F. Couperin, "Les Calotins," *Ordre* 19, mm.10-12.

The melodic aspect of the mordent can range from milder accentual forms to slow and languorous treatment, with either one or several repercussions. For instance, the mordent opening Example VI-18 is perhaps most

EXAMPLE VI-18.
J. S. Bach, French Suite in G, Sarabande, m.1.

effective with a slow realization, lingering slightly on the first tone. Such mordents can be made both gentler and more sonorous by overlegato. Varied execution of a single ornament, perhaps ranging from one to several repercussions and with varying degrees of melodic or accentual quality, is a possible approach to Example VI-19, in which the composer supplies mordents on each iteration of the soprano D.

EXAMPLE VI-19.
J. H. d'Anglebert, Gavotte "Ou estes vous allé?" m.3.

The long mordent is used both for its rhythmic and melodic qualities and to sustain notes. In the latter capacity it resembles the trill and can benefit equally from varied realizations. François Couperin's ornament table is unusual in that it makes specific reference to long, short, and prolonged mordents (Example VI-20a). The last (*pincé continu*) is rarely specified as such in Couperin's works (Example VI-20b) but it is perhaps applicable to similar contexts (Example VI-20c).

EXAMPLE VI-20.
F. Couperin: a. Mordents from the ornament table of 1713. b. "L'Insinüante," *Ordre* 9, mm.33-36. c. Les Folies Françaises, "La Langeur," *Ordre* 11, mm.5-7.

Like trills, simultaneous mordents can be varied; a slow, melodic mordent paired with a rapid, accentual one can sound very effective, and in tender pieces it prevents the abrupt quality so easily generated by this ornament. Occasionally one of two simultaneous mordents (or trills) must be played ahead of the beat or the two must be otherwise staggered to avoid parallel fifths or octaves (Example VI-21).

EXAMPLE VI-21.
F. Couperin, "Les Vieux Seigneurs," *Ordre* 24, m.23.

EXAMPLE VI-22.
D. Scarlatti, Sonata in E♭, K. 193, mm.1-2.

The mordent is sometimes combined with other ornaments, most frequently an upper or lower *appoggiatura*. The former often appears in Italian music and Scarlatti's sonatas (Example VI-22) and is usually highly accentual. The mordent with lower *appoggiatura* was often used by the French in lyrical contexts; in its melodic and accentual functions, as well as in its varying notations, the figure may fall on, before, or across the beat.

The preceding remarks concerning the *appoggiatura*, trill, and mordent also apply to the turn and the slide. These can be both emphatic (stressing a single note) and connective (moving from one note to another).

The way in which ornaments may be realized is affected by overall tempo as well as by local rhythmic factors. Tempo is sometimes influenced by the need for flexibility in the rendition of ornamentation and of embellishment.

ARPEGGIOS

Broken chords are essential to the harpsichordist's technique. The flexible clavichord is not as dependent on arpeggio effects as the harpsichord, although both instruments can create considerable diversity of accent and dynamic flux through this device. (The role of arpeggiation in timing and beat perception is treated in chapter 5.)

Arpeggiation is rarely indicated in keyboard literature before the early seventeenth century. Italian scores of this period show some written-out, usually descending, broken-chord figures; a few samples appear in Example VI-23. Some of them suggest a rhythmically free rendition. They convey the impression that the Italians often treated the harpsichord as an instrument to be attacked aggressively and made to resonate to its fullest.

EXAMPLE VI-23.
a. Giovanni de Macque, Toccata, mm.1-2. b. G. de
Macque, *Capricio sopra re, fa, mi, sol*, mm.105-106.
c. G. Picchi, Toccata, m.1.

In the Italian style, chords containing dissonances were often arpeggiated and/or reiterated to make the sonority and dissonance as full and sustained as they naturally are on the organ. Frescobaldi refers to such repetition and figuration in the Preface to his Toccatas:

> The beginnings of the toccatas should be played slowly and arpeggiated. In suspensions or [other] dissonances, as well as in the middle of the work, [the notes] should be struck together in order not to leave the instrument empty; and this striking may be repeated as the player likes.[11]

Luigi Tagliavini comments:

> In the written music of the period dissonant notes are not generally represented as being struck with the notes of the chord with which they clash: one or the other is usually held—in the case of *ligature* (suspensions) the dissonant note is tied and held; and *durezze* ("harshnesses," in this context "dissonant passing notes") occur while consonant notes are held. Given the brevity of sound of quilled instruments, one must strike the held notes again in order to maintain the effect and flavour of the dissonance. This technique should be used not only for dissonances, but also elsewhere in the course of a piece ("in the middle of a work") to keep the sound of the instrument alive and full. Frescobaldi's aim was, as Diruta puts it, to "produce the same effect of holding the harmony on the quilled instrument as the air does in the organ." "Striking together" need not be construed exclusively as prescribing absolute

simultaneity and thus does not necessarily preclude the arpeggio. Indeed, in the foreword to the *Capricci* (1624), Frescobaldi advises that "in some dissonances one should pause, arpeggiating them, so that the following passage comes out more spiritedly."[12]

Such reiterations were occasionally notated, as in Example VI-24, (given by Tagliavini). The freedom with which the Italians treated suspensions may explain the frequent omission of ties in music of the period, particularly in works by the Italian-influenced Froberger.

EXAMPLE VI-24.
G. Frescobaldi, Toccata 7 (manuscript version),
mm. 13-15.[13]

EXAMPLE VI-25.
L. Couperin, patterns of broken chords from preludes.

The French harpsichordists and lutenists of the seventeenth century frequently employed broken-chord figures, whether in the actual figuration of the music (one aspect of *style brisé*), indication by sign, or in unmeasured notation. The variety of broken-chord patterns available to notation by sign is limited, but the unmeasured repertory shows a wide range of figurations, some of which appear in Example VI-25, culled from Louis Couperin's preludes. Some of these patterns could surely have been used in the performance of measured repertory as well. The brilliant rattle of some of Couperin's figurations is perhaps echoed in Example VI-26a. Froberger occasionally goes to the trouble of writing out broken-chord patterns more

complicated than up or down motion (Example VI-26b), but they are generally cumbersome to notate. In any case, the figures appearing in the unmeasured style are extremely sonorous, and it is not surprising to hear Nicolas
Lebègue (and later, Saint Lambert) recommending, as did the Italians,
restriking chords for greater resonance:

> I have tried to present the [unmeasured] preludes as simply as possible,
> with regard to both conformity [of notation] and of harpsichord technique,
> which separates or repeats [the notes of] chords instead of holding them in
> units as on the organ.[14]

Lebègue's approach to restriking appears in Example VI-27a. Since the reiterations are supposed to have the effect of a single sustained chord on the
organ, the rhythmic realization of the example should perhaps unite the
chords in a single gesture.

EXAMPLE VI-26.
a. J. S. Bach, Toccata in d, mm.14-15.
b. J. J. Froberger, *Lamento,* m.2.

EXAMPLE VI-27.
a. N. Lebègue, Prelude in F, mm.1-4. b. Perrine,
illustration of broken chords.

Various seventeenth- and eighteenth-century sources illustrate broken-
chord realization with examples showing the chord members distributed

over much or even all of the full duration of the chord itself: for instance, four sixteenth-note divisions in the time of a four-note chord lasting a quarter note. (See Example VI-28a, below. This kind of realization is shown by d'Anglebert, Gaspard le Roux, Charles Dieupart, C. P. E. Bach, and others.) Such realization is of course subject to musical context; the intent of the examples is more to show a pattern of breaking than a rigid rhythmic formula. The most frequent occasion for pronounced division of the available time among chord members is in breaking two-note intervals. Saint Lambert remarks that "when there are several [broken intervals] in sequence, the notes are more graceful when noticeably separated, such that the second [notes] are reduced even to half their value."[15] Such treatment is also suggested in several French ornament tables and in Perrine's staff notation of lute music (in place of tablature) for use by lute or harpsichord (1680), in which arpeggios are indicated with oblique lines. In his preface, Perrine shows breaking patterns for two- and three-note arpeggios[16] that always crowd the last note into the last sixteenth-note value of the available time (see Example VI-27b). These, like other examples, are presumably intended only as approximations, to be modified according to musical context, but it is notable that none of Perrine's examples show restrictions of arpeggio timing to the first subdivisions of even the longest chord's duration (the longest of Perrine's illustrations being a dotted quarter-note value). This style, which is rarely suggested by other sources, can be extremely elegant if it is well integrated into the overall pacing of a phrase, but in some circumstances the illustrated patterns can create a splintered texture and a fussy surface rhythm that impair the integrity of individual lines.

The first two broken chords of Example VI-27a contain passing tones, called *mordente* by the Italians and *coulés* by the French. The French normally indicated them by slanting lines or brackets, as in Example VI-28a. These extra tones are to be released immediately upon sounding, while the chordal tones are sustained. Italian composers often notate such extra notes as full-sized notes, and it is not always clear whether they are meant to be released or sustained (see below). Variation in the precise duration of the nonchordal tones and of the speed with which the notes are crushed together provides an interesting range of color and accent. These passing tones can also help the timing of broken chords, for instance, if one of the chords in a rhythmically realized pattern has fewer tones than the others. *Coulés* and *mordente* appear frequently in both measured and unmeasured music, were encouraged in accompaniment, and appear even late in the eighteenth century.

Introduction of consonances or dissonances that are to be released immediately upon sounding (other than *coulés*) occasionally appear in French music as notated in Example VI-28b. Similarly, it is sometimes advantageous to add resonance to a chord by briefly sounding more than the written chord members and quickly releasing them. Often merely doubling the fifth of a chord will suffice. This technique varies so much from instrument to instrument and from one interpretation to another that such extra notes could hardly be notated in usual practice. Example VI-28c shows an unusual case of such added notes, distinguished by small noteheads.

EXAMPLE VI-28.
a. J. H. d'Anglebert, ornament table (1689), coulés sur une tièrce, cheutes. b. F. Couperin, Passacaille, *Ordre* 8, mm.104-105. c. Pancrace Royer, Courante, "La Majesteuse," m.3.

The term *acciaccatura* refers to held (or partly held) tones extraneous to the basic harmony of a chord: the French *coulé* in a sustained form. The Italian style of accompaniment in the later seventeenth century and the eighteenth favored free use of *acciaccaturas*, presumably to give greater volume or plain noise to the continuo. (Both Neumann and Peter Williams give examples of them.[17]) The most famous cases of *acciaccaturas* in the solo literature occur in the sonatas of Scarlatti (see Example VI-29).

EXAMPLE VI-29.
D. Scarlatti, Sonata in a, K. 175, mm.21-26.

The Italians seem to have favored a highly active motion of broken chords in accompaniment, of which C. P. E. Bach and others complained. In the later eighteenth century this style apparently gave way to more or less unbroken chords (see chapter 7). In both styles, *mordente* and *acciaccaturas* were generously employed. The Germans and French disliked the held *acciaccaturas* and preferred the *mordente* style; they also seem to have disliked the constant activity of the Italian arpeggio style.

Arpeggiation is useful in sustaining tones, "filling" the instrument, and accenting beats, depending on the speed, figuration, dissonances, and so forth. Baroque and *galant* music sometimes notate bare chords, the elaboration of which is left to the player. In such passages the harpsichordist has every opportunity to create a full wash of sound, whose volume and stresses can be varied by judicious selection of sustained versus released tones and changes of speed and pattern. Useful patterns include simple up-and-down motion, sounding of the outermost notes with up-and-down motion continued by the inner parts, rising left-hand and descending right-hand figures (simultaneously or in succession), beginning each hand's group of notes together and moving up and down, simultaneous motion in each hand but at different speeds, or the technique of batteries (Example VI-30). Accent can be produced in broken passages by a change of pattern, an isolated held note, or "whipping" a chord up and down, perhaps after pausing on the bass note. A *forte–subito piano* effect can be produced on the harpsichord by striking a chord abruptly and then repeating it at once, slowly breaking it. Release of all but essential harmonic tones can further assist a *piano*. Although the clavichord lacks the rustle and brilliance of the harpsichord, it can vary the volume in the course of a single arpeggio—a device of infinite flexibility.

EXAMPLE VI-30.
J. K. F. Fischer, Suite "Polyhymnia," Harpeggio,
mm.1-4.

VIBRATO AND PORTATO

The clavichord's sensitivity to pitch inflection is one of its best-known features. Minute adjustments of pitch can color the sound in many ways, but pronounced use of *vibrato* and *portato* is ornamental in nature. Vibrato was often specified as an ornament, with a sign, in Baroque string music (see Marin Marais's gamba music), and this usage developed for the clavichord in *galant* repertory.

Ornamental pitch variation on the clavichord is divided into two categories, vibrato (*Bebung*) and portato (*Tragen der Töne*). (Production of these effects is described in chapter 2.) Of the two, portato is by far the more limited. It consists of weighty execution of notes with an extra pulse of pressure into the key after the note is sounded. Türk describes it in detail:

The playing of notes which are slurred and yet detached [*Tragen der Töne*] is signified either as shown in *a* [Example VI-31] or by the word *appoggiato*. The dot indicates the pressure which every key must receive and by the curved line the player is reminded to hold the tone out until the duration of the given note has been completed. One should guard against the overexaggeration of a tone ... which some call howling.[18]

EXAMPLE VI-31.
J. D. Türk, notation of *portato*.

EXAMPLE VI-32.
Vibrato, illustrated by J. D. Türk (a, b, c, d) and
C. P. E. Bach (e).

Vibrato is much more variable than portato. Eighteenth-century scores show fairly frequent instances of notated vibrato on short notes, but its most characteristic use was on long, plaintive tones. It is in this capacity that Türk describes it:

> The *Bebung* ... can only be used over long notes with good effect, particularly in compositions of melancholy character and the like. It is indicated by the sign at *a* or by the word *tremolo* (*b*) [see Example VI-32]. The execution must be approximately as in *c* or *d*.
> The finger is allowed to remain on the key for as long as is required by the duration of the given note and attempts to reinforce the tone with a repeated and gentle pressure. I scarcely have need of mentioning that after each pressure there is a lessening, but that the finger should not be completely lifted off the key. Besides, everyone knows that this ornament can be achieved only on the clavichord, indeed, only on a very good clavichord.
> In general, one ought to beware of the frequent use of *Bebung* and when it is used, one must guard against ugly exaggeration of the tone by too violent a pressure.[19]

C. P. E. Bach supports Türk's comments, with a qualification about when to begin the vibrato (a remark added in the edition of 1787):

> A long, affettuoso tone is performed with a vibrato. The finger that depresses and holds the key is gently shaken. The sign of a vibrato appears in [Example VI-32e]. The best effect is achieved when the finger withholds its shake until half the value of the note has passed.[20]

Türk's remark that vibrato "attempts to reinforce the tone" is not musical illusion but plain acoustic fact. Vibrato, or even a single pitch inflection, can actually prolong a tone or very minutely renew it. This phenomenon is related to the use of pressure in sustaining the tone, as described in chapter 2, p.29.

Vibrato has both ornamental and colorational capacities. Ornamental vibratos usually exhibit greater pitch modification than those that discreetly color the tone. They can vary in speed, degree of pitch inflection, and placement in the tone's overall duration. Uniformly rapid, slow, accelerating, or otherwise regular or irregular vibratos each have particular uses. The vibrato of a responsive clavichord can be nearly as flexible as a supple human voice.

Mainly in the realm of tone color, vibrato can be employed on full chords as well as on single notes. Discreetly used, it can impart a warm glow to what might otherwise be a dull or heavy sound. Vibrato can be useful in absorbing the percussive aspects of attack and tone on chords, and it can enliven long, forcibly struck bass tones.

Vibrato can be used in conjunction with trills, mordents, and other ornaments; this combination is particularly successful in slow contexts. C. P. E. Bach notates several instances of ornaments with vibrato (see Example VI-33).

EXAMPLE VI-33.
C. P. E. Bach, Sonata in F, mm.33-37.

In very soft passages, some notated trills or even mordents may be unmanageable on the clavichord, for a controlled rendition is sometimes difficult at a soft level. A vibrato coloring of the ornamented notes is often a useful alternative. Of course, such a procedure is not applicable to highly characteristic and recurrent ornaments.

✿ Embellishment

Embellishments cannot be codified in the manner of ornaments, and in a certain sense they embrace all subsidiary notes from the simplest rhythmic subdivisions to wide-ranging and virtuosic flourishes. Late medieval and especially Renaissance embellishments often lean toward regular rhythmic

subdivisions and strong rhythmic impetus, in contrast to the irregular adornments of much Baroque music. The earlier styles, too, are sometimes
grounded in formulas to a greater extent than are many Baroque examples.
Renaissance instruction books contain multitudinous formulas for rhythmic
subdivisions (diminution) of different melodic intervals and sample melodies; Example VI-34 is somewhat representative.[21]

EXAMPLE VI-34.
Diego Ortiz, sample embellishments on a melodic
fragment.

A player drew on such formulas and examples when improvising
diminution structures on any appropriate music. This style continued
well into the Baroque. In late seventeenth-century France, factions developed between the adherents of the diminution style and those who
adopted the "newer" *agrémens*, the latter being championed by Lully.[22]
The dispute centered on vocal music, but the distinction and attitude are
worth noting. For keyboard music, the most important realms for the
diminution style are the vast repertory of intabulations (keyboard arrangements of chansons and motets) from the late Gothic and Renaissance eras,[23] the diminution style of repeat embellishments, and some
Spanish solo repertory. The Renaissance embellishment manuals and
many intabulations can serve as guides to the application of diminutions
to keyboard music; some examples are discussed below in the account of
specific style features. The French Baroque *doubles* with even rhythmic
values are among the last remnants of the old diminution style. The constant motions of diminutions in much Renaissance keyboard music (e.g.,
Antonio Valente's variation sets) may appear to be tediously regular to
the newcomer. However, in many cases the surface uniformity actually
provides a fluid, dynamic continuity open to delicate dynamic molding
and/or time adjustments.

The more rhapsodic, rhythmically variegated style of Baroque embellishment is characteristic of much vocal and string music and appears in
keyboard repertory as well. This style is often a looser, more *rubato*-ori-
ented phenomenon than the often drivingly rhythmic diminution style. In
any embellishment style, but particularly in richly irregular elaborations,

the player must recognize, and differentiate in performance, the embellishing from the fundamental notes. Although elaborate figurations often fulfil important stress functions, their individual notes are weak in the sense described in chapter 5. Large flourishes and elaborate lines are always based on a few structural tones, and most of the component notes must be subsumed in the larger gesture; and the complexity of the surface motion should be proportional to the overall phrase. The suggestions of dynamic fluctuation made by some embellishments' varying density of rhythmic activity should be brought out; the flexible, highly subdivided beats can be strongly adjusted to bring out strong and weak aspects of phrasing. These facets of embellishment must be conveyed in performance whether the decorations are improvised by the player or specified by the composer. Such proportioning of emphasis is more likely in the former case, as the player will be well aware of the role of the improvisations. In playing fully embellished scores, particularly of famous works that one has heard in a variety of performance traditions, there is the danger of giving equal weight to every note—and by emphasizing everything, nothing is stressed or delineated. In J. S. Bach's music, everything essential is often written in, occasionally more than is essential, as in the Sarabande of the Partita in e. Indeed, Bach's habit (particularly marked in his later works) of writing everything out was criticized by one of his contemporaries, the musician and writer Johann Adolph Scheibe:

> Every ornament, every little grace, and everything that one thinks of as belonging to the method of playing, he expresses completely in notes; and this not only takes away from his pieces the beauty of harmony but completely covers the melody throughout.[24]

Scheibe was incensed, not only at the supposed affront to the performer's common sense and abilities but also at the occasional difficulty of seeing the forest for the trees. Which notes were fundamental and which were the embellishments? Bach's notation does not always make this distinction clear, and indeed the degree to which embellishments are logically integrated into his lines does not readily allow reduction to a "simple" version. Some of Bach's examples of embellished repetitions are discussed below.

Although Handel only sketched out the skeletons of many movements, some of his harpsichord suites provide beautiful models for embellishment. Their place in the keyboard repertory is analogous to that of Corelli's embellished movements in the violin repertory.[25] The opening Adagio from Handel's Suite II in F is a case in point. Not only is it fully ornamented and embellished, but in the original edition (1720) the embellishing notes are printed in smaller type to distinguish them from the main notes. (Surely Scheibe would have been grateful to Handel—or to his engraver.) The excerpt in Example VI-35 is representative of the movement. The strength of various beats (and hence their timing) is suggested by varying distribution of embellishments on beats 1, 2, 3, and 4 of each measure. Usually the embellishing notes are organized around conjunct motion; the skeletal notes are circled in mm.6 and 8. In this kind of line, certain intervals or single notes can be stressed by leaving them unadorned, for instance the leap to a″ in m.7. Note the *rubato* dots in m.7 as well. The intermingling of ornaments (that is, conventional figures, whether written out or indicated by sign) with free embellishment, as in this example, is typical of all periods, from the florid upper lines of the Faenza Codex through music of the eighteenth century and after. The line of demarcation between ornamentation and embellishment is sometimes more verbal than musical; the distinction is made for ease of discussion.

EXAMPLE VI-35.
G. F. Handel, Suite in F, Adagio, mm.6-9.

There was no completely international style for ornamentation and embellishment; within any one period and school, the practice of different composers and players varied. One must seek as closely as possible the habits of specific composers or their circles in rendering the works associated with them. Most if not all schools of composition include works in which all necessary graces are indicated in full, and others in which only the bare essentials are shown; of course, many pieces occupy a middle ground. Handel's works include both extremes of presentation. Most of the famous works in the literature are already fully ornamented and embellished. (C. P. E. Bach remarked that many pieces are fully written out and that additions made to the score "must relate to the piece's affect, and they must always be at least as good as, if not better than, the original."[26])

Fully realized pieces are usually a reliable guide to the decoration of sketchier works in the same style.

IMPROVISED GRACES AND VARIED REPEATS

The habit of varying reiterated material is perhaps as old as music itself. Varied repetitions, whether of phrases or of large sections, can range from alterations in interpretive details to changes in the notes themselves. While preserving the original note picture, the player might make variations in articulation, timing, and emphasis, perhaps phrasing more in terms of the overall picture in one rendition and, upon repetition, phrasing so as to emphasize details. At the other extreme, one may create elaborate figural (rhythmic) embellishments and/or copious ornamentation and free (*rubato*-like) embellishment. There are vast areas of style and many valid choices (for many pieces) between these two extremes.

Written-out embellishments and varied repeats are extant for most of the early schools of keyboard writing, the virginalists being the first to leave a large body of music that juxtaposes simple and elaborated versions of the same material. Studying illustrations left by a particular school of playing and composition can be of immense help when one is preparing to make embellishments and varied repeats in works of similar style.

Two approaches to varied repetitions may be discerned. They are not mutually exclusive, although one style usually predominates in each surviving example. Of general use in different schools and periods is the technique of embellishing the diverse rhythms of the original statement with a fairly constant, even run of rapid notes, often half of the beat value, sometimes faster. They may run in one part or, more frequently, meander among several voices; the even surface rhythm is often an interaction among the different lines, essentially *style brisé*. The bass and lower parts rarely participate in this activity or in that of the second style. The second approach encrusts the original version with various ornaments and embellishments, creating great rhythmic diversity. These two styles relate to the diminution technique and the later Baroque *rubato*-like embellishments discussed above.

More than any other repertory, that of the virginalists supplies us with numerous examples of written-out repeats. As might be expected, they are nearly all for dance forms. These embellishments follow the division style; the passages (original and embellished versions) shown in Example VI-36 are typical. A faster and generally more uniform surface rhythm is usually found, either in one part (for at least one measure at a time) or frequently divided between parts. Brief points of imitation may appear upon repetition, even if they are not suggested in the first statement. Cadences are sometimes decorated with a sudden flourish of rapid notes, most commonly in long, extended sections and passages. In lighter, brief pieces, the repeated notes and even figuration shown in Example VI-37 are useful devices.

EXAMPLE VI-36.
Peter Philips, *Pavana Pagget.* a. mm.1-2. b. mm.9-11.

EXAMPLE VI-37.
John Bull, *The Duke of Brunswick's Alman.* a. mm.9-10. b. mm.17-18.

Varied repeats appear less commonly in seventeenth-century Italian music than in the English repertory. Their infrequency is hardly surprising, as dances were less fundamental to Italian keyboard writing of this period. The variation set and particularly the toccata were the leading forms, and as a rule they contain fully realized embellishments. These, too, show the diminution style. It is the basis of the relatively few instances of written-out dance repetitions. Several examples make especial use of broken (*spezzata*) chords in a manner again analogous to *style brisé*, often showing a very uniform surface rhythm created by interchange among the parts. Note that in Example VI-38 the bass is varied, sometimes as much as the upper parts.[27]

Some of the changes in the *spezzata* version involve omission of certain line fragments and figures that were in the original statement. The movement becomes on the whole less linear and more vertical in conception, not to mention less dancelike. The same style of constant eighth-note motion appears in five correnti with written-out *spezzata* repetitions in the second of Martino Pesenti's books of harpsichord dances (1630). One of J. S. Bach's *doubles* is reminiscent of this style (see below).

EXAMPLE VI-38.
G. Frescobaldi, Corrente seconda, Book II, mm.1-2.
a. Original statement. b. Repetition.

EXAMPLE VI-39.
G. Picchi, *Ballo Ongaro*, Prima parte, mm.1-7.

To be sure, diminution style with rapid notes was also used in dances. The variation in Example VI-39 is entirely confined to the right hand. Giovanni Picchi's print of 1621 includes many varied repetitions, specified *alio modo*.

The French masters were well known for being the most systematic in their notation of ornaments and for the sensitive role taken by ornaments and embellishments in their music, whether the graces were written out or improvised. (The French composers of the high Baroque were often taken as models by German composers, and their ornamental/embellishmental style often applies to German music as well.) Mr. le Gallois (1632-1707) said of J. C. de Chambonnières, the found of the French Baroque keyboard school, that every time he played a piece, he introduced new beauties, with grace notes, passages, and various embellishments, including *double cadences*. In a word, he so diversified them with all these different adornments that he disclosed ever fresh graces in them.[28]

Of the "virtuosos" who exhibit poor taste in playing, le Gallois remarked:

One hears nothing in their playing but a perpetual trill, which prevents one from hearing the medody of the piece distinctly. And they continually add passages, particularly from one note to its octave [*tirades*], which Chambonnières used to call "tinkering."[29]

Despite the complexity of the French ornamental style (it has been said that the French gave up music and took up ornamentation), the basic line, clarity, and mood of a work should be not compromised but enhanced by the added embellishments and ornaments. Many pieces are fully written out and require no additions, but even some of these can be heightened in expression by further additions. Many other works require ornamentation even on first reading. Some of Chambonnières's music is fully realized, some relatively bald and in need of added graces. Louis Couperin's scores are often spare, but comparison with some of his own and his contemporaries' music suggests that adding to his note picture is not out of the question. (His unmeasured preludes and some allemandes, courantes, and chaconnes seem to be fully realized; but many sarabandes, for instance, are rather bare.) D'Anglebert's and François Couperin's compositions are for the most part fully realized. Couperin remarks in the Preface to his third book of pieces (1722) that his music is to be played precisely as written, without adding or removing anything; this instruction was presumably in reaction to careless performances that he describes. His first book (1713) includes written-out embellished versions of movements that were ornate to begin with. It is possible that they were meant as models for similar procedures in other pieces, and that the composer's attitude changed subsequently. Saint Lambert, by the way, remarks that ornaments may be changed, added, or omitted at will, a habit Couperin must have considered to be indulged excessively. Whatever Couperin's own preferences, both his and Saint Lambert's comments give a fair picture of the prevalent attitude and practice.

The varied repeats usually found in seventeenth-century French music are usually based on diminution style, showing generally uniform rhythmic flow in smaller note values than in the first statement. In the French examples, the varied material is most often confined to a treble line, and the lower parts remain unaltered. Some of the surviving seventeenth-century examples are highly energetic and even virtuosic (Example VI-40); they appear along

EXAMPLE VI-40.
Anonymous, Rigaudon, mm.1-3. a. Original. b. *Double*
by L. Couperin.

EXAMPLE VI-41.
F. Couperin, Menuet in g, *Ordre* 1, mm.1-6.
a. Original statement. b. *Double*.

with gentler, more flowing variations. The latter style continued through at least the early eighteenth century, with specimens printed by F. Couperin (1713; Example VI-41) and Rameau (1724).

To judge from le Gallois's comments, the thornier, rhythmically varied style of added ornaments and embellishments, more complex than simple rhythmic subdivision, must have been employed in the seventeenth century, but most examples of repeats written out in this style appear in the eighteenth century. These elaborations are generally limited to sarabandes and courantes. With some exceptions, lighter or more melodic dances tended to receive diminution-style embellishments (as in Example VI-41); moderate or grave movements were given the more complex adornment. Example VI-42 contains a sample of François Couperin's treatment of a repetition in this style. Note the unusual variation of the bass. The fundamental outlines of the varied parts are not changed in any way.

J. S. Bach seems to have imitated Couperin's example in providing the graces for a number of movements in his English Suites: the second Courante of Suite I and the Sarabandes of Suites II, III, and VI. In line with Couperin's procedure, usually only the upper part is varied, the bass remaining the same. In the Courante from Suite I, Bach outdoes Couperin by providing two *doubles*, both of which make more substantial changes than anything Couperin demonstrated, including variations on the bass. In this case, the composed *double* possibly goes beyond what was expected of an improvised repetition. (Indeed, this issue is relevant to most very elaborate written variants. Do they represent particular complexity beyond the improvised norm? Are they perhaps written as examples for imitation at a simpler level? Or were variations of this complexity commonly improvised? To judge from le Gallois's comments, they may often have been attempted, but with indifferent success by some players.)

EXAMPLE VI-42.
F. Couperin, Sarabande "La Majesteüse," *Ordre* 1,
mm.17-20. a. Original statement. b. Varied repetition.

EXAMPLE VI-43.
J. S. Bach, English Suite in d, Sarabande, mm.1-4.
a. Original statement. b. *Double*.

Bach's sarabande *doubles* show two styles of variation. Those in Suites II and III add various ornaments and small embellishment figures, similar to the treatment in Example VI-42. The Sarabande of Suite VI is strongly reminiscent of sarabandes by Froberger and its *double* of Italian *spezzata* treatment (see Example VI-43); it shows continual eighth-note motion in 3/2 meter that occasionally infiltrates the left-hand parts. Such an approach can be taken successfully in similar sarabandes, such as some of Froberger's and that of Handel's Suite VII in g, also in 3/2. A typically French sarabande, such as that in Bach's English Suite IV, which is notated rather sparely, would be amenable to treatment in the manner of the sarabandes from English Suites II and III.

A number of sarabandes by Bach and from the French school are fully written out with complex ornamentation and embellishment without any alternative simple versions. Noteworthy examples are the sarabandes of Bach's English Suite I and Partita VI, and Couperin's sarabande "La Lugubre," *Ordre* 3.

❀ Ornamentation and Embellishment in Particular Schools

Much of the virginalist repertory is copiously ornamented and embellished with signs and written out formulas. Use of the single- and double-slash signs ⫻ and ⫽ as well as other musical details sometimes vary enormously from one manuscript version of a piece to another. One gets the impression that the English were far less particular than some other schools about ornamental detail. Comparing the different versions of a work can provide insight into certain stylistic variables. (The Musica Britannica edition of John Bull's keyboard music offers comparison of four different manuscript versions of *My Jewel*.)

The realizations of ⫻ and ⫽ are not fully described by contemporary documents. It seems likely that the single slash can mean an *appoggiatura*, a mordent, or a slide. The double slash apparently indicates a trill, a mordent, or even an inverted mordent; and the sign ⫽ persisted in English usage to notate trills until the early eighteenth century. (The inverted mordent was used by contemporary Spanish players, whose music and style were known in England.) Desmond Hunter has pointed out that the positioning of single and double slashes above or below a note may sometimes indicate the upper or the lower auxiliary respectively, but this distinction is not always observed by the manuscript copyists and is rarely reproduced in modern editions.[30] A continuous ornament, such as a trill with termination, is sometimes suggested by double and single slashes on consecutive notes.[31]

The virginalists' signs may generally indicate emphatic, accentual ornaments in contradistinction to the lyrical, written-out trills and similar
figures. The sign ornaments often seem to be less essential and less delicately
integrated into the musical line than many written-out graces, and the variation of signs among manuscript versions of a given work suggests a certain
carelessness of approach. Occasionally the signs occur in great profusion,
creating a *crescendo* of rhythmic activity, as in example VI-44, whose ornaments require rapid treatment and few repercussions. (As the tension heightens in the course of such a passage, the ornaments can also be realized with
progressively greater speed and intensity.)

EXAMPLE VI-44.
Robert Johnson, arranged by Giles Farnabye, Pavane,
mm.24-27.

Occurrences of single or double slashes on simultaneous notes in one
hand are interesting both musically and technically (Example VI-45a). It is
possible to realize such cases with one ornament ahead of the beat and the
other on it, a solution that is clearer and technically easier than some simultaneous realizations. The latter, for Example VI-45a, might take the
form of Example VI-45b. A double trill or perhaps simultaneous mordents
or inverted mordents are possible when the parallel ornaments are a third
apart. Hunter suggests that in some cases of ornaments paired on a beat,
one below and one above, one sign qualifies the other to indicate a lower
or upper auxiliary in contradistinction to that suggested by the placement
of a single sign.[32] If this is the case, it is still unclear which sign qualifies
the other.

EXAMPLE VI-45.
John Bull, *The King's Hunt*, m.23. a. Original notation.
b. Possible realizations of the double ornament.

Some modern writers have suggested Italian influence on virginal ornaments, particularly regarding the main-note trill shown by Diruta (♫♫♫♩).
The main-note style, as mentioned, may apply to short trills indicated by

sign, but those that are written out invariably begin on the auxiliary note, even when a main-note start is contextually possible (Example VI-46). The nearest to Diruta's trill is the written-out figure . Of the Italian *trillo* (; see below) there is no trace known to this writer in the virginal literature.

EXAMPLE VI-46.
Francis Tregian (?), *Heaven and Earth,* m.42.

The trill figures in Example VI-47 are typical of the virginalists' written-out ornaments. A gradual acceleration rather than a literal realization of the rhythmic values shown on long trills (Example VI-47a) can sometimes suggest a *crescendo* on a single note, as though rendered by a stringed or wind instrument or a singer. Some trills may have been written out to show a prefix or suffix or to show that the trill lasted for the full duration of the note. Descending chains of trills often appear as in Example VI-47b. Sextupulet trills (Example VI-47c) frequently occur in this literature, and perhaps some ornament signs can be realized on this model.

EXAMPLE VI-47.
a. G. Farnabye, Pavana, mm.54-55. b. Ibid., mm.71-72.
c. John Bull, *Queen Elizabeth's Pavane,* mm.1-2.

The Italians never worked out so complete a system of ornament notation as the French; sign indications are altogether sparser and sketchier. The literature often inclines more to embellishmental figures (whether written out or improvised) than to complex ornamentation.

Neumann provides a wide sampling of Italian trills of the late sixteenth and the seventeenth century and gives the impression that the majority of them begin on the main note.[33] Perhaps this is so, but the issue seems largely to depend on the composer's preference: Picchi, for instance, favors the trill beginning on the upper note, both in his published pieces (1621) and in the excerpt in Example VI-48a, from a work of his in the *Fitzwilliam Virginal Book*. Frescobaldi shows instances of both types, although he inclines toward the main-note type (Example VI-48c), as did his pupil Johann Jakob Froberger (Example VI-48d). Froberger often writes out main-note trills, and the contexts in which he uses trill signs often suggest them as well.

EXAMPLE VI-48.
a. G. Picchi, Toccata, m.21. b. G. Frescobaldi, Toccata 7, Book I, m.40. c. G. Frescobaldi, Toccata 12, Book I, mm.43-44. e. J. J. Froberger, Capriccio in a, mm.90-92.

EXAMPLE VI-49.
G. Frescobaldi, *Partite sopra l'aria della Romanesca*, Var. 4. m.1.

The most important aspect of Italian ornaments generally and trills particularly is the immense diversity of figures found in both the music and the treatises. With this variety, the lack of signs is hardly surprising: the numerous forms require writing out. An extremely cumbersome set of signs would be necessary for Frescobaldi's music alone. The notation, then, may often be approximate, indicating only the general shape and rhythm of the ornament; again, the player probably has some freedom in choosing the number of repercussions.

Example VI-49 illustrates a special type of written-out Italian trill. It shows acceleration (in common with descriptions of trills by authors from many nations) made in conjunction with dotted figures at the beginning. The main note is almost always the dotted note, favored by both rhythm and metric positioning. This treatment is extremely useful in many contexts in which the trill is not written out. The rhythmic balance between the main and the auxiliary notes is open to infinite variation.

The Italian variety in trills largely died out by the eighteenth century, at least in regard to notated instances. The music of della Ciaja, for instance, makes extensive use of several signs (sometimes rather crassly; see Example VI-50a) and shows nothing like the earlier plethora of written figures. One interesting passage shows a repeated major second (see Example VI-50b), which is a unique occurrence in della Ciaja's publication.

EXAMPLE VI-50.
Della Ciaja: a. Canzone, mm.1-2. b. Sonata I, Toccata, mm.2-3.

EXAMPLE VI-51.
J. J. Froberger: a. Suite in D, Allemande, mm.1-2.
b. Suite in c, Sarabande, mm.1-2.

Della Ciaja's figurations in Example VI-50b may relate to the *trillo*, a figure of varied pattern but always involving rapid repetition of one pitch. Its first keyboard appearance was in the early seventeenth century, probably as a keyboard imitation of the vocal ornament. It was known in Germany as well as Italy and was described by Praetorius in 1619. Froberger used it in two famous instances, shown in Example VI-51. Most of the written keyboard examples date from the later seventeenth century; Examples VI-51 and VI-52 show some typical instances. Examples VI-52a and b include both the sign *tr* and brief, *trillo*-like figures. Probably the sign is present not to indicate the addition of further, unwritten notes but to clarify the nature of the written-out ornament and to assure the proper freedom and nuance in its rendition. Whether an oscillating trill or a single-note *trillo* is meant by the *t* signs in Example VI-52c is unclear.

EXAMPLE VI-52.
a. G. Frescobaldi, *Toccata avanti la Messa delli Apostoli* (1635), mm.7-9. b. Gregorio Strozzi, *Ancidetemi dell' Arcadelt,* mm.32-33. c. G. Frescobaldi, Toccata 11, Book II, m.1.

The *trillo* survived, after a fashion, into the eighteenth century as the *tremolato* (♫), described by Pasquali (see Appendix 2). It is a possible solution to some of the *tremolo* indications in several Scarlatti sonatas, although it is not satisfactory in all contexts.[34]

The ornamental and embellishmental style preferred by Spanish composers and players from the sixteenth through the eighteenth century is in many ways distinct from those of the rest of Europe. Unfortunately, there are few sources from which to draw conclusions, whether theoretical writings or repertory containing written-out illustrations of actual graces.[35] Through the seventeenth century, the information on ornaments (*adornos*) is more limited than that on embellishments (*glosas*), but examples of the latter technique are to be found in variation works by Antonio Cabezon and others.

Most seventeenth-century Spanish trills begin on the main note. Ornaments using the upper auxiliary were preferred to those using the lower (such as long mordents). The ornament realizations shown in the treatises are generally only approximations of the more flexible performance usage; Correa d' Arauxo (1626) states that *redobles* (trills) and *quiebros* (mordents, inverted mordents, and turned trills) have no fixed number of repercussions. Expressively varied speed is as appropriate in this style as in others.

Variation in ornament patterns seems to have occurred as frequently in sixteenth- and seventeenth-century Spain as in Italy. For instance, certain of Correa's realized *redobles* in his actual music differ from his model examples in their extended prefixes, surrounding florid movement, or placement of the auxiliary note on the beat. Similar variety is found in the completely written-out ornaments of Cabanilles (eighteenth century), whose ornamentation is very close to the earlier styles.

The musical use of embellishment and ornamentation in Spanish repertory varied from one instrument to another. The music was often played interchangeably on the organ or the clavichord (the harpsichord seems to have been used less often), and the sources often recommend that ornament realizations on the clavichord continue their rhythmic activity for the full note value. Shorter realizations are recommended for the organ's sustained tone. Long, sustained tones were to be decorated, especially on the clavichord, and as far as possible all statements of a contrapuntal subject were to be ornamented or embellished in the same manner. Spanish clavichord style made up in rhythmic/ornamental activity what it lacked in sustaining power, while organ music was ornamented in a more restrained manner.

❧ Conclusion

In approaching the decoration of a movement, school and style must be one governing factor, but from the standpoint of expressivity, the following criteria might be considered in adding and realizing ornaments and embellishments:

Are extra adornments necessary? Is the movement fully notated already, or only sketched?

Should the ornaments and embellishments, in accordance with other factors in the piece, try to imitate the voice, the violin, or other instruments?

What are the dynamic implications of the range and rhythms of the written or improvised decoration?

How do variations in the surface rhythm caused by embellishments or ornaments suggest dynamic stresses and fluctuations? What additions can assist various dynamic implications and time stresses?

Do any added embellishments accentuate or reduce the effect of a particularly striking interval or passage? Is this desirable?

Do added decorations accentuate or obscure certain significant rhythms or beat stresses of the original? How do they relate to motives and motivic development? Do written embellishments incline toward driving rhythms or a *rubato* quality?

Do changes in the surface rhythm made by added decorations empha-size or undermine the phrase structure of the original?

Ornaments and embellishments are most effective when added or real-ized as an outgrowth of the intended expression. Whatever the style or pe-riod, ornamentation and embellishment—improvised or written out, simple or elaborate—should always further, never hinder, the musical expression.

7

Accompaniment

IN EARLIER TIMES SOLO PLAYING WAS often the exception rather than the rule for keyboard players, whose usual employment was as accompanists. The modern harpsichordist who eschews group playing is missing one of the great pleasures the instrument affords and one hardly to be emulated by other keyboards, for the harpsichord's powers in supporting and blending with an ensemble are unique. Accompanying is also instructive, for in attempting to match and blend with the varied nuances of other parts, one learns the dynamic powers of the instrument and gains a better understanding of the varied textures of solo literature, whose origins often lie in the practice of thoroughbass playing.

Many original treatises on accompanying are now available in facsimile, translation, or both. Among modern studies, F. T. Arnold's pioneering work, *The Art of Accompaniment from a Thorough-Bass*,[1] offers a digest of many sources and a variety of practical suggestions. Arnold's book is very useful, but his attempts to synthesize an accompaniment style of general applicability must be viewed with skepticism. Robert Donington devotes a substantial portion of his *Interpretation of Early Music*[2] to a helpful account of the accompanist's problems. Peter Williams's *Figured Bass Accompaniment*[3] is extremely useful, particularly in that it presents the accompanying styles of various countries, periods, and situations. The text is copiously illustrated with musical examples.

Newcomers are faced with two issues: a concern for historical and musical validity; and the need to deal in an immediate, practical way with figured basses. While research can give some guidelines on historical styles, one should bear in mind that every accompanying situation is open to greatly diverse solutions. As with other performance practices, historical information should guide, rather than inhibit, musical creativity. For one and the same piece, every ensemble situation (differing in harpsichord, solo instruments or voices, size of ensemble, musical interpretation, room size, and acoustics) will require a different realization. Thus, the figured bass is more than a musical shorthand: it is the only way to allow the accompanist sufficient latitude. One can vary the realizations provided by music editors according to circumstance, and this skill is often necessary when no unrealized part is available. However, the skill of reading a figured (or often unfigured) bass is necessary for full freedom in accompaniment. Facility in chord realization is also necessary for solo repertory, such as some of Telemann's fantasies, that requires fuller harmonization in places.

In learning to realize the figures, the novice should begin by practicing common cadences and progressions, first in four strict parts, then with more freedom. After gaining some confidence with chords, one can dive into actual music. A good deal of repertory employs a narrow harmonic vocabulary, and the beginner will find real pieces more stimulating than a constant diet of exercises.

The discipline of working with four strict parts is useful for some musical situations and necessary for training; skill in four-part playing develops awareness of which parts may be doubled or omitted in more varied textures. However, the harpsichordist should learn early how to thin out and thicken the realizations in accordance with dynamic nuance. Generally, Baroque authors describe strict four-part style as suitable for the organ and varied textures as most effective on the harpsichord. Often an accompaniment that is impressive on paper is ineffective in practice. Good realizations often revel in variations between thin and heavy textures that are anything but models of academic voice leading. What kinds of texture are successful in a given circumstance? Certain traits seem to be common among the early treatises and written-out examples; others seem to be more or less associated with particular schools.

The early authors who discuss thoroughbass approach their subject from varying perspectives, of wide or narrow application. Lodovico da Viadana, for instance, is mainly concerned with the accompanying styles suited to his *Concerti ecclesiastici* (1602), which are prefaced by remarks on accompaniment. Giulio Caccini's remarks (1601/2) are in reference to monody. Eighteenth-century authors usually speak from a more general standpoint; their often lengthier accounts try to deal with many possible musical situations. Although there are numerous differences among the musical styles that each author expected the accompanist to deal with, and although their recommendations often vary with respect to those styles and to the overall stress laid on particular approaches, there is some consistency among authors of various countries and periods regarding the musical materials with which the player has to work. Textures for large versus small ensembles, plain or embellished accompaniment, doubling of parts or lines, considerations regarding soloists, the range of the accompaniment, certain uses of dissonances: these and similar fundamental points receive similar coverage from diverse early writers.

The treatises are in general agreement on the subject of range. In most instances the accompanist should not play high enough to interfere with the important top voices of a composition. A low range, restricted to the bottom and middle areas of the keyboard, seems to be the usual practice. When the keyboard cannot help embracing the range of a solo line, it must provide a transparent texture that does not interfere with the solo.

How much the accompaniment may double parts of the ensemble varies with the period and with the size of the group. Renaissance and Baroque ensembles were often divided into foundation and ornamental functions. Foundation instruments (keyboard, lute, theorbo, harp, chittarrone) played supporting harmonies in a low range, leaving ornamental instruments (violins, winds) to play solo lines in higher ranges. The keyboard (organ or harpsichord) was often used in both capacities. In the sixteenth and the early seventeenth century, the keyboard often doubled ensemble parts as literally as possible, whether accompanying an ensemble or replacing it. (In the latter capacity, Diego Ortiz in 1553 mentions the possibility of performing a chanson or madrigal with a harpsichord playing all the lines, including that of a solo viol, which would play elaborate divisions on its line. Changing an ensemble piece into a solo with keyboard and one voice or instrument was a frequent practice.) The keyboardist would make an intabulation of the ensemble piece and use it to accompany. In such cases, of course, the range of the accompaniment was the same as the ensemble's; Michael Praetorius (1619) mentions that the ensemble must be accompanied in its own range. The practice of writing out full intabulations was gradually replaced by the short score, showing only the two outer parts. The player filled in the middle parts, relying on his ear and common sense. From such semi-improvised accompaniment to the use of the bass alone was not a great step, and one wonders to what degree the full or short score was literally followed when it was used. To be sure, Agazzari, Praetorius, and others mention exchanges of embellishments between accompaniment and soloist(s). The literalness of the accompaniment probably depended on the circumstances: a plain support is appropriate for massive choruses; and lighter, more diversely textured music could accommodate more variety from the accompanist. Accompanists were warned not to abuse the use of improvised embellishments, but to suit them to the occasion.

Doubling of upper parts, embellished or not, between the keyboard and the other ensemble members became less frequent in the course of the seventeenth century, and by the eighteenth century it was quite unusual. (For example, Alessandro Poglietti in 1676 and Francesco Gasparini in 1708 warn against it.) That is possibly the reason that the coincidence of solo and accompaniment in Example VII-1 had to be written out. On the other hand, Lorenzo Penna (1656; 1672) advises the accompanist to double at least the principal notes of a solo singer's line, evidently feeling that the singer would be in need of help.

EXAMPLE VII-1.
J. S. Bach (?), Sonata for flute and continuo in C,
Menuet, mm.1-5.

Interweaving of the upper parts in a heterophonic manner characterizes Example VII-2, a French work from the late seventeenth century.[4] This style may represent a common practice.

EXAMPLE VII-2.
G. Nivers, Motet *Veni de Libano:* original version and
contemporary accompaniment part, mm.1-2.

The foregoing examples are presumably unusual. Most early authors recommend close-textured four-part writing as a starting point, but as Quantz remarks,

> The general rule of thorough-bass is that you always play in four parts; yet if you wish to accompany well, a better effect is often produced if you do not bind yourself very strictly to this rule, and if you leave out some parts, or even double the bass an octave higher with the right hand. For just as a composer is neither able nor compelled to set a three-, four-, or five-part instrumental accompaniment to all melodies, lest they become unintelligible or

obscure, so not every melody allows an accompaniment of full chords upon the keyboard; hence an accompanist must govern himself more by the individual case than by the general rules of thorough-bass.[5]

Quantz is conservative. Variations of texture were so much a norm of accompaniment, at least by mid-century, that C. P. E. Bach simply remarks that accompaniments are realized in one, two, three, four, or more parts. Heavier textures, says Bach, are for large ensemble pieces that are not particularly delicate. A thinner keyboard realization is more suited for accompanying solos and to adjustments of dynamics through fine gradations of texture.

In the Baroque period, harmony and voice leading were often taught at the keyboard. In the treatises, the teaching of basics is often inextricably entwined with discussions of actual accompaniment. Consequently, many written-out realizations (in, for example, Saint Lambert's publication of 1707, or Heinichen's of 1728) show uniform, stodgy textures (see Example VII-3). They may typify a certain level of amateur accomplishment but are hardly consistent with accounts of the fine points of accompaniment.

EXAMPLE VII-3.
Saint Lambert, thorough-bass realization.

Some authors differentiate between simple accompaniments (such as the uniform four-part examples) and styles with nuances of texture. Johann Friedrich Daube (1756) enumerates three style divisions: simple or common, with plain three- or four-part chords in the right hand against the bass played in the left; "natural," which follows the mood of the solo, using arpeggios and broken chords; and "artificial," or "composite" (limited to the accompaniment of one or a few performers) in which the right hand plays counterpoint against the solo part, above and below it, using imitations, embellishments, suspensions, and countersubjects, and even embellishments of the bass line.[6]

The sources describe and illustrate many styles of accompaniment for different circumstances. Their full diversity can hardly be outlined here, but some representative approaches to realization are described below.

1. A four-part realization may be divided so that there are two parts in each hand. No large gap should be allowed between the hands. This type of

accompaniment appears in several mid-seventeenth-century German treatises, as well as in the eighteenth century. Praetorius even shows instances of three parts in the left hand and one in the right, with some parts occasionally migrating between the hands. Gasparini (1708) shows examples of "embellished accompaniment," in which the left hand plays chords (indicated by figures) and the right hand plays figurations.

2. Realizations in two or three parts must often be close-textured in order not to sound thin. C. P. E. Bach's examples of two-part accompaniments are low in range and contain many parallel thirds and sixths. Parallel tenths are also frequently useful.

3. *Tasto solo* (bass alone, as written) or *all' unisono* (bass doubled up, or occasionally down an octave), are used when marked in the music, often when all instruments are playing in unison or *pizzicato*. The single or doubled bass is also useful in cases when the harpsichord is otherwise redundant or intrusive. C. P. E. Bach remarked that the Italians would often omit the harpsichord altogether, rather than play *tasto solo* or *all' unisono*:

> [The Italians] do not care to have the tinkling sounds of their keyboardists in such places; the more so because it is known that they can scarcely play any chord without rolling it.[7]

4. Five or more parts are employed when dynamically necessary. Sources throughout the Baroque show many examples of the two hands playing as many parts as possible. When playing dense textures such as those shown in Example VII-4, the oft-cited rule was that care in voice leading applied only to the two outermost parts. Variation from one to a multitude of parts is entirely possible in the same movement. Authors mention

"pour remplir des deux mains"

In Cembalo erlaubt

EXAMPLE VII-4.
Textures for full-voiced accompaniment. a. Example by J. H. d'Anglebert (1689). b. Example by Georg Muffat (1699).

adding extra parts as necessary, first doubling the chord root, then the fifth, adding *acciaccaturas*, arpeggiating, or doubling the bass an octave up or down in addition to the parts played by the right hand. The last is mentioned by many authorities throughout the seventeenth and eighteenth centuries. Quantz suggests an approximate *crescendo* of textures:

On a harpsichord with one keyboard, passages marked Piano may be produced by a moderate touch and by diminishing the number of parts, those marked Mezzo Forte by doubling the bass in octaves, those marked Forte in the same manner and also by taking some consonances belonging to the chord into the left hand, and those marked Fortissimo by quick arpeggiations of the chords from below upwards, by the same doubling of the octaves and the consonances in the left hand, and by a more vehement and forceful touch. On a harpsichord with two keyboards, you have the additional advantage of being able to use the upper manual for the Pianissimo. But on a pianoforte everything required may be accomplished with the greatest convenience, for this instrument, of all those that are designated by the word keyboard, has the greatest number of qualities necessary for good accompaniment, and depends for its effect only upon the player and his judgment. The same is true of a good clavichord with regard to playing, but not with regard to effect, since it lacks the Fortissimo.[8]

Quantz later adds that when the bass rises to the tenor range, the right hand should play close to it, in few parts.

Volume can be decreased not only by reducing the number of parts and registers but by playing fewer chords when possible and by adjusting details of voice leading. C. P. E. Bach advises that a *cantabile* accompaniment can best be accomplished by tying over common chord tones as much as possible. He also suggests ways of playing softly and warns against seeking to reduce sound mass through an overly detached touch:

Of all the instruments that are used in the playing of thorough bass the single-manual harpsichord is the most perplexing with regard to forte and piano. To make amends for the imperfection of the instrument in this respect the number of parts must be increased or reduced. But care must be exercised to include all necessary tones and avoid incorrect doublings. Some resort to a highly detached touch in order to express a piano, but the performance suffers tremendously by this; and even the most detached staccato performance requires pressure. It is better to reduce the volume by using the right hand less frequently over passing tones [that is, play fewer chords].[9]

In the interests of dynamics, an accompanist can quickly learn to sort out essential chords from inessential. Depending on the harmony, the latter can be passed over with rests or by one or two notes that harmonize with the bass. Dynamic variation is frequently more important than a complete rendering of the harmony. This principle even extends to voice leading: as Telemann remarks, not all dissonances in accompanying have to be prepared and resolved.

Chords used in the course of ordinary accompaniment usually cannot accommodate the degree of break and time stress that might be employed in a harpsichord solo. Much breaking of chords makes the instrument obtrusive and confuses the other parts more than it softens the attack of the chords. Very rapidly rolled chords at strong points often have an invigo-rating rhythmic impetus, which is helpful to the ensemble, but, as mentioned in chapter 4, the relativity of stress devices effective on the solo harpsichord largely disappears in conjunction with other instruments. Recitative is an exception to these remarks (see below).

5. Notes must often be omitted from the accompaniment, even when the figures and reasonable voice leading require their presence. Quantz rec-ommends omitting notes that are out of tune between the keyboard and other instruments. (In some circumstances, the harpsichord may be tuned so as to accommodate special cases; see chapter 9.) Leading tones and thirds of chords often need to be deleted on this account; and even when they are tuned together, the ensemble is often clearer when the accompaniment does not double them. The figures sometimes act as a short score, to indicate what is going on in other parts, and the player need not realize every har-mony. For instance, parallel 4–3 suspensions played by both the soloist and the accompanist often lack delicacy and transparency; the keyboard is best confined to the root and fifth of each chord.

Some active basses are idiomatic for the cello, gamba, or other melodic instruments. When a great deal of bustle is necessary, the keyboard can dou-ble the other bass instrument(s) to fine effect, but it is sometimes better off playing only the essential notes and leaving the filigree to others. The reverse of this procedure can also be employed, for example, when the bass uses Alberti figurations, which are natural to the keyboard but can sound awk-ward on stringed instruments.

6. Truly contrapuntal realizations were known in early practice, but this style must suit the music at hand. Saint Lambert suggests imitations on the harpsichord for accompanying another single part. J. S. Bach is said to have accompanied in a highly contrapuntal idiom, changing trios into quar-tets with independent right-hand melodies, but this art was regarded as ex-ceptional. (Bach's written-out accompaniments to the second movements of the Sonata in b for flute and harpsichord and of the cantata *Amore Traditore* perhaps illustrate his accompanying style in a more homophonic vein.) As a rule, contrapuntal complexity in accompaniment diminishes as the ensemble texture becomes more complicated; and when accompanying very large forces, the best textures will often place full chords on strong beats, the harpsichord providing mainly rhythmic support. The treatises suggest that for most situations, however, good continuity if not melodic independence was appreciated in the top part of accompaniments. According to Johann David Heinichen, who is very conservative in matters of textural variation,

The art of ornamented thoroughbass consists of this: that one does not always play the chords in an ordinary manner, but introduces here and there an embellishment in all the parts (especially in the top voice in the right hand which stands out very prominently). One thereby gives more grace to the accompaniment, which is ordinarily performed very perfunctorily in a four-part—upon occasion five- and six-part—accompaniment.[10]

7. Eighteenth-century authors (including Mattheson, Heinichen, Gasparini, and C. P. E. Bach) show examples of *style brisé*, which was probably much more frequent in accompaniment than true counterpoint. Some specimens appear in Example VII-5. Example VII-5a perhaps shows broken style at its best, in a realization by the composer.

EXAMPLE VII-5.
a. De la Barre, Allemande "La Mariane," for flute and harpsichord, mm.1-3.[11] b. Example by J. Mattheson.

8. Authorities from the early seventeenth century through the eighteenth remark that one of the goals of the accompanist is a flowing, continuous sound, for which legato and overlegato are often necessary. Lorenzo Penna, for instance, recommends that "It is at all times a very good thing to play legato, in order not to interfere with the vocal part."[12] (Quantz speaks of the need to link notes as much as possible on the harpsichord.) Also, the realization should employ textures and rhythmic activity that will overcome the harpsichord's natural lack of sustaining power. In many contexts, chords can be distributed in broken figurations. According to Francesco Geminiani,

the Art of Accompaniment chiefly consists in rendering the Sounds on the Harpsichord lasting, for frequent interruptions of the Sound are inconsistent with true melody. The Learner is therefore to observe not to exhaust the Harmony all at once, that is to say, never to lay down all his fingers at once upon the Keys, but to touch the several notes whereof the chords consist in Succession.[13]

This style is not limited to the eighteenth century; it is also mentioned in seventeenth-century commentaries on sustaining the harpsichord's tone through chordal figurations (see chapter 6, pp.156-59). Geminiani's remarks do not refer as much to the quick rolling of chords as to rhythmically broken patterns, as his examples make clear. Example VII-6 offers three selections from his many samples of different realizations of a given bass.

EXAMPLE VII-6.
Textural examples by Francesco Geminiani.

9. Ornaments can be used in accompaniment. C. P. E. Bach advocates mordents in the bass as an easy and effective way to stress notes. Most authors allow trills in right-or left-hand parts, some preferring the right. Saint Lambert remarks that both can be of use, but that simultaneous trills in both hands sound too "affected." Of course, when the accompaniment imitates a soloist's line, the ornaments must be included.

The *acciaccatura* (often sustained through all or most of a chord) was frequently used in Italy as a way of adding accent and volume (sometimes, perhaps, sheer noise) to the accompaniment. Roger North, in England, wrote of the frequent use of dissonances in accompanying full ensembles. This English practice probably stemmed from Italian influence. The French also employed *acciaccaturas*, but in the form of rapidly released dissonances, sometimes called *mordente* by the Italians (see chapter 6, pp.159-60).

The French seem on the whole to have been less flamboyant in their accompaniment style than the Italians. Le Cerf, writing in 1725, comments that the best French accompanying styles do not show the Italian faults of continual figurations and broken chords, constantly rolling arpeggios, technical display, and chaotic embroidery of parts in both hands.[14] C. P. E. Bach apparently agreed; witness his remark about the Italian penchant for arpeggiation. In general, Italian accompaniment may have been less restrained than that of other nations; the Italians differed from French style particularly in recitative, which was, to begin with, universally regarded as a distinct style.

EXAMPLE VII-7.
Giulio Caccini, *T'amo mia vita,* mm.1-3.

The vast topic of recitative can only be touched on here. Early Baroque vocal accompaniments, sometimes written out for plucked instruments such as the lute or cittern, are often quite simple (see Example VII-7).[15] In the late sixteenth and early seventeenth century, strummed (*battuta*) textures were usual for vocal accompaniment on plucked instruments. Perhaps the harpsichord followed suit, although it may have shown more varied textures than are necessary for strumming on the dynamically variable lute, cittern, or guitar. Textures with more linear interest developed in the accompanying style of plucked instruments in the course of the seventeenth century, single tones alternating with chords as the harmonic style grew more complex than that of early monody. Some written-out keyboard accompaniments may have been intended as a short score, to be used only as a point of departure and a clue to the movements of the other parts.

Caccini (1602) refers to striking and reiterating chords to sustain them in recitative, a practice mentioned by other authors, including Saint Lambert and C. P. E. Bach (see also chapter 6). Arpeggiation and reiteration of chords is characteristic of recitative accompaniment in all periods and countries, but different times and places show variations in approach. The Italians, as mentioned, seem to have favored more or less continual washes of arpeggiation. Nicolo Pasquali (1757)[16] remarks that the harmony must be filled up as fully as possible in both hands. He shows arpeggios in continual upward and downward sweeps, to be rendered quickly or slowly, depending on the text, with pauses or abrupt accents generally occurring only at full stops. Gasparini[17] shows arpeggios with a multitude of *acciaccaturas* (Example VII-8) as well as upward and downward, inward and outward patterns. Italian style seems to have changed later in the eighteenth century: Rameau (1760) and Rousseau (1782) remark that arpeggios are necessary in recitative, but that the Italians play plain chords. Perhaps this observation is in reference to the lighter style of opera *buffa*, rather than *seria*.

EXAMPLE VII-8.
Francesco Gasparini, broken chords with *acciaccaturas*.

The French approach to recitative was more varied than the Italian style; so was the German practice, despite the German addiction to Italian opera. Saint Lambert recommends variety in arpeggiation as well as pauses and silences in the accompaniment during the course of the recitative:

> When one accompanies a long Recitative, it is sometimes good to dwell a long time on one chord, when the Bass [i.e., harmony] permits, and to let the voice sing several notes without accompaniment; then to strike a second chord, and then to pause upon it again; and to give no accompaniments except by long intervals, supposing as I said that the Bass has only long notes, which is quite usual in Recitative.
>
> At other times after having struck a full chord on which one pauses for some time, one restrikes one or another note quite by itself, but in such a way that it seems that the Harpsichord played it by itself, without the consent of the Accompanist.
>
> At other times doubling the Parts one strikes all of the notes one after another in continual repetition, making at the Harpsichord a crackling rather resembling musketry fire; but after having made this agreeable racket for

three or four measures, one stops abruptly on some great Harmonic chord, that is to say without dissonance, as if to rest from the effort of making such a noise.[18]

This approach is certainly much more flexible than that attributed to and described by Italian players.

It is hoped that this brief survey will give the newcomer some idea of the historical approaches to continuo playing and of the diversity possible in this, perhaps the most stimulating and creatively challenging, facet of the harpsichordist's art.

8
Harpsichord Registration

THE ROLE OF REGISTRATION IN THE ART
of harpsichord playing is secondary to the matters discussed in previous
chapters. The primary expressive resources of the instrument are variations
of articulation, legato, and timing. However, well-chosen registration can
enhance the effects sought by the player. Stop choices should be determined largely by the type and range of articulation desired. Some music
(e.g., pieces imitating orchestral *tutti* and *soli*) requires strong dynamic
contrasts, but in most repertory these and coloristic effects are of little
importance.

The player should be aware of the dispositions of typical harpsichords
of any time and place (see Bibliography, "Instruments"). Of equal or greater
importance is the fact that an instrument of restricted registrational means
often benefits from its limitations: with fewer strings encumbering the
soundboard, a small single-manual instrument may possess a more resonant
tone than a larger, more complex instrument. While double-manual harpsichords became common during and after the late seventeenth century, sin-
gles with simple dispositions continued to be made throughout the
eighteenth century and remained the typical instrument in Italy and the Iberian peninsula. Even when elaborate dispositions became more common,
there was apparently little or no repertory that required them. Quirinus van
Blankenburg, writing in 1708 of a large Flemish double with four registers,
praised its variety of tone colors but commented that no repertory required
it and that one had to improvise music to show off the instrument's capabilities.[1] Handstops rather than pedals remained the standard means of changing stops. They were often located above the keyboard(s) but were
sometimes accessible only at the side of the instrument or on the wrestplank
near the tuning pins (a characteristic of even elaborate German harpsichords
with many registers).

Pedals for changing stops were known by the late seventeenth century and were praised by Thomas Mace (1676) and C. P. E. Bach (1753). The fact that pedals did not pass into general use may mean that they were not found necessary musically, at least until the harpsichord began to compete with the piano in the late eighteenth century. At this time, English and French builders began to add a multitude of "expressive" devices, more or less extraneous to the instrument's usual designs and previous requirements. Leather plectra of hard and soft varieties, pedals or knee levers for stop changing, the "machine stop," the Venetian swell, and the nag's head swell are among the extras often found on late instruments. On the other hand, certain features extraneous to the essential 8′ stop design (4′ stop, buff stop, nasale) appeared with sufficient frequency in the seventeenth and eighteenth centuries to suggest that they were employed on a regular basis, for builders and players were nothing if not practical.

Timbral variety was greatly overemphasized by both builders and players during the first stages of the harpsichord revival. Instruments were built for maximum differentiation of tone color among the stops and frequently produced a poor ensemble tone. This approach may have developed in part because some of the best-known antique instruments were from the late eighteenth century, when stops were sometimes designed for solo colors more than for blending characteristics, as in most earlier harpsichords. (Cf. the late eighteenth-century use of quill on upper-manual 8′ stops and leather on the lower 8′. English builders sometimes used hard leather for a rounder tone on the lower 8′; the French would provide two rows of jacks for the same stop, one in quill and the other in soft *peau de buffle* leather.) In a way, it is curious that the marked changes of timbre that often occur from bass to treble in an old harpsichord (helping to clarify counterpoint and coloring the musical textures) were generally minimal in the first attempts at reconstruction. Since these instruments were often lacking in resonance and insensitive to the finer shades of articulation available on early instruments, it is hardly surprising that many players sought variety through frequent manipulation of stops. The tone colors on historical harpsichords are usually close enough to blend well. Even if kaleidoscopic, pedaled registrational variation were possible, there would be little use for it, for the many colors and sometimes uneasy blendings of the revival harpsichords are absent. Apart from special effects like the buff stop or nasale, changes of stop combinations on historical harpsichords before the late eighteenth century generally offer different shadings of one or two basic timbres rather than striking contrasts.

On a modern instrument of any design there is the danger that use of pedals will distort the dynamic balances that are often built into a musical texture and that more or less depend on the flat dynamic background ordinarily provided by the harpsichord. If used at all, variety of registration, whether pedaled or not, should be carefully chosen to reinforce the dynamic implications of the musical texture. As the texture becomes heavier, so may the registration, and vice versa, although many dynamic implications of texture are too small and fluctuate too frequently to benefit from mechanical reinforcement. To oppose a thickening texture with lighter registration is to undermine the effect probably intended by the composer. The harpsichordist should take advantage of all that a single register setting can provide before working out more elaborate registrational schemes.

Changes of registration within a movement are perhaps best reserved for long pieces, especially those with strong contrasts that could be undermined by lack of register change, or works whose textural variety needs registrational reinforcement because of the particular harpsichord or other factors. Much of the repertory consists of brief movements, as in suites of dances, and registrational contrast between movements or even groups of movements is often more effective than changes within short single movements. Sometimes it is effective to use a different registration for the repeats of binary movements.

With harpsichords whose sonority relies a great deal on variety of pedaled changes, it is advisable to play the instrument in the manner for which it was designed. Mechanical adjustment must to some extent replace subtlety of tonal response.

Several uses for register changes are terrace dynamics, which make clear opposition of loud and soft combinations; color contrasts; and graded dynamic changes. The last can subtly reinforce textural changes and in such cases are best confined to 8′ stops; they can often be effected by manual changes without making much noticeable variation in timbre. Terrace dynamics are often suited to music in concerto style, involving alternation of two or more types of musical material with different volume levels or timbres. Color contrasts can range from terraced effects, to imitation of small instrumental ensembles, to timbral contrasts between phrases or sections (e.g., from one variation to another). One should always seek a consistent parallel between musical structure and its registrational framework, except in many cases of graded dynamic effects.

Models of "concerto-style" terraced registration can be found in some of J. S. Bach's pieces that contain indications for manual changes. The *Italian Concerto* and the Partita in b are specified for a two-manual harpsichord and exhibit orchestral contrasts between solo and tutti groups represented by the different dynamic levels of the two keyboards. The composer's concern that no individual line be broken illogically between manuals is of particular importance. Bach's careful approach to independent voices leads to at least one slight tangle, shown in Example VIII-1. (The fingering is suggested by the present author to allow smooth negotiation of the passage.)

It is valuable to study the registrational treatment specified in these pieces and in several organ works that also appear to bear the composer's own markings: the "Dorian" Toccata, the "Saint Anne" Prelude, and some of the concerto arrangements. The style of tutti/solo contrasts shown by Bach can easily be applied to the large, orchestral-style preludes to his English Suites, arrangements of concertos by Italian composers, and similar movements.

Bach's registration, indicated by dynamic markings (and hence manual changes) alone, seems intended to *suggest* the different bodies of an orchestra by means of dynamic contrast, and no more. Historical harpsichords are rarely capable of any suitable variety of colors to compete with the versatility of Bach's actual orchestration, and any analogies of color between the two will emerge with little success in actual execution. As mentioned previously, the contrast of any decisive coloristic devices with the varieties of light and shade inherent in the harpsichord's normal technique can unbalance any sound image otherwise suggested by refinements of timing and articulation. Even when a performance is strongly based on variety of registration, the player should keep in mind the relationship of color to other expressive criteria.

EXAMPLE VIII-1.
J. S. Bach, Partita in b, Overture, mm.89-92.

Manual changes made in the course of an ongoing passage (as in Example VIII-1) should always be effected smoothly, never so as to lose continuity. In gliding between keyboards, one finger can often lead the hand so that it momentarily plays on both. The finger must extend from the lower manual to upper or curl down from the upper to the lower. The thumb is sometimes a useful pivot; both thumbs can even pivot at once, to make a smooth change in a passage like that in Example VIII-2. Such motions are limited on some antique doubles, whose keyboards are sometimes separated by a considerable distance.

EXAMPLE VIII-2.
J. S. Bach, English Suite in F, Prelude, mm.69-71.

EXAMPLE VIII-3.
J. S. Bach, *Goldberg Variations*, Var. 5, mm.29-32.

Bach's *Goldberg Variations* is, of course, another important source of original registrational markings. No contrasts are shown within variations (their brevity hardly requires that, in any case), but each bears directions for use of one or two keyboards, sometimes with the choice left to the performer. All of the canonic variations (Variations 3, 6, 9, etc.) save the last (the only one without an independent bass) are for a single manual, suggesting that Bach may have wanted a common tone color for these movements, although several can be played with the bass on another keyboard. Most of the duet variations are for two keyboards; a few leave a choice for performance on one or two manuals. All contain hand crossings. As the choice of single- or double-manual performance is sometimes left to the player, hand crossing is obviously not an infallible sign that two keyboards are required. Many such passages in the literature would suffer dynamically by reduction to single opposed 8′ stops. Even Variation 5, whose texture sometimes appears to require two manuals (see Example VIII-3), is specified "for one or two keyboards." Possibly in the course of the variation one could change from one to two keyboards in accordance with textural or dynamic implications.

In a manner analogous to concerto style, duet or trio textures can be suggested by contrast of manuals and/or dynamic levels. If the division of parts allows, a bass line can be played on one stop while another is used for one or two lines above. Should a middle part be divided between the hands, one hand can often cover both manuals briefly to preserve the timbral integrity of the line (see the circled notes in Example VIII-4).

EXAMPLE VIII-4.
J. S. Bach, Prelude in c♯, *WTC* II, mm.1-4.

Dynamic and/or color contrasts can often be effective on a scale smaller than that of concerto-like movements, but they should not disturb other facets of registration, articulation, or phrase groupings. Pieces such as Sweelinck's echo movements or the Echo from Bach's Partita in b are structured around dynamic contrast of tiny motives or occasional larger-scale phrase opposition, but such indications of dynamic change rarely reduce reiterated phrases to continual statement-and-echo. Echoes can be charming but must not be allowed to trivialize. Scarlatti's Sonatas K. 70, 73, 88, 287, 288, and 328 (for organ) bear directions for manual changes, and although reiterated phrases are fairly frequent, they are never treated so as to lose the force of their larger groupings. Strongly contrasted registrational colors should also be employed with regard to musical structure. A coloristic approach is often effective with sequences of short movements. The C. P. E. Bach variations, discussed below (p.203), is a case in point.

A significant proportion of eighteenth-century French pieces have *petites reprises* marked *p*; this seems to have been a typical procedure. A few other suggestive indications appear. Pancrace Royer indicates that upon recapitulating the opening of his *Le Vertigo* (an ABA form) the first four measures should be played softly. In another of Royer's pieces, a single note is to be played on the upper keyboard ("petit clavier"). This passage appears in Example VIII-5; the note in question is even expressively delayed

EXAMPLE VIII-5.
P. Royer, *La Marche des Scythes,* mm.64-65.

(marked with the sign ⌃). Such instances, and other criteria discussed below, suggest that in eighteenth-century France at least, a two-manual harpsichord was fairly common.

Overall dynamics can often be modified successfully by moving one hand to another keyboard. Such a change can create a partial echo effect on phrase repetition and can also be used to reduce volume over an essentially unchanging tone color. In the latter usage, the effect should not be noticeable as a change of register and should not disrupt linear or textural continuity. Such variations of dynamic rather than of color can often be achieved on instruments whose 8' stops are fairly similar in quality. A passage open to such treatment appears in Example VIII-6, in which the single upper-manual 8' can be opposed to coupled 8' stops below. The opening measures of the example can be played with a full tone, sustaining chordal notes together; as the solo soprano line begins, the bass can fade back dynamically by means of drier articulation in m.2 and by moving quietly to the upper manual after the opening of m.3. The combination of 8' stops helps to bridge over what might otherwise be a more noticeable change in timbre. This kind of keyboard change is not related to delineation of phrase endings but is entirely dynamic. Such an effect is often more successful in a large hall (where it may also be more necessary) than in a room.

EXAMPLE VIII-6.
J. S. Bach, Partita in D, Sarabande, mm.8-10.

Isolated notes can sometimes be unobtrusively emphasized by sounding unison keys on both manuals when the keyboards are otherwise uncoupled. This device is of limited application and is most often useful on bass notes and in a large performing area.

Effective as changes of manual or register can be, they are mainly expressive of large-scale contrast and should never overbalance the often smaller-scale dynamic implications of articulation, timing, and musical texture. (Textures that remain constant and yet specify dynamic gradations are probably written for clavichord or fortepiano.) A useful working technique is to annotate a score with dynamic markings rather than with specific register indications. The dynamics can be realized by whatever means suggest themselves on different occasions or under different circumstances. Nothing will be so quickly discarded as yesterday's registrations. Another advantage of marking dynamics is that they keep the player's mind on the musical image. They can include *crescendo* and *diminuendo*–any effects to be implied.

A player should be familiar with the possibilities of registration available on instruments of different epochs, knowing the norms, if any, of a period or country and what exceptions could generally be expected. The limitations of a particular era need not be followed, but they can serve as a useful starting point. Unfortunately, we have little data on typical use of registers. Some information is suggested in a letter dated August 23, 1712, from Thomas Day to Edward Hanford. Day comments on the care and use of a harpsichord; he mentions that the three stops "may be played on either all together, or every one by itself . . . all together are only a thoroughbass to a Consort: for Lessons, any two sets of the three are more proper."[2] One wonders whether two stops together were the norm. Since English doubles were normally doglegged (i.e., the upper 8′ jacks played from the lower manual as well, eliminating the need for a coupler), use of solo stops may often have been restricted to the upper manual: disengaging the upper 8′ to allow a solo lower 8′ would mute the upper manual unless a nasale were present. However, the same approach is suggested by French registration directions, despite the fact that French doubles typically provided a coupler instead of a dogleg. David Fuller has pointed out that French instructions for playing unusual repertory, such as *pièces croisées*, are always couched in terms that imply that the coupler and even the 4′ were habitually engaged.[3] Among other examples, Fuller cites François Couperin's directions for playing "Les Bagatelles" (*Ordre* 10):

> To play this piece, it is necessary to withdraw [i.e., uncouple] one of the keyboards of the harpsichord, retire the little octave, place the right hand on the upper keyboard and place the left on the lower.[4]

Saint Lambert speaks in the same terms: "[To accompany] extremely delicate voices, one can as we have said retire one or two stops of the harpsichord. . . ."[5] One is always told to disengage stops, as if they were normally kept engaged. Such descriptions may simply have followed a customary form of phraseology, but they can give us pause to wonder, in view of the aspects of English registration just mentioned, or in light of early Italian harpsichords. On the latter, two unisons were frequently provided with no stop-moving mechanism at all and could be played independently only for tuning purposes. On a double, was the upper manual 8′ the customary stop for a single 8′ sound? Were French pieces marked "tendrement" usually heard on the upper 8′? Even if the 4′ was removed from time to time, was the lower 8′ generally heard in conjunction with the upper? While the approach suggested by the descriptions may have been customary, there must have been exceptions according to individual taste. An example of registration from C. P. E. Bach, at least, illustrates use of the solo lower 8′ (see below). As far as gentle pieces are concerned, however, the likelihood of customary performance on the upper manual (or front 8′) stop is reinforced by the usual terminology applied to the different registers. In eighteenth-century France, the back or lower manual 8′ was generally termed the "grand jeu" and the front or upper 8′ the "petit jeu." Several instruments show such labeling,[6] and Saint Lambert refers to the upper manual as the "petit jeu." Another letter from Thomas Day describes an instrument by John Player: "the upper set of keys is an Eccho, very soft and in my opinion a little snaffling; but the other set has two Unisons like Mrs. Stratford's belonging to it, but a more noble sound."[7] Whether the snaffling upper-manual stop was a lute register or one of the two unisons (doglegged to the lower manual) is not clear. Hubbard infers that the harpsichord was a three-stop instrument (no lute) with dogleg, which is what Mr. Hanford eventually acquired. This suggests a soft voicing for the upper 8′ and possibly reflects English taste of the period. The French terms "grand jeu" and "petit jeu" certainly suggest contrast of loud and soft stops. If the ensemble in France and/or England was dominated by a relatively loud lower 8′, the upper 8′ was likely to be more sympathetic for delicate solo work, and the ensemble itself would emphasize the fundamental and the mellowness of the back 8′ more than the wiry overtones of the upper 8′.

The relative strengths of the 8′ stops depend finally on the player's taste and the use intended for the harpsichord. Two 8′ registers disposed on one manual can usually be voiced so that one is strong (usually the back 8′) and the other more delicate. Thus, a *piano* stop, a more robust stop, and an ensemble reinforced by the fuller back 8′ are all available. If maximum volume is necessary, equal strength for the two 8′ stops is a likely requirement. Two-manual instruments, for purposes of polyphonic playing on the two stops, seem to require equal or nearly equal strength from them. The duets of the *Goldberg Variations* are a case in point. (No German commentary on register balance in known to this writer.) In the past, as now, strong contrast between register strengths, equality, or the shades between probably depended on personal taste and the use for which an instrument was intended.

Apart from the French pieces and the Bach examples mentioned above, there are few extant indications of seventeenth- or eighteenth-century harpsichord registrations. This is hardly surprising since harpsichords varied so widely, and register choices are not as crucial as on the organ. Rameau occasionally suggests manual changes by indicating *fort* and *doux* (e.g., in "La Poule"). Fuller[8] cites a few other instances, notably in two chaconnes by

Nicolas Lebègue (second collection, 1687); as in most examples, manual changes are indicated. A notable exception, directing which stops are to be employed, is C. P. E. Bach's *Sonata per Cembalo a due tastature* (Wq. 69, 1747). This piece contains full registrational directions for a two-manual, four-stop instrument with coupler. The stops are designated as Flöte (lower 8'), Octava (4'), Cornet (upper 8'), and Spinett (nasale). The work specifies one stop setting for each movement and for each variation of the Finale, including several combinations for different *fortes* and *pianos,* such as full harpsichord, upper 8' + 4', lower 8' + 4' (*fortes*); and upper 8' solo, nasale solo, upper 8' + nasale (*pianos*). The variations use the buff stop on the upper 8', alone and with the 4'; opposition of solo 8' stops; solo 4' opposed to the buffed upper 8'; solo lower 8'; and various oppositions of hands and registers on the two keyboards. (Note that coupled upper and lower 8' stops do not appear.) Fuller gives a complete account and shows some extracts from the music.[9]

Although such full registrational indication is highly unusual, there is no way of knowing if C. P. E. Bach's Sonata or J. S. Bach's *Italian Concerto,* Partita in b, and *Goldberg Variations* reflect common practice or represent unusually varied registrations. If such changes are indicated in some scores, can we infer that none are intended where none are marked? This does not seem likely. Again, the variation among instruments would make many registrational indications useless. In the case of most printed collections, use of a two-manual harpsichord could not be presupposed, and the music might be played on a different instrument altogether. C. P. E. Bach's Sonata may represent an unusual case in which specific colors were desired by the composer; a performer might otherwise have arranged a different but equally colorful registration. J. S. Bach's *Clavierübung* II registrations are a logical outcome of the composer's concern with emulating orchestral effects; this collection and the *Goldberg Variations* are unusual in being specified for a two-manual harpsichord, which is not indicated for Bach's other keyboard music. These pieces most likely represent special and illustrative cases, rather than limitations (due to lack of indications) on other repertory.

Employment of registers is an extremely subjective matter, depending on individual interpretation, instrument, and acoustic. Nonetheless, to conclude, a few suggestions may be offered regarding stops and stop combinations:

1. A single 8' stop, particularly a back- or lower-manual 8', is often best for *cantabile* movements. Playing with one hand on each 8' of a two-manual instrument is usually not as successful as playing with both hands on the same stop, even if the parts are consistently accommodated, unless a duet or trio contrast is to be suggested. The divided sonority of different stops in a

homophonic or even polyphonic texture sometimes distracts from the balances otherwise set up in the music.

2. Two 8' stops used in combination are useful for both *cantabile* and brilliant movements. The increased fullness of the sound generally offers greater flexibility than a single 8' can provide in realizing the dynamics of textural variation. Overall manipulation of tone and dynamics is usually more varied with combined 8' stops, whereas a single 8' is often preferable for delicate linear adjustments of articulation and legato. A combination of two 8' stops is perhaps the most generally useful and flexible disposition for a small harpsichord.

3. The combination of the 4' with a single 8' is brittle and inflexible when their overtones do not blend properly. In such a case, a solo 8' with 4' is often best reserved for special coloring. When an instrument carries only two choirs of strings, a single 8' often retains more tonal fullness and reveals better blending powers and articulatory sensitivity with the 4' than in a similarly designed harpsichord with two 8' stops and a 4'. This combination is mentioned in some sources as typical of solos, and it is employed in the C. P. E. Bach registrations mentioned above.

4. Solo use of the 4', at either 8' or 4' pitch level, can produce lovely and plaintive effects, although to blend with the 8' stop(s) of some instruments, the 4' must be voiced so softly as to endanger its usefulness as a solo. In the late Renaissance and early Baroque, a separate ottavino (a small spinet at 4' pitch) was sometimes used on top of a larger instrument, a practice mentioned by Praetorius.[10] It appears that some seventeenth-century French doubles were disposed with only a 4' on the upper manual, but the organological evidence is unclear.[11] Some sources mention the same thing for German harpsichords even in the eighteenth century,[12] although no German instruments showing such a disposition have survived. In any case, it seems that use of 4' as a solo stop and perhaps for echo effects was widespread though perhaps not habitual.

5. The buff stop can be cloying when used for long stretches, and it does not allow much subtlety of touch. Used discreetly in thin textures, it can have a charming effect. Extreme overlegato is often useful with this stop, whether it is used to accompany a line or for all parts. Its least obtrusive employment is in left-hand accompaniments.

6. The lute, or nasale, is also easily heard to excess, although a fine one can be ravishing in tone. Its nasality is best voiced *piano*, and thus it can provide a welcome change of volume. In seventeenth-century England the lute was apparently often used to brighten the ensemble in place of the 4', and its use in this capacity should not be overlooked.

7. The 16' stop can provide grandeur in tutti passages and solemnity when combined with single or combined 8' stops, but it can easily render

textures opaque; and its long sustaining power limits the diversity of articulation and legato. The 16' is perhaps best employed at a grand climax to extend the apparent limits of an instrument's resources, or as a color stop by itself or in conjunction with the 4'. It must be remembered that, historically, the 16' appears only on three extant instruments by Hass, which seem to be rarities for their time, and on two other quite atypical instruments from very late in the eighteenth century. Michael Mietke, Gottfried Silbermann, and Johann Heinrich Harrass are also said to have built harpsichords with the 16' register, but no specimens have survived. Interest in the stop seems to have been restricted to Germany.

A unique three-manual harpsichord by Hass (1740) places a 16' stop on the bottom keyboard with a 2'. The middle manual controls 8' and 4' stops and shares a dogleg 8' with the top keyboard, which also has a nasale. This arrangement allows easy solo use of the 16'. More importantly, when the middle keyboard is coupled to the bottom, the 16' can reinforce the bass line of a piece while the right hand plays with one or another registration on the middle manual or even on the top. Thus, texture permitting, a full ensemble can be achieved, yet with the 16' only on the bass line. This is perhaps the ideal arrangement for use of the stop.

8. The *peau de buffle* stop of soft buffalo hide plectra, invented by the French in the 1760s, belongs entirely to late French repertory by composers such as Balbâtre. Its rather frequent appearance on modern reproductions parallels the general overemphasis that has been given to the French harpsichord. The stop is lovely in quality but of limited non-anachronistic use; it is perhaps at its best in broken-chord accompaniments. It is very difficult to keep in regulation, and since it adds weight to the action, there should also be a device on the harpsichord to raise the jacks when the stop is not in use.

❦ Conclusion

A registration should be selected for musical value, not for superficial variety of color. Stop changes should be logically integrated into a larger registrational scheme and coordinated with the dynamic levels built into the musical texture. Orchestral opposition of manuals should be consistent in regard to *tutti* and *soli*. Changes of manual made purely for dynamic effect should be made smoothly and calculated for the least alteration of timbre. Although some historical sources imply a rather unadventurous approach to registration, some (van Blankenburg and C. P. E. Bach) give precedents for using the instrument's potential for varied sonorities. A piece registered in the manner of C. P. E. Bach's *Sonata* operates on a somewhat different level from the delicate timing and range of articulations predicated on conservative use of registers: instead of a flat dynamic plane and many dynamic suggestions, a full realization occurs in terms of variegated timbre. Both are valid approaches musically and historically, but they should perhaps be kept segregated to some degree. In the course of a generally staid registrational scheme, the possibility of overbalancing musical suggestions and implications by a sudden dash of purely coloristic effect should be weighed carefully.

Temperament

ALL PLAYERS OF THE HARPSICHORD AND clavichord should be able to tune and regulate their instruments. Beyond the matter of practical upkeep, the variations possible in musical temperament profoundly affect the music to be played. Since several books and a number of articles have appeared on the subject of keyboard temperament, the present discussion will be limited to the description of a few useful temperaments and consideration of the treatment of temperament generally.

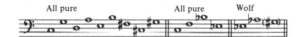

EXAMPLE IX-1.
Pythagorean tuning pattern.

Pythagorean temperament is most suitable for late medieval and early Renaissance music. Fifths are tuned absolutely pure (beatless), with the natural acoustical inequality of the cycle of fifths placed on one particular fifth of the tuner's choice, called the "wolf." (A pure tuning of the complete cycle of fifths returns to a starting note considerably sharper than the one that began the cycle. In most temperaments, the inequality is spread over several fifths, to make them all usable; in equal temperament, the inequality is divided uniformly over all twelve fifths of the cycle.) Pythagorean temperament features eight very sharp (wide) major thirds and four that are essentially pure. For primarily linear music, the high leading tones provided by the wide thirds are an advantage. The tuning cycle in Example IX-1 may be used; it sets the wolf interval on E♭–G♯ and results in nearly pure thirds on B, F♯, C♯, and G♯. An alternative placement of the wolf in a Pythagorean system is on B–F♯, with resultant pure major thirds on D, A, E, and B; this system is more useful for much early literature.[1]

For music based more on vertical sonorities but without enharmonic requirements, meantone temperament is often the most successful, and it was widely used from the Renaissance through the early nineteenth century. Its basic form (quarter comma, in which four consecutive fifths are flattened equally to produce a pure major third) involves pure major thirds and narrow fifths, although modifications are possible. The easiest way to tune it is illustrated in Example IX-2. A cycle beginning on F is shown; it is the easiest to set using an A fork, although a bearing set from C is frequently useful.

EXAMPLE IX-2.
Meantone tuning pattern.

Following Example IX-2, F should be tuned beatless to A; then the three intervening notes in the cycle of fifths (C, G, and D) must be tuned so that the four intervals F–C, C–G, G–D, and D–A are all beating equally, with narrow fifths and wide fourths. (Thus, all intervals in an ascending pattern of fifths and fourths are tuned slightly flat.) This is the only difficult part of the temperament; the remaining notes of the chromatic scale are then tuned in pure major thirds to the already established pitches: B is tuned pure to G, E to C, and so forth. In setting the accidentals, choices must be made according to the music: C♯ or D♭, E♭ or D♯, etc. No enharmonic usage is possible, and for this reason some keyboards were built with a few divided accidentals, for freer modulatory range and to avoid the necessity of retuning.

EXAMPLE IX-3.
L. Couperin, Chaconne in d, mm.1-4.

The natural harmonic stresses and relaxations are increased with this temperament, and it does well by most seventeenth-century music and much early eighteenth-century repertory. Even some of its harshness can be expressive, for instance, the wide-beating F♯–B♭ and the pure B♭–D in Example IX-3.

Mark Lindley describes a variant of normal meantone, which was probably known by the mid-seventeenth century:

> To set a nicely shaded form of what became known in the eighteenth century as *tempérament ordinaire*, tune the diatonic notes and F sharp in a regular meantone pattern, with the initial G–E beating four or five times per second; make D sharp/E flat (below middle C) beat equally fast with low B and with G; tune B flat as nearly pure as possible with both E flat and F; make C sharp pure to F sharp, and G sharp pure to C sharp; and then raise F sharp very slightly, just enough to make it impure with C sharp, but not enough to make it pure with B.[2]

Such an adjustment can accommodate some degree of enharmonic use and has many of the virtues of pure meantone temperament; it is very useful for the mid-Baroque. Andreas Werckmeister's famous third temperament, by the way, is derived from quarter comma. Beginning from C, the first three fifths and the sixth fifth of the cycle (C–G, G–D, D–A, and B–F♯) are each flattened by a quarter comma, and then the rest are tuned pure. This tuning is most easily set by beginning with a normal quarter-comma bearing on the opening fifths C–G–D–A–E, then tuning E pure to A, B pure to E, and finally tuning pure fifths backward through the cycle, C–F–B♭–E♭–A♭–D♭–(C♯)–F♯. The interval B–F♯ should beat at the same rate as the fifths that opened the cycle. This temperament is colorful and useful for enharmonic music.

A great many temperaments were described by theorists of the Renaissance and Baroque periods, and considerable variation in temperament occurred at any time or place. It is difficult or impossible to assess to what degree some of the temperaments described by theorists entered actual practice. Some appear so frequently in treatises that their common use seems likely; and some, like quarter-comma meantone, are described by certain authors as being in general usage. In deciding on a temperament for a specific work or set of works, one must consider what association, if any, can be found between the composer and the source of a given temperament, and what musical grounds justify the choice of temperament. In the former case, association of time and place between theorist and composer is often the extent to which a relationship can be ascertained; in the latter, subjectivity of choice is inevitably a factor. This is not necessarily a disadvantage, and no one choice needs to be regarded as final. Since various shadings of certain basic temperaments appear in early treatises, it seems reasonable to suppose that minor adjustments might be made for special cases. Different temperaments applied to the same work may highlight various aspects of it, just as different performances do.

Within the same historical framework, several different temperaments are possible. Most music of the sixteenth, seventeenth, and eighteenth centuries does not stray far from the "natural" tonalities (C major, D major, etc.), and unexceptional music in the common range of keys may have employed whatever temperament to which an instrument was habitually tuned: a kind of temperament that a performer might expect, just as a pianist today expects a piano to sound in equal temperament. (Apparently some form of meantone often filled the role of such a standard temperament. Certainly clavichord fretting was often set up for meantone and allows limited variation of temperament.) On the other hand, certain tonalities are quite unusual in the repertory, and one wonders to what degree they were accommodated by the "usual" temperament of the composer's or performer's locality. The vast majority of Scarlatti's 555 sonatas are in "natural" keys. Did the composer have particular key colors in mind (aside from any associations with absolute pitch) when he wrote in c♯ (Sonatas K. 246-247), f♯ (K. 447-448), or F♯ (K. 318-319)? F♯ minor was the *ton de la chèvre* to a seventeenth-century French musician because of its "bleating" intervals: for Louis Couperin's Pavanne in f♯, how much did intervals actually bleat? How much was a "usual" temperament adjusted, if at all? Was adjustment necessary? In single works that modulate widely, such as John Bull's hexachord fantasy *Ut, re, mi, fa, sol, la (Fitzwilliam Virginal Book*, #51) or J. S. Bach's *Chromatic Fantasy and Fugue*, to what degree were modulations colored by inequalities of temperament? The same can be asked for collections that span a wide range of keys, such as J. K. F. Fischer's *Ariadne Musicae* (nineteen tonalities), J. S. Bach's *Well-Tempered Clavier* (twenty-four tonalities), and Bach's *Inventions* and *Sinfonias* (fifteen tonalities). Do such collections presuppose a constant temperament, or might adjustments be made throughout? (Fischer's collection is primarily for the organ, which is much harder to adjust than the harpsichord or clavichord.)

Answers to such questions can in most cases only be conjectural. Little information is extant concerning composers' own preferences (Rameau is a notable exception), and it is questionable to what degree certain systems proposed by theorists actually entered common practice. One must depend on secondhand material: descriptions stemming from a composer's environment and clues offered by the music.

In the broadest terms, several kinds of temperament can be categorized, based on the manner in which the comma is distributed. Mark Lindley divides temperament into meantone, equal temperament, and irregular systems.[3] It is possible to form a continuum from Pythagorean, through meantone and well-tempered systems, to equal temperament with respect to acceptable ranges of modulation and tonality. The fifths in irregular temperaments vary in size so that none are left unusable and so that the most frequently used thirds are rendered most nearly pure. Infinite shadings are possible. Equal temperament, of course, favors no one key over any other. In musical terms, one is concerned with temperaments that are primarily linear (i.e., with a high leading tone, as in Pythagorean temperament) or primarily harmonic (with generally pure chords, as in meantone). Obviously, historical knowledge can to some extent delimit the range of possible temperaments for a given work, but in musical terms, the following criteria are important for further narrowing of the possibilities: Is the music primarily melodic (e.g., with strongly independent lines as in medieval motet intabulations) or primarily harmonic in texture? Are there any enharmonic relationships? With or without enharmonic relationships, do chromatic passages suggest roughly equal division of semitones? Do different pieces in the output of one composer or school suggest that certain intervallic colorings were associated with specific tonalities? When tuning for a specific, perhaps unusual work, what temperament will best enhance the tension and repose between the tonic key and modulatory areas?

The prevalence of horizontal over vertical factors is most characteristic of some medieval repertory, in which voices were often composed one at a time rather than simultaneously. (Keyboard repertory of this period generally consists of intabulations of vocal works.) As mentioned, some fifteenth-century theorists recommend Pythagorean temperament for keyboard instruments; it suits the repertory by virtue of its sharp leading tones and the pure fifths which, along with the octave, are the most important consonances of the period.

For music with a strong harmonic orientation and limited chromaticism, meantone is extremely useful; quarter-comma, the basic form, was apparently a standard temperament during much of the Renaissance and Baroque periods. Its main limitation is that it does not permit enharmonic relationships. Most keyboard repertory of the sixteenth and early seventeenth century is accommodated by meantone; most virginal music does not even require retuning of accidentals, the repertory usually employing only C♯, E♭, F♯, G♯, and B♭. Retuning is mentioned in only one source;[4] possibly the enharmonic equivalents were used at times in place of the written note. This usage can have an expressive effect on some chord voicings and on the mood of a piece, but it is of course entirely a matter of taste. (For example, an E♭ instead of a D♯ in William Tisdall's *Pavana Chromatica, Fitzwilliam Virginal Book* No. 214, creates a harsh effect that is perhaps in keeping with the mood of the piece. See Example IX-4.) The fact that quarter-comma will accommodate certain repertory, however, does not mean that it is the only possibility. The character of some pieces might benefit from sharper major thirds, etc. (The major thirds of quarter-comma are pure; wider thirds result from spreading the comma over five or more fifths. Such temperaments were known during the sixteenth century, but not all source tuning instructions are clear.)

EXAMPLE IX-4.
William Tisdall, *Pavana Chromatica,* mm.1-4.

Quarter-comma meantone accommodates even the extravagant harmonic experiments of the early seventeenth-century Italian school, for, strangely enough, this repertory does not show enharmonic relationships as a rule. Neither are they frequent in the works of Frescobaldi, whose music is generally suited to meantone. However, a few pieces do show enharmonic relationships (E♭ and D♯, A♭ and G♯ appear in the *Cento partite sopra gli passacagli* of his first book, 1637 edition; and a few enharmonic relationships appear in toccatas from the second book) and may be indicative of the interest Frescobaldi is said to have shown in equal temperament toward the end of his life.[5]

The contrast of wide and pure major thirds characteristic of meantone tuning makes striking variation in the coloring of the augmented triads sometimes employed by Froberger and the French harpsichord composers, for example. Some augmented triads in quarter-comma consist of two pure major thirds; others contain one pure and one harsh third. Such varied effects could never be achieved by equal temperament and may be one reason why equal temperament, although recommended by several seventeenth-century theorists, was not generally adopted. More importantly, the irregular systems, the shades of grey between meantone and equal temperament, allow variety of color from one tonality or modulation to another, unlike equal temperament, which allows no such variety. Irregular temperaments were apparently adopted in its place as modulatory needs expanded, perhaps often beginning as adjustments to basic meantone. By slightly compromising the purity of some major thirds, a wider range of tonalities and even some enharmonic relationships could be accommodated without sacrificing much of the sonority and varied colors of meantone. A great number of irregular ("well-tempered") temperaments developed along these lines. Their general use and the variety of their color is implied by Johann Heinichen's preference for keys with two or three accidentals, which he saw as the most expressive.[6] Probably the keys on either side of such a tonic would be most varied in intonation. From the centrally located keys with two or three flats or sharps, it was a short step to modulate to tonalities on either side with few or many accidentals. In an irregular temperament, these keys would vary the most in color.

The position of equal temperament, which was known at least theoretically in the Renaissance, is rather equivocal from the Renaissance through the Baroque. Lindley suggests that J. J. Froberger, who was a pupil of Frescobaldi, made use of equal temperament,[7] and enharmonic relationships are sufficiently noticeable in some of his music to make this plausible. (For instance, the *Lamentation* for Ferdinand III uses both D♭ and C♯ in exposed contexts.) Even a piece such as Froberger's hexachord fantasia can benefit from equal temperament or something approaching it. No enharmonic relationships appear, but different sizes of semitone create an odd effect in a chromatic line such as that in Example IX-5.

EXAMPLE IX-5.
J. J. Froberger, *Fantasia sopra ut, re, mi, fa, sol, la,*
mm.146-49.

By the early eighteenth century, equal temperament was beginning to be accepted. Its use was encouraged by its unlimited modulatory possibilities, but its lack of individual key colors continued to be a major drawback. Its advantages and disadvantages apparently affected musicians in different ways. Rousseau said that François Couperin, after having worked with equal temperament, eventually abandoned it; Rameau, on the other hand, began as an advocate of an unequal temperament and later preferred equal temperament.[8] By the mid-eighteenth century, some (mainly German) musicians, such as Marpurg and C. P. E. Bach, were in favor of equal temperament; and others, including Johann Philipp Kirnberger, were opposed to it. Certainly the wide range of modulation employed by the *galant* composers required, if not equal temperament, something closely approximating it. The position of equal temperament in Germany during the earlier eighteenth century is of particular interest because of the music of J. S. Bach.

The issue of temperament in Bach's music has attracted much attention and is perhaps the more fascinating since there are no grounds for definite conclusions. The story of Bach's annoying the organ builder Gottfried Silbermann by playing in tonalities not accommodated by Silbermann's sixth-comma meantone,[9] and of course the range of modulations and tonalities often employed by the composer, indicate that Bach preferred a temperament or temperaments allowing unlimited enharmonic modulation and perhaps use of all keys as the tonic. Unfortunately we have no precise data on the system or systems used by Bach. Equal temperament is a possibility, and its validity is perhaps borne out by the fact that Bach transposed certain preludes and fugues from their original keys to more remote ones to fill out the scheme of twenty-four tonalities in the *Well-Tempered Clavier*. For example, the Prelude in C♯, Book 2, was originally written in C. If individual key color in an unequal temperament was an important concern for Bach, such a change seems unlikely. Some transpositions in a setting of unequal temperament might enhance the original conception, but this lyrical Prelude could hardly benefit from the change from its original key of C to the undoubtedly harsher quality of C♯ in an unequal temperament. Early eighteenth-century German authors such as Mattheson, Sorge, and Neidhardt considered equal temperament to be most apt when many keys were employed. On the basis of such writings, Rudolf Rasch has made a convincing argument for equal temperament in the *Well-Tempered Clavier* and similar collections.[10]

Of course, composers are no less open than the rest of humanity to diverse solutions for a given problem. At least some degree of inequality in Bach's tuning preferences might be indicated by the approach advocated by his pupil Kirnberger. In the 1770s, when equal temperament had become increasingly common, Kirnberger held out against it because he preferred the additional interest that an unequal temperament gives to modulations and to pieces in different keys:

> through equal temperament, the variety of the tonalities is thrown away, because it unfortunately allows only two characteristics; on the one hand all the major keys and on the other all the minor tonalities are made the same.[11]

If Kirnberger does reflect Bach's preferences, the implications of the transpositions in the *Well-Tempered Clavier* remain enigmatic; but there are no grounds for suggesting that Bach's attitude to keyboard temperament remained constant throughout his life or that he would not tune differently for different occasions when he might employ a wide or narrow range of tonalities.

Certainly, particular keys appear to have had special significance for Bach. B minor often portrays tragic or noble sentiments (Prelude and Fugue in b, *WTC* I; parts of the Mass in b), but there are exceptions (for example, the passepied-like Fugue in b, *WTC* II). E♭ is often lyrical (cf. movements of French Suite IV; the Prelude, Fugue, and Allegro in E♭; and the two prelude/fugue pairs in E♭ from *WTC*). D major is festive (examples from *WTC*; Concerto in D for harpsichord and strings); G major is often virtuosic (examples from *WTC*; the *Goldberg Variations*). Such descriptions are, of course, subjective and insufficient for constructing or reconstructing a temperament.

Choice of temperament is frequently an interpretive decision and this was often the case in earlier times as well. For example, Johann Mattheson provided a list of seventeen different tonalities and their respective emotional qualities.[12] His descriptions presuppose a specific temperament, with major thirds of varying purity or sharpness. Heinichen, in his thoroughbass treatise, criticized Mattheson for assigning a specific character to each key, remarking that such qualities are entirely dependent on the particular temperament employed.[13] This criticism suggests that at least a fair variation in particulars of temperament was often expected at the time.

Usually, a keyboard performance of the seventeenth or eighteenth century would be centered about a group of pieces in one key: a suite or a set of variations, for example. Such works are generally in common keys and limited in modulation; remote keys, which are so problematic for those concerned with temperaments for the pieces touched on above, would occur only in passing, if at all. Therefore, when playing in and around one or a few tonic areas, the specific music may determine the keys to favor in the temperament. The tuner/player should be familiar with at least the more important tuning systems of earlier times, but indiscriminate application of them may fail to serve the harmonic points of tension and repose in the particular music being performed. On the other hand, one may easily set a temperament (whether newly invented or based on a particular old temperament) to favor a tonality or some specific work.[14]

The purity of the major thirds is achieved at the expense of the fifths. Therefore, when beginning a bearing from the tonic note of the tonality to be accommodated, the first four fifths should be flattened sufficiently to make the first major third (the one above the starting point) discernably pure (i.e., nearly beatless). The four fifths will usually be flattened equally, although one or more may be modified subsequently; how close the major third is to being beatless depends on other requirements of the music. Obviously, if it is made absolutely pure, the resulting temperament will be quarter-comma meantone. The more tolerable one must make the remote keys, the less purity is possible on the tonic and its related keys. Usually at least two more fifths will require flattening; but other factors in creating a temperament cannot be set forth abstractly, as they depend too closely on circumstances. In general, the more enharmonic relations and sweetly intoned distant keys are required, the more compromise will be necessary on the intonation of the tonic and related keys. However, some unpleasantly exposed wide major thirds may be disguised by judiciously added ornamentation if they do not occur too often; then the tonic area can be left more consonant. When tuning for more general usage, some variations of key color can be retained by slightly favoring the natural ("white key") tonalities. All keys will remain usable, yet the neutrality of equal temperament will be avoided.

When a keyboard instrument is used in ensemble, its temperament should match that of the other instruments. Lutes and viols often tend toward equal temperament; early flutes often work very well with some form of meantone, depending further, of course, on the needs of the music. Members of the violin family rarely use tempered fifths. Pythagorean temperament is hardly usable for string repertory, but a temperament allowing pure fifths on D and especially on A are useful for accompanying stringed instruments. Werckmeister III is flexible for general usage, and its pure fifth on A recommends it for playing with strings. As with solo keyboard literature, experimentation with temperament by soloists and their accompanists or ensemble players is often rewarding.

The complexity of the clavichord's tone often favors the purities available in an unequal temperament: the uniformly wide major thirds of equal temperament often sound harsh on the instrument. (The sonority of a good harpsichord is similarly promoted by consonant temperaments.) Nonetheless, equal temperament or something close to it is often necessary for the clavichord's important *galant* repertory.

It is necessary to tune the clavichord with uniform pressure on the keys, since the pitch varies with the player's touch. Notes in the extreme bass of some instruments require that their usual volume be taken into account: a gentle attack on the slack strings will not raise the pitch as much as a strong attack, unless special care is taken with a soft touch. The minute spreading of octaves in the extreme bass, a common feature of modern piano tuning and mentioned by Michel Corrette (1753) in regard to the harpsichord, is sometimes useful on the clavichord. The octaves are widened infinitesimally so that conflicting overtones are less noticeable, increasing the overall consonance of the tuning. This adjustment is another that depends on the individual instrument. Ralph Kirkpatrick describes a subtlety that can be used to great tonal advantage on the clavichord; it was also practiced by Arnold Dolmetsch:

There are minute differentiations that can be set up in the tuning of unisons when and if desirable by tuning one string infinitesimally higher [than the other]. This often serves to give a certain life and warmth to the upper registers of the instrument that will help to balance its weakness against the ... strings of the bass. None of this should be perceptible to the ordinary listener, and its application varies greatly from instrument to instrument.[15]

Similarly, this brief coverage of a vast subject can be summarized by remarking that gradations of temperament and other adjustments of tuning (such as the treatment of octaves and unisons) can and should vary from instrument to instrument, from piece to piece, and from one musical interpretation to another.

APPENDIX I

Exercises for Facility and Accuracy

A GOOD PORTION OF EARLY KEYBOARD music is not technically very strenuous. However, the greater the player's facility, the more delicate will be rhythmic (and, on the clavichord, dynamic) control in such matters as finely modulated ornaments and embellishments. Control of slow motions as well as rapid ones improves as one gains mechanical dexterity. The most important aspect of technical skill is that it allows such intimate contact with the instrument that the performer feels at one with it, rather than playing "at" it. The fingers should learn every detail of coping with the keys so as to achieve any desired aural effect.

The most far-reaching aspects of facility and sometimes the most difficult to analyze are the physical responses absorbed in the course of years of practice. Good or bad habits, whether physical or mental or both, become deeply ingrained; the bad habits can be extremely difficult to eradicate, even if they are comprehended intellectually. (For the same reason, difficult pieces learned at one point in a player's development will often continue to present problems that have since been overcome in other, newer contexts. The difficulties have been "practiced in.") The development of good habits and the correction of poor ones relate to learning and cognitive processes as well as to purely physical motions. Fluent sight-reading, for example, indicates a combination of good physical and perceptual habits. To root out some bad habits, it may be necessary to rebuild a technique from fundamentals; during the process, difficult repertory must be limited in order to achieve new freedom, however advanced the player may be in other musical matters.

Another aspect of facility concerns techniques consciously learned and deliberately applied to a specific musical context: perhaps a new way of trilling or a new way of positioning the hand for a certain kind of passage. Concepts that are understood intellectually and applied to musical or digital requirements can make a sudden and dramatic change in the ease with which technical problems are overcome.

It is often necessary to study the physical motions of playing apart from purely musical matters and even apart from technique in its larger sense, as the means by which a performer projects through the instrument. An incomplete technique segregates these elements to some degree, because of the limits of physical dexterity or poor habits of concentration. One may be capable of isolated technical feats—rapid passage work, for instance—but remain unable to employ this facility with much musical subtlety: that is, with any fine control of inflection. Or, certain movements may seem to be mastered in isolation but are not assimilated into overall patterns of endurance. The player so limited must search for the basis of such problems and work from there to eliminate them. It is best to master scales, arpeggios, and other basic figurations at an early point in one's study so that they do not present problems later.

Comprehension of musical processes, from fundamentals to the most sophisticated analysis, is extremely helpful to the development of physical facility. Every player, however occasional or amateur, should have some theoretical comprehension of music; concentration on matters of musical organization is often more conducive to fluency in playing than concentration on the mechanical level. A firm grip on the structure of a piece, from the large units to the small details, and definite ideas on projecting the structure in performance will often ease the negotiation of its technical requirements. The understanding of harmonic organization from the bass line, developed in the study of thoroughbass, is particularly helpful in this regard. It is also useful to become familiar with the typical figurations of each school of keyboard writing. Clear intellectual perception of note patterns can greatly aid accuracy in playing and expedite the physical learning process. For this among other reasons, silent score study and analysis away from the keyboard is highly advantageous in learning a work. Players who struggle to learn note by note should return to simpler repertory and rebuild and reorganize their approach to learning and playing. One should strive through practice and other musical study toward the ideal level, where attention to musical matters causes the physical matters to take care of themselves.

For players with reasonable hands and no particular handicaps, facility is often as much an intellectual as a physical matter, once basic musical patterns and physical motions have been learned securely. One must understand both the music and the ways of using the hands to fullest advantage. Digital limitations can sometimes be overcome almost instantly with clearer comprehension of the musical concept or of the proper physical motions. Although physical responses should become largely automatic, all players need to be conscious of the negative or positive effects of different modes of attack: hand and arm angles, wrist levels, finger positions. Beginners, particularly, must concentrate on a relaxed attack and be aware of every joint of each finger. Ignoring all but the fingers immediately employed can lead to poor hand positions, tension, and sluggish response. A strong tactile awareness aids both accuracy and touch sensitivity and should be a goal for every beginner.

Most players will agree that accuracy is one of the first things to go when given attention *per se*, and that attention to the mechanical level of playing distracts one from musical concentration. Practice for accuracy should serve that end specifically and not interfere with musical work. Slow practice is usually best in working on accuracy, but exaggeratedly slow playing is not always advisable for entire movements or even long stretches; the physical motions can easily become distorted and so lose the flexibility of more normal speeds. Slow practice should in any case be relaxed practice, and it is most successful if the musical interpretation is adapted to the slow tempo, however ludicrous that might at first seem. Much can be learned musically in this way, and the technical aspect will become more relaxed and natural. This approach holds even for practice in different rhythms.

It can also be useful to practice occasionally at speeds above performance tempo. This approach should not become habitual or be allowed to breed carelessness or physical tension. However, fast tempi can suggest new aspects of the overall phrasing of a movement; and from a technical standpoint they can be useful for checking that the player's machinery is running smoothly, so to speak. They can also suggest new approaches to keyboard facility. Whether the practice tempo is fast or slow, tension must not accumulate through either physical strain or, at fast speeds, the visceral excitement of brilliant playing. Practice is often most successful when adapted to one's nervous state. Slow practice when the player is tense can be more destructive than helpful. Periods of low energy are often best utilized for slow, careful work on exercises or especially difficult passages. Musical or technical practice must never become mechanical or it will cease to be productive. Lack of concentration can even make work time counterproductive. Time and distribution of emphasis should be divided according to needs and capacities, never so as to shortchange the former or overstrain the latter.

Technical progress moves in waves over long periods of time. Sudden improvements occur, as do plateaus and even periods of seeming regression. For some players, a time of no practice at all, from several days to even two or three months, can actually work to advantage by "letting the kinks out." When practice is resumed, it should be managed without strain. The amount of progress that suddenly appears after such a hiatus is at times astonishing.

It is often helpful to watch the fingers in an awkward passage. Sometimes one can see what is not felt, such as fingerings or motions that block the smooth negotiation of a passage. Much can often be cleared up by simply taking a careful look.

One should learn the natural capabilities of the individual fingers. Although their differences are more pronounced on some individuals than on others, each finger has particular advantages and weaknesses. In developing fingering and hand motions, it is often useful to work from this premise, which was the basis of keyboard technique up through the eighteenth century. In the nineteenth century, piano technique developed the ideal of equality among the fingers. Frederick Chopin, for one, considered this concept to be unrealistic, and felt that the advantages of each finger should be pursued on their own terms. The pursuit of absolute equality is indeed unrealistic for many hands, but one may adopt aspects of both approaches. While cultivating the advantages of the earlier technique, building up the weaker fingers need not be neglected, and they should in any case develop their own potentials to the fullest. Players can compensate for fingers of pronounced inequality by careful exercise and by judicious angling of the hand to allow maximum freedom of motion. (The clavichord often requires such adjustment of hand position; it teaches the "handing" as well as the fingering of many passages almost automatically.)

Basic to velocity and endurance is the conservation of effort. Passages that lie naturally under the hand should be allowed to flow; any special effort exerted should be limited to the most awkward passages. Every level of endurance has its limit; and the skillful player learns to delay the inevitable breakdown (i.e., the need for repose and the rallying of forces) until the danger points are passed and the music has reached the safe haven of a sectional ending, a slower surface rhythm, or a rest. With care, these rest points can be found even in the course of an ongoing rush of notes. The aural effect is constant, but the player is alternating between relative difficulties and places of ease.

Difficulties on the harpsichord and clavichord can be divided into two rough categories: those of dexterity (e.g., jumps, rapid passages, complex figuration, ornamental figures, repeated notes) and those of finger independence (e.g., playing several polyphonic voices, delicately manipulating the sound). The first requires technical work relatively independent of musical considerations. The second category is by far the more complex, and it must be cultivated in largely musical study and practice: at all times by careful and critical listening to the sound being produced.

Several exercises are included and discussed below. Some (Nos. 2 and 4, for example) are not directly applicable to repertory but will develop finger strength and sensitivity. Others relate to standard figurations found in repertory (compare No. 6 to *Goldberg Variation* 28). The player should develop similar exercises from the literature. The exercises given below that present complete patterns should be transposed to different keys, refingered as necessary, and practiced in various meters and rhythms with different articulations. These patterns are offered only to suggest a starting point for technical work, not as a complete method.

The first exercises show a few basic patterns intended to develop sensitivity to the keyboard. The two-finger Exercise 1 should not be scorned even by advanced players, for careful practice of this kind of pattern can always lead to new awareness of the fingers and of their weaknesses. When practicing, shift the hand position slightly, if necessary, to allow each pair of fingers maximum freedom when in use and each finger equal access to the keyboard. This usually requires a slight drawing in of the hand toward the ends of the keys for the long central digits and moving the hand minutely into the keyboard for the shorter extremities. On some hands, of course, the fingers vary more in length than on others.

Exercise 2 begins with simultaneous depression of five adjacent keys. They are held throughout the exercise (a variant of Exercise 1) except when a new finger is raised to depress its key again. All notes are to be held down as much as possible; particular care must be taken to avoid a buildup of tension. The pattern must usually be learned at a slow tempo.

The parallel thirds in Exercise 3 can be practiced with varied articulations in different lines in each hand and/or between hands. Exercise 4 shows parallel chromatic thirds, major and minor, using finger sliding for smoothness and rapidity. This figuration is rarely found in the literature, but it is an excellent discipline for finger independence, for the use of different pairs of fingers, and for sliding.

Players with small hands will find stretching exercises helpful. Many books of piano exercises offer useful stretching procedures (as well as other exercises that can be useful on early keyboards); Exercise 5 is a good starting point, as its intervals can be adjusted to individual need. It must be played legato. The pattern must be preserved, but the size of the intervals should be chosen with regard to the size and other requirements of the individual hand, for this exercise can cause strain if it is overpracticed or if the intervals are too large. Practice should begin with the smallest intervals that allow any degree of stretching.

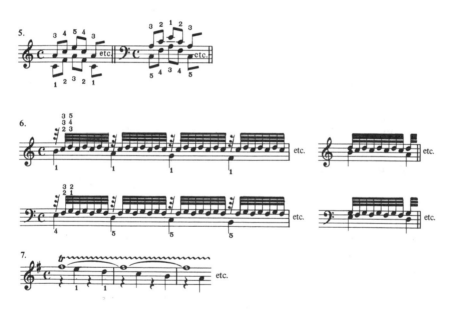

Ways of increasing rapidity and lessening tension in trills are described in chapter 2, and a number of trill fingerings are suggested in chapter 3. Exercises 6 and 7 can help further with trilling and also promote facility in trilling while playing another part in the same hand. In many cases it is most comfortable to incline the hand slightly in the direction of the trilling fingers. The thumb must cultivate lightness, both in trills and in scalar crossings, as it is naturally more resistant to rapid motion than the other digits.

In scales played with the thumb passing under, the thumb rarely moves with the speed of consecutive fingers. Velocity practice of scales up to, from, and finally beyond the thumb-passing junctures will increase the overall speed of scales and contribute to the thumb's general facility. Exercises 8 and 9 show scale divisions for work on these thumb junctures; they should be practiced with a light hand for maximum fluency and speed. Each segment should be played as rapidly as possible in a single movement. The rhythmic thrust and any pressure from the hand or the finger should arrive on the last note of each unit.

In playing rapid harpsichord passages such as scales and arpeggios, a high, loose wrist will often allow maximum freedom: playing with what is in effect a "controlled runaway" sensation in the fingers. The natural tendency to tense up for greater "control" is usually as destructive as it is deceptive. (For some players, brief passages are sometimes conquered only with tight fingers, but the choice must be made consciously; nor should tightness become a frequent recourse.) Once accustomed to the increased flexibility and rapidity available from some hand positions, the player can quickly gain control of the new freedom and consequently achieve greater velocity.

Scalar finger crossings (as opposed to thumb-under technique) are often facilitated by turning the hand slightly in the direction of the motion. For instance, the right hand may turn slightly to the right when ascending 3–4–3–4. The finger beneath the crossing finger must be drawn in toward the palm to allow fleet and smooth negotiation of the line. *Ad hoc* practice of scales with many crossings can easily lead to pattern blindness and carelessness. The passages shown in Exercise 10 are a useful starting point for practice, as they show a clear conclusion to every passage. Scales should be practiced for placement of the crossing finger on and off the beat.

Other figures, such as those in Exercise 11, should also be practiced with finger crossing. This type of practice pattern and fingering is useful for developing closed-hand clavichord touch.

Patterns of repeated notes, if using the thumb, also provide a means of working on its lightness. Different groupings of fingers (3–2–1–3–2–1, 3–2–3–2, 2–1–2–1) can assist the rhythmic articulation of groups of repeated notes, but a rhythmically smooth rendition is often desirable, and perfect evenness should be striven for in practice. (A well-regulated harpsichord is essential.) The hand can sometimes tense up in the course of long passages of repeated notes (which occur very frequently in Scarlatti sonatas); easy lightness should be cultivated as with trills. The player should find a position for approaching the key that allows maximum accessibility to it for all fingers involved in the repetition. Once that position is found, it is best to aim all the fingers at the same spot on the key and to work for an easy finger rotation with respect to it. The "chicken-scratch" finger withdrawal is of course necessary for even moderately fast repetitions.

Arpeggios on the harpsichord and clavichord call for a more active wrist and sometimes arm than are necessary with most other figurations. The fingers must guide the position of the arm and wrist. Once again, the thumb must pass rapidly and lightly. Some fingerings and practice patterns are shown in Exercises 12–14. In Exercise 14, for two manuals, one may improvise changing harmonies to derive the most use and variety from the pattern.

Broken intervals occur frequently in the literature; a few basic patterns are given in Exercises 15-18. They should be fingered so that the hand shifts position as little as possible, unless special emphasis is sought by means of fingering. Alternatively, a light flow can often be achieved by using the same pair of fingers, such as 4–2–4–2 on broken thirds.

Accuracy in hand crossings and leaps can be improved by glancing at the key with which the hand is to connect, even if the eye must move away before the connection is actually made. When numerous leaps occur in succession, the eye can stay a step ahead of the hand, particularly on long-range jumps and hand crossings. For smaller leaps to-and-fro, a spread hand centrally located between the notes involved can minimize movement and improve accuracy. (The second and fifth fingers are best for leaps.) Some jumps require a circular hand motion and a feeling for rebound, which most pianists acquire but which is rarely called for in the early literature. The works of Domenico Scarlatti and Antonio Soler contain some notable

a. D. Scarlatti, Sonata in D, K. 299, mm.27-31.
b. A. Soler, Fandango, mm.35-37.

exceptions. Note that the tone of the harpsichord necessitates that notes played in rapid skips must be held long enough for the actual pitch to assert itself.

The scope of this book does not permit a wide range of exercises. It is hoped that the preceding remarks will suggest ways of analyzing individual technical problems and devising exercises to work on them. The exercises by Isolde Ahlgrimm and Anthony Newman cited in the Bibliography are very helpful; so are selections from the standard piano volumes by Brahms, Czerny, Hanon, Hummel, Isidor Phillip, and Pischna.

APPENDIX II

Nicolo Pasquali on Harpsichord Touch

FROM NICOLO PASQUALI, *THE ART OF Fingering the Harpsichord* (London, 1758), concluding remarks, "Of the different touches":

As I would not conclude this work without communicating to the Learner all I know of the Power of the Harpsichord, I thought proper to insert in it its various Touches, which, when judiciously applied, must greatly contribute to the different Expressions so necessary in many musical Performances.

These Touches are five in Number, viz. *Legato*,—Tied or equal. *Staccato*,—Distinct or pointed. *Sdrucciolato*,—Sliding [i.e., *glissando*]. *Staccatissimo*,—Very distinct or pointed. *Tremolato*,—Quavering. [This may be relevant to some passages marked *Tremolo* in the sonatas of Domenico Scarlatti.]

The *Legato* is the Touch that this Treatise endeavors to teach, being a general Touch fit for almost all Kinds of Passages, and by which the Vibration of the Strings are [*sic*] made perfect in every Note.

The *Staccato* is expressed by purposely lifting up the Fingers sooner than the Length of the Notes require, in order to give a certain Distinction to some particular Passages, by way of Contrast to the *Legato*; but, in my Opinion, it is to be used seldom, and only when a good Effect is expected from it.

The *Sdrucciolato* is never used but in Scales of natural Notes, without any short Keys interfering betwixt them. And it is performed by sliding the Nail of the Fore-finger over the Keys in ascending, or the Nail of the Thumb in descending. It is recommended here only as a Whim, which, if applied in a Lesson of Humour, may afford a pleasing Variety.

As is likewise the *Staccatissimo*, which being played by striking every successive Key with the Point of one and the same Finger (generally the first) makes a great Contrast with the *Sdrucciolato*, being, as it were, a Caricature of the fine Contrast that is found between the *Legato* and the *Staccato*.

The *Tremolato* is played by touching the same Key with three different Fingers, one after the other, viz. 3d, 2d and 1st Fingers, as quick as the Quill which strikes the String will permit. This Touch is also whimsical.

In the Lesson XIV all these Touches are used, *St.* signifies *Staccato; Sdr.* *Sdrucciolato; Stmo. Staccatissimo*; and *Trem. Tremolato*. All those Passages that have none of these Marks must be played *Legato*, i.e., in the usual Way.

Lesson XIV, mm.11-16.

Notes

1. Instruments

1. See Edwin Ripin, "The Two-manual Harpsichord in Flanders before 1650," *Galpin Society Journal* 21 (March 1968):33.
2. William Dowd, "The Surviving Instruments of the Blanchet Workshop," *The Historical Harpsichord*, edited by Howard Schott (New York: Pendragon, 1984), p.65.
3. Reproduced in Frank Hubbard, *Three Centuries of Harpsichord Making* (Cambridge: Harvard University Press, 1965), Plate XL.
4. Dowd, "Blanchet Workshop," p.56.
5. Ibid.
6. Charles Burney, *The Present State of Music in France and Italy* (London: Becket, 1771), p.38.
7. Excerpts from Girolamo Diruta, *Il Transilvano*, translation by Carol Mac-Clintock in *Readings in the History of Music in Performance* (Bloomington: Indiana University Press, 1979), p.91.
8. Saint Lambert, *Nouveau traité de l'accompagnement du clavecin* (Paris: Ballard, 1707; facs. ed. Geneva: Minkoff, 1972), p.61. My translation.
9. Carl Phillip Emanuel Bach, *Essay on the True Art of Playing Keyboard Instruments*, translated by William Mitchell (New York: Norton, 1949), p.37.
10. Ibid., p.379.
11. Johann Joachim Quantz, *On Playing the Flute*, translated by Edward Reilly (London: Faber, 1966), p.259.
12. Quoted in Philip James, *Early Keyboard Instruments* (London: Peter Davies Ltd., 1930), p.42.
13. See comments by Johann Friedrich Agricola, quoted in Arthur Mendel and Hans T. David, *The Bach Reader*, rev. ed. (New York: Norton, 1972), pp.258-59.
14. Quoted by Hugh Boyle, "From London," *The Harpsichord* 1, no.3 (August 1968):18-19.
15. Edwin Ripin, "The Early Clavichord," *Musical Quarterly* 53 (1967):536-38.
16. See Edwin Ripin, "A Reassessment of the Fretted Clavichord," *Galpin Society Journal* 23 (August 1970):46.
17. Translation by Emily Anderson, *Letters of Mozart and His Family*, 2d ed., edited by A. Hyatt King and Monica Carolan (London: MacMillan, 1966), p.366.
18. C. P. E. Bach, *Essay*, p.172.

2. Approach to the Keys

1. Jean-Philippe Rameau, *Pièces de clavecin* (Paris: author, 1724), p.6. My translation.
2. Ibid., p.4.
3. Johann Joachim Quantz, *On Playing the Flute*, translated by Edward Reilly (London: Faber, 1966), pp.259-60.
4. Julia Aranguren and Orpha Ochse, "Thomas de Sancta Maria, c. 1515-1570, How to Play with Complete Perfection and Excellence," *The American Organist* 13, no.11 (1979):32.

5. Ibid.

6. Ibid.

7. Quoted in Arthur Mendel and Hans T. David, *The Bach Reader*, rev. ed. (New York: Norton, 1972), p.308.

8. Quoted in Raymond Russell, *The Harpsichord and Clavichord, an Introductory Study*, rev. 2d ed., edited by Howard Schott (New York: Norton, 1973), p.25.

3. Fingering

1. The information in this and the following three paragraphs is based on Richard Troeger, "Speculations on Bach's Clavichord Technique," *Diapason* 73, no.12 (December 1982):12.

2. Quoted in the Introduction to Johann Daniel Türk, *School of Clavier Playing*, translated by Raymond H. Haggh (Lincoln: University of Nebraska Press, 1982), p.xvii.

3. See Richard Troeger, "Source Fingerings in Elizabethan Keyboard Music," *Performance Practice Journal* 1 (1983):47.

4. See Robert Parkins, "Keyboard Fingering in Early Spanish Sources," *Early Music* 11, no.3 (1983):323.

5. The first edition of the *Wegweiser* (1689) presented little on keyboard fingering. An interesting account of the *Wegweiser*'s position in the eighteenth century is provided in Paul Walker, "Fingering, Bach, and the *Wegweiser*," *Early Keyboard Studies Newsletter* 1, no.3 (June 1985):1.

6. See Sandra Soderlund, *Organ Technique: An Historical Approach* (Chapel Hill: Hinshaw, 1980), pp.80-81. On p.122, Soderlund shows some specimens of the Wegweiser's fingerings, including Example III-29.

7. Saint Lambert, *Les principes du clavecin* (Paris: Ballard, 1702; facs. ed. Geneva: Minkoff, 1972), p.65. My translation.

8. Glyn Jenkins, "Fingering," section 4, *The New Grove*, vol.6, p.572.

9. C. P. E. Bach, *Essay on the True Art of Playing Keyboard Instruments*, translated by William Mitchell (New York: Norton, 1949), p.58.

10. Isolde Ahlgrimm cites some examples in "Current Trends in Performance of Baroque Music," translated by Howard Schott, *Diapason* 73, no.4 (April 1982):8, 10.

11. Ibid., p.10.

12. Ibid.

13. Cited in Carol MacClintock, *Readings in the History of Music in Performance* (Bloomington: Indiana University Press, 1979), p.90.

14. Ahlgrimm, "Current Trends," p.6.

15. Ibid.

16. See Barbara Sachs and Barry Ife, *Anthology of Early Keyboard Methods* (Cambridge: Gamut, 1981), p.69.

17. Ibid., p.67.

18. Quoted in Peter le Huray, "Fingering," section 1, *The New Grove*, vol. 6, p.567.

19. Clifford Curzon, "Epilogue," in *The Book of the Piano*, edited by Dominic Gill (Ithaca: Cornell University Press, 1981), p.264.

4. Articulation and Legato

1. Cf. Isolde Ahlgrimm, "Current Trends in Performance of Baroque Music," translated by Howard Schott, *Diapason* 73, no.4 (April 1982):1.

2. Translated by Carol MacClintock, *Readings in the History of Music in Performance* (Bloomington: Indiana University Press, 1979), p.136.

3. Ibid., p.90.

4. Ibid., p.92.

5. Saint Lambert, *Nouveau traité de l'accompagnement du clavecin* (Paris: Ballard, 1707; facs. ed. Geneva: Minkoff, 1972), p.63.My translation.

6. François Couperin, *L'Art de toucher le clavecin* (Paris: author, 1717; facs. ed. New York: Broude, 1969), p.60.

7. Jean-Philippe Rameau, *Pièces de clavecin* (Paris: author, 1724), p.4. My translation.

8. Nicolo Pasquali, *The Art of Fingering the Harpsichord* (Edinburgh: Bremner, 1758), p.19.

9. Ibid., p.21.

10. Ibid., p.26.

11. Johann Joachim Quantz, *On Playing the Flute*, translated by Edward Reilly (London: Faber, 1966), p. 259.

12. Julia Aranguren and Orpha Ochse, "Thomas de Sancta Maria, c. 1515-1570, How to Play with Complete Perfection and Excellence," *The American Organist* 13, no.11 (1979):32.

13. Translated by William Pruitt, in "The Organ Works of Guillaume-Gabriel Nivers (1632-1714)," Ph.D. diss., University of Pittsburgh, 1969, p.162.

14. C. P. E. Bach, *Essay on the True Art of Playing Keyboard Instruments*, translated by William Mitchell (New York: Norton, 1949), p.157.

15. Friedrich Wilhelm Marpurg, *Anleitung zum Clavierspiel* (Berlin: Haude and Spener, 1765), translated and edited (with Marpurg's *Principes du clavecin*) by Elizabeth Loretta Hays, Ph.D. diss., Stanford University, 1976, pp.VII-9-VII-10.

16. C. P. E. Bach, *Essay*, p.154.

17. Ibid., p.149.

18. Translated by David Fuller, in "French Harpsichord Playing in the Seventeenth Century–after le Gallois," *Early Music* 4 (1976):23-24.

19. Johann Daniel Türk, *School of Clavier Playing*, translated by Raymond H. Haggh (Lincoln: University of Nebraska Press, 1982), p.347.

20. Ibid., p.348.

21. Some illustrations of the figural approach to composition are provided by Peter Williams in "J. S. Bach's Well-Tempered Clavier: A New Approach," part 2, *Early Music* 11 (1983):332.

22. Saint Lambert, *Principes du clavecin* (Paris: Ballard, 1702; facs. ed. Geneva: Minkoff, 1972), pp.12-13. My translation.

23. Donald Francis Tovey, Preface to Ludwig van Beethoven, *Sonatas for Pianoforte* (London: Associated Board of the Royal Schools of Music, 1931), vol.2, p.7.

24. Peter Williams, "Need Organists Pay Attention to Theorists of Rhetoric?" *Diapason* 73, no.4 (April 1982):4.

5. Timing

1. Girolamo Frescobaldi, *Preface to Capricci fatti sopra diversi soggetti* (Rome, 1624), translated by Carol MacClintock, *Readings in the History of Music in Performance* (Bloomington: Indiana University Press, 1979), p.135.

2. A useful article on Frescobaldi's time notation is Karin Paulsmeier, "Temporelationen bei Frescobaldi," *Alte Musik, Praxis und Reflexion* (Winterthur: Amadeus, 1983), p.187.

3. Johann Philipp Kirnberger, *The Art of Strict Musical Composition*, translated by David Beach and Jurgen Thym (New Haven: Yale University Press, 1982), p.377.

4. Ibid., p.400.

5. Saint Lambert, *Principes du clavecin* (Paris: Ballard, 1702; facs. ed. Geneva: Minkoff, 1972), p.25. My translation.

6. Kirnberger, *Art*, p.396.

7. Ibid., p.391.

8. Ibid., pp.387-88.

9. See Raoul-Auger Feuillet, *Choréographie* (Paris: author, 1701; facs. ed. New York: Broude, 1968); Wendy Hilton, *Dance of Court and Theatre: The French Noble Style 1690-1725* (Princeton, N.J.: Princeton Book Co., 1981); Helen Meredith Ellis Little, "The Contribution of Dance Steps to Musical Analysis and Performance: La Bourgogne," *Journal of the American Musicological Society* 28 (1975):112; Richard Troeger, "Dance, Dance Music and the Baroque Keyboard Suite," in Anthony Newman, *Bach and the Baroque* (New York: Pendragon, 1985), pp.138-51; Pierre Rameau, *Le Maître à danser*) Paris: Villette, 1725; facs. ed. New York: Broude, 1967; translated by Cyril Beaumont, New York: Dance Horizons, 1970); Anne L. Witherell, *Louis Pecour's 1700 Recueil de dances* (Ann Arbor: UMI Research Press, 1983).

10. Translated by Hans Lenneberg, "Johann Mattheson on Affect and Rhetoric in Music," *Journal of Music Theory* 2 (1958):65.

11. Ibid., p.66.

12. Johann Joachim Quantz, *On Playing the Flute*, translated by Edward Reilly (London: Faber, 1966), p.125.

13. Translated by Newman Powell, "Kirnberger on Dance Rhythms, Fugues, and Characterization," in *Festschrift for Theodore Hoelty-Nickel* (Valparaiso: Valparaiso University, 1967), p.67.

14. Ibid., p.66.

15. C. P. E. Bach, *Essay on the True Art of Playing Keyboard Instruments*, translated by William Mitchell (New York: Norton, 1949), p. 164.

16. Quantz, *On Playing*, p.123.

17. Perrine, *Pièces de luth en musique* (Paris: author, 1680; facs. ed. Geneva: Minkoff, 1982), p.9.

18. Etienne Loulié, *Elements ou principes de musique* (Paris: Ballard, 1696); English translation by Albert Cohen (New York: Institute of Mediaeval Music, 1965), pp.27-28.

19. Johann Gottfried Walther, *Musicalisches Lexicon* (Leipzig: 1732; facs. ed. Kassel: Bärenreiter, 1953), p.507. My translation.

20. Saint Lambert, *Nouveau traité de l'accompagnement du clavecin* (Paris: Ballard, 1707; facs. ed. Geneva: Minkoff, 1972), p.58.

21. Johann Daniel Türk, *School of Clavier Playing*, translated by Raymond H. Haggh (Lincoln: University of Nebraska Press, 1982), p.326.

22. Ibid.

23. Ibid., pp.327-28.

24. See Newman, *Bach and the Baroque*, pp.59-60

25. Kirnberger, *Art*, pp.398-99.

26. See Newman, *Bach and the Baroque*, pp.58-84.

27. Ibid., pp.66-71.

28. Kirnberger, *Art*, p.390.

29. C. P. E. Bach, *Essay*, p.106.

30. On overdotting, see Michael Collins, "A Reconsideration of French Over-Dotting," *Music and Letters* 50 (January 1969):111; Robert Donington, *The Interpretation of Early Music*, rev. ed. (New York: St. Martin's Press, 1974), pp.441-51; David Fuller, "Dotting, the 'French style' and Frederick Neumann's Counter-Reformation," *Early Music* 5 (1977):517; and several articles on the subject included in Frederick Neumann, *Essays in Performance Practice* (Ann Arbor: UMI Research Press, 1982).

31. A useful summary of the French style of inequality is included in Wilfred Mellers, *François Couperin and the French Classical Tradition* (London: Dobson, 1949), pp.294-301. Judith Caswell, "Rhythmic Inequality and Tempo in French Music between 1650 and 1740," Ph.D. diss., University of Minnesota, 1973, quotes and translates all passages from French sources up to 1740 that are relevant to inequality.

32. Girolamo Frescobaldi, *Toccate e partite d'intavolatura*, Book 1 (Rome: Borboni, 1615, 1637), translated by Carol MacClintock, *Readings*, p.134.

33. Michael Praetorius, *Syntagma musicum*, translated by Carol MacClintock, *Readings*, p.151.

34. Frescobaldi, *Toccate e partite*, ibid., p.134.

35. François Couperin, *L'Art de toucher le clavecin* (Paris: author, 1717), pp.18-20. My translation.

36. Louis-Claude Daquin, "Avertissement" to *Pièces de clavecin* (Paris: author, 1735; facs. ed. Geneva: Minkoff, 1982), pp. [v-vi]. My translation.

37. Pierre-Claude Fouquet, Preface to *Pièces de clavecin*, vol. 2 (Paris: author, [1751]; facs. ed. Geneva: Minkoff, 1982), p. [ii].

38. Antoine Forqueray, *Pièces de clavecin*, edited by Colin Tilney (Paris: Heugel, 1974), p.94. My translation.

6. Ornamentation and Embellishment

1. Frederick Neumann, *Ornamentation in Baroque and Post-Baroque Music: With Special Emphasis on J. S. Bach* (Princeton: Princeton University Press, 1978). This book is an essential reference tool, containing much factual information on ornaments.

2. David Fuller, "An Unknown French Ornament Table from 1699," *Early Music* 9 (1981):55.

3. Ibid., p.57.

4. C. P. E. Bach, *Essay on the True Art of Playing Keyboard Instruments*, translated by William Mitchell (New York: Norton, 1949), p.101.

5. François Couperin, *L'Art de toucher le clavecin* (Paris: author, 1717; facs. ed. New York: Broude, 1969), p.24.

6. Saint Lambert, *Les principes du clavecin* (Paris: Ballard, 1702; facs. ed. Geneva: Minkoff, 1972), p.43.

7. Girolamo Frescobaldi, *Toccate e partite d'intavolatura*, Book 1 (Rome: Borboni, 1615, 1637), translated by Carol MacClintock, *Readings in the History of Music in Performance* (Bloomington: Indiana University Press, 1979), p.134.

8. Saint Lambert, *Principes*, p.43. My translation.

9. Neumann, *Ornamentation*, pp.263-86.

10. Julia Aranguren and Orpha Ochse, "Thomas de Sancta Maria, c. 1515-1570, How to Play with Complete Perfection and Excellence," *The American Organist* 13, no.11 (1979):36.

11. Girolamo Frescobaldi, *Toccate e partite*, Book 1, translated by Luigi Ferdinando Tagliavini in "The Art of 'Not Leaving the Instrument Empty': Comments on Early Italian Harpsichord Playing," *Early Music* 11 (1983):300.

12. Ibid.

13. Example VI-24 is also given by Tagliavini, "The Art;" this version of the piece is found in the German organ tablature manuscript, vol. 1, Turin, Biblioteca Nazionale, Raccolta R. Giordano, 1, ff.44-46.

14. Nicolas Lebègue, *Les pièces de clavessin* (Paris: author, 1677), Preface. My translation.

15. Saint Lambert, *Principes*, p.55. My translation.

16. Perrine, *Pièces de luth en musique* (Paris: author, 1680; facs. ed. Geneva: Minkoff, 1982), pp.6-8.

17. See Neumann, *Ornamentation*, p.486.

18. Johann Daniel Türk, *School of Clavier Playing*, translated by Raymond H. Haggh (Lincoln: University of Nebraska Press, 1982), p.343.

19. Ibid., p.281.

20. C. P. E. Bach, *Essay*, p.156.

21. Among many primary and secondary sources illustrating Renaissance diminutions, good starting points are provided by Sylvestro Ganassi, *Opera intitulata Fontegara* (Venice: author, 1535); and Richard Erig and Veronika Gutmann, *Italian Diminutions* (Zürich: Amadeus, 1979).

22. Neumann, *Ornamentation*, pp.526-31.

23. Many instructive parallel presentations of intabulations against their vocal orginals are to be found in Otto Kinkeldy, *Orgel und Klavier in der Musik des 16. Jahrhunderts* (Leipzig, 1910; reprint Hildesheim: Georg Olms, 1968).

24. Quoted in Arthur Mendel and Hans T. David, *The Bach Reader*, rev. ed. (New York: Norton, 1972), p.238.

25. See Hans Marz, "Some Unknown Embellishments of Corelli's Violin Sonatas," *The Musical Quarterly* 56 (1970):65.

26. C. P. E. Bach, *Essay*, p.165.

27. Tagliavini, "The Art of 'Not Leaving the Instrument Empty'," gives a clear account of *spezzata* treatment and includes Example VI-38.

28. Quoted in David Fuller, "French Harpsichord Playing in the Seventeenth Century—after le Gallois," *Early Music* 4 (1976):23.

29. Ibid.

30. Desmond Hunter, "The Position of Grace Signs in MS. Sources of English Virginal Music," *English Harpsichord Magazine* 3 (1983):82.

31. Ibid., p.86.

32. Ibid., pp.88-90.

33. Neumann, *Ornamentation*, pp.287-95.

34. On this subject, see Joel L. Sheveloff, "The Keyboard Music of Domenico Scarlatti," Ph.D. diss., Brandeis University, 1970; and Neumann, *Ornamentation*, pp.352-55. Neumann suggests that Scarlatti's *tremolo* is the *tremolo di sotto*, or long mordent. Sheveloff assesses the evidence, lists the sonatas involved, and arrives at no conclusion.

35. An excellent summary of the available material is given in Robert Parkins, "Cabezon to Cabanilles: Ornamentation in Spanish Keyboard Music," *Organ Yearbook* 11 (1980):5. Much of the material presented here is derived from or included in this article.

7. Accompaniment

1. Franck Thomas Arnold, *The Art of Accompaniment from a Thorough-Bass* (London: Oxford University Press, 1931; reprint New York: Dover, 1965).

2. Robert Donington, *The Interpretation of Early Music*, rev. ed. (New York: Saint Martin's Press, 1974), pp.288-372.

3. Peter Williams, *Figured Bass Accompaniment*, 2 vols. (Edinburgh: Edinburgh University Press, 1970).

4. The full piece in both the original and the accompanied versions is reproduced in Jean Nicolas Geoffroy, *Livre d'orgue*, edited by Jean Bonfils (Paris: Heugel, 1974), pp.95-98.

5. Johann Joachim Quantz, *On Playing the Flute*, translated by Edward Reilly (London: Faber, 1966), p.251.

6. Derived from Williams, *Figured Bass*, vol.1, p.29.

7. C. P. E. Bach, *Essay on the True Art of Playing Keyboard Instruments*, translated by William Mitchell (New York: Norton, 1949), p.316.

8. Quantz, *On Playing*, p.259.

9. C. P. E. Bach, *Essay*, p.368.

10. Quoted in Hermann Keller, *Thoroughbass Method*, translated and edited by Carl Parrish (New York: Norton, 1965), p.47.

11. Example VII-5a appears in Williams, *Figured Bass*, vol.2, p.97.

12. Quoted in Arnold, *Art of Accompaniment*, p.153.

13. Francesco Geminiani, *A Treatise of Good Taste in the Art of Musick* (London, 1749; facs. ed. New York: Da Capo, 1969), p.2.

14. See Williams, *Figured Bass*, vol.1, p.29.

15. An excellent account of early Baroque Italian continuo is in John Hill, "Realized Continuo Accompaniments from Florence *ca.* 1600," *Early Music* 11 (1983):194. Example VII-7 is taken from this article.

16. Nicolo Pasquali, *Thorough-bass Made Easy* (London: Bremner, 1757), pp.47-48.

17. Francesco Gasparini, *L'Armonico pratico al cimbalo* (Venice: Bartoli, 1708), pp.91-95.

18. Saint Lambert, *Nouveau traité de l'accompagnement du clavecin* (Paris: Ballard, 1707), pp.62-63. My translation.

8. Harpsichord Registration

1. Frank Hubbard, *Three Centuries of Harpsichord Making* (Cambridge: Harvard University Press, 1965), pp.239-40.

2. Ibid., p.153.

3. David Fuller, "Harpsichord Registration," *Diapason* 69, no.7 (July 1978):6.

4. François Couperin, *Pièces de clavecin*, vol.2 (Paris: author, 1717; facs. ed. New York: Broude, 1973), p.62. My translation.

5. Saint Lambert, *Nouveau traité de l'accompagnement du clavecin* (Paris: Ballard, 1707), p.61. My translation.

6. See G. Grant O'Brien, Michael Thomas, and W. Rhodes, "A Clavichord, a Harpsichord and a Chamber Organ in the Russell Collection, Edinburgh," *The Organ Yearbook* 5 (1974):93.

7. Hubbard, *Three Centuries*, p.152.

8. Fuller, "Registration," p.6.

9. Ibid., p.7.

10. See Hubbard, *Three Centuries*, p.168.

11. Ibid., p.102; and William Dowd, "The Surviving Instruments of the Blanchet Workshop," *The Historical Harpsichord*, edited by Howard Schott (New York: Pendragon, 1984), p.30.

12. See Hubbard, *Three Centuries*, p.168.

9. Temperament

1. Described in Mark Lindley, "Instructions for the Clavier Diversely Tempered," *Early Music* 5 (1977):19.

2. Ibid., p.22.

3. Mark Lindley, "Temperaments," *The New Grove*, vol. 18, p.661.

4. Ibid., p.667.

5. Ibid., p.665.

6. Ibid., p.668.

7. Ibid., p.665.

8. Ibid., p.668.

9. Arthur Mendel and Hans T. David, *The Bach Reader*, rev. ed. (New York: Norton, 1972), p.290.

10. Rudolf Rasch, "Does 'Well-Tempered' mean 'Equal-Tempered',," in Peter Williams, ed., *Bach, Handel, Scarlatti: Tercentenary Essays* (Cambridge: Cambridge University Press, 1985).

11. Johann Philipp Kirnberger, *Die Kunst des reinen Satzes in der Musik* (Berlin: Decker and Hartung, 1776/79), part 1, p.19. My translation.

12. Johann Mattheson, *Das neu-eröffnete Orchestre* (Hamburg: Schiller, 1713).

13. Lindley, "Temperaments," pp.668-69.

14. See Richard Troeger, "Flexibility in Well-Tempered Tuning," *Diapason* 73, no.6 (June 1982):6. The information in this and the ensuing paragraph is derived from this article.

15. Ralph Kirkpatrick, "On Playing the Clavichord," *Early Music* 9 (1981):305.

Bibliography

PRIMARY SOURCES

Adlung, Jacob. *Anleitung zur musikalischen Gelahrheit.* Erfurt: J. D. Jungnicol, 1758; facs. ed. Kassel: Bärenreiter, 1953.
———. *Musica mechanica organoedi.* Berlin: F. W. Birnstiel, 1768; facs. ed. Kassel: Bärenreiter, 1931.
Agazzari, Agostino. *Del sonare sopra 'l basso....* Siena: Domenico Falcini, 1607; facs. ed. Bologna: Forni, 1969.
Ammerbach, Elias Nicolaus. *Orgel oder Instrument Tabulatur.* Leipzig: J. B. Erben, 1571.
Anonymous. *The Harpsicord Master,* Book 1. London: D. Wright, 1697; facs. ed. Oxford: Oxford University Press, 1982.
———. *The Harpsicord Master,* Books 2 and 3. London: Walsh and Hare, 1700 and 1702; facs. ed. New York: Boethius Press, 1980.
Arbeau, Thoinot. *Orchesography.* Translated by Mary Evans. New York: Dover, 1969.
Bach, Carl Philipp Emanuel. *Versuch über die wahre Art das Clavier zu spielen.* Berlin: G. L. Winter, 1759/62. English translation by William Mitchell, New York: Norton, 1949.
Bacilly, Bénigne de. *Remarques curieuses sur l'art de bien chanter.* Paris: Ballard, 1668. English translation by Austin B. Caswell, Brooklyn: Institute of Mediaeval Music, 1968.
Banchieri, Adriano. *Conclusioni nel Suono dell' Organo.* Bologna: Heredi di G. Rossi, 1609; facs. ed. New York: Broude, 1975.
Bermudo, Juan. *Declaración de instrumentos musicales.* Ossuna: Juan de Leon, 1555.
Brossard, Sebastien de. *Dictionaire de musique.* Paris: Ballard, 1703.
Burney, Charles. *The Present State of Music in Germany, the Netherlands and United Provinces.* London: Becket, 1775; facs. ed. New York: Broude, 1969.
Caccini, Giulio. *Le nuove musiche.* Florence: Marescotti, 1601; facs. ed. New York: Broude, 1973.
Correa de Arauzo, Francisco. *Facultad Orgánica.* Alcala: Antonio Arnao, 1626.
Corrette, Michel. *Les amusemens du Parnasse.* Paris: Boivin, le Clerc, 1749.
———. *Le maître de clavecin.* Paris: author, 1753; facs. ed. Geneva: Minkoff, 1976.
Couperin, François. *L'Art de toucher le clavecin.* Paris: author, Boivin, 1717; facs. ed. New York: Broude, 1969.
Dalla Casa, Girolamo. *Il vero modo di diminuir ...,* vols.1 and 2. Venice: Angelo Gardano, 1584.
Dandrieu, Jean-François. *Principes de l'accompagnement du clavecin.* Paris: author, [ca. 1719]; facs. ed. Geneva: Minkoff, 1972.
Daquin, Louis-Claude. *Pièces de clavecin,* vol.1. Paris: author, Boivin, le Clerc, 1735; facs. ed. Geneva: Minkoff, 1982.
Denis, Jean. *Traité de l'accord de l'espinette.* Paris: Robert Ballard, 1650; facs. ed. with an introduction by Alan Curtis, New York: Da Capo, 1969.
Diruta, Girolamo. *Il Transilvano.* Vol.1, Venice: Vincenti, 1593. Vol.2, Venice: Vincenti, 1609. English translation by Edward J. Soehnlein, Master's thesis, University of Michigan, 1975.

Feuillet, Raoul-Auger. *Choréographie*. Paris: author, 1701; facs. ed. New York: Broude, 1968.

Foucquet, Pierre-Claude. *Pièces de clavecin*, vols.1 and 2. Paris: author, Boivin, le Clerc, Castagneri, de Bretonne, [1751]; facs. ed. Geneva: Minkoff, 1982.

Frescobaldi, Girolama. *Toccate e partite . . .* , vol.1. Rome: Borboni, 1615, 1637.

Ganassi, Sylvestro. *Opera intitulata Fontegara*. Venice: author, 1535.

Gasparini, Francesco. *L'Armonico pratico al cimbalo*. Venice: Bartoli, 1708.

Geminiani, Francesco. *A Treatise of good Taste in the Art of Musick*. London, 1749; facs. ed. New York: Da Capo, 1969.

Hartong, P. C. *Dess Musici Theoretico-Practici*, Part 2. Nürnberg: A. J. F. Erben, 1749.

Heinichen, Johann David. *Der Generalbass in der Composition*. Dresden: author, 1728; facs. ed. Hildesheim: Georg Olms, 1969.

Hotteterre, Jacques. *Principes de la flute traversière*. Paris: author, 1707. English translation by David Lasocki, New York: Praeger, 1968.

Kirnberger, Johann Philipp. *Clavierübungen mit der Bachischen Applicatur*, vol.4. Berlin: F. W. Bünstiel, 1761.

_____. *Die Kunst des reinen Satzes in der Musik*. Berlin: Decker and Hartung, 1776/ 79. English translation by David Beach and Jurgen Thym, New Haven: Yale University Press, 1982.

Löhlein, Georg Simon. *Clavier-Schule*. Leipzig: Züllichau, Waisenhaus und Frommannische Buchhandlung, 1765.

Loulié, Etienne. *Elements ou principes de musique*. Paris: Ballard, 1696. English translation by Albert Cohen, New York: Institute of Mediaeval Music, 1965.

Mace, Thomas. *Musick's Monument*. London: Radcliffe and Thompson, 1676; facs. ed. Paris: Centre National de la Recherche Scientifique, 1958.

Marpurg, Friedrich Wilhelm. *Anleitung zum Clavierspiel*. Berlin: Haude und Spener, 1765. English translation (together with Marpurg's *Principes du clavecin*) by Elizabeth Loretta Hayes, Ph.D. diss., Stanford University, 1976.

Mattheson, Johann. *Critica Musica*. Hamburg: author, 1722-25.

_____. *Grosse general-bass-Schule*. Hamburg: Kissner, 1731.

_____. *Grundlage einer ehren-pforte*. Hamburg: author, 1740.

_____. *Das neu-eröffnete orchestre*. Hamburg: Schiller, 1713.

_____. *Der Vollkommene Capellmeister*. Hamburg: Christian Herold, 1739. English translation by Ernest C. Harris, Master's thesis, George Peabody College, 1969.

Mersenne, Martin. *Traité de l'Harmonie Universelle*, vol.2. Translated by John B. Egan, Ph.D. diss., Indiana University, 1962.

Montéclair, Michel Pignolet de. *Nouvelle méthode pour apprendre la musique. . . .* Paris: author, 1709.

_____. *Principes de musique. . . .* Paris: Boivin, [1736].

Mozart, Leopold. *Versuch einer gründlichen Violinschule. . . .* Augsburg: J. J. Lotter, 1756. English translation by Edith Knocker, London: Oxford University Press, 1948.

Muffat, Georg. *An Essay on Thoroughbass*. Edited by Hellmut Federhofer. Rome: American Institute of Musicology, 1961.

_____. *Floregium Secundum*. Passau: Höller, 1698.

Nassarre, Pablo. *Escuela Musica segun la practica moderna*. Zaragoza: de Larumbe, 1724.

North, Roger. *Roger North on Music*. Edited by John Wilson. London: Novello, 1959.

Ortiz, Diego. *Tratado de glosas. . . .* Rome: Dorico and Hermano, 1553; edited by Max Schneider, Kassel: Bärenreiter, 1936.

Pasquali, Nicolo. *The Art of Fingering the Harpsichord*. Edinburgh: Bremner, 1758.

————. *Thorough-bass made Easy.* London: Bremner, 1757.

Penna, Lorenzo. *Li primi albori musicali.* . . . Bologna: Giacomo Monti, 1672.

Perrine. *Pièces de luth en musique.* . . . Paris: author, 1680; facs. ed. Geneva: Minkoff, 1982.

Petri, J. S. *Anleitung zur practischen Musik.* Lauban: J. C. Wirthgen, 1767.

Praetorius, Michael. *Syntagma musicum,* vol.2. Wolfenbüttel, 1619; facs. ed. Kassel: Bärenreiter, 1958.

Prencourt. *Short, Easy and Plaine Rules.* London: British Library, Add. Ms. 32,351.

Printz, Wolfgang Caspar. *Phrynis Mitilenaeus.* Dresden and Leipzig: Mieth und Zimmermann, 1696.

Purcell, Henry. *A Choice Collection of Lessons for the Harpischord or Spinet.* London: Mrs. Henry Purcell, Playford, 1696; facs. ed. New York: Broude, 1972.

Quantz, Johann Joachim. *Versuch einer Anweisung die Flöte traversière zu spielen.* Berlin: Johann Friedrich Voss, 1752. English translation and edition by Edward R. Reilly, London: Faber, 1966.

Rameau, Jean-Philippe. *Code de musique pratique.* . . . Paris: Imprimerie royal, 1760; facs. ed. New York: Broude, 1965.

————. *Dissertation sur les differentes méthodes d'accompagnement pour le clavecin ou pour l'orgue.* Paris: Boyvin, le Clerc, 1732.

————. *Pièces de clavecin.* Paris: author, Boivin, Hochereau, 1724; facs. ed. New York: Broude, 1967.

Rameau, Pierre. *Le maître à danser.* Paris: Villette, 1725; facs. ed. New York: Broude, 1967. English translation by Cyril Beaumont, New York: Dance Horizons, 1970.

Reichardt, Johann F. *Briefe eines aufmerksamen Reisenden die Musik betreffend.* Frankfort and Leipzig, 1774; Frankfort and Breslau, 1776.

Rigler, Franz. *Anleitung zum Klavier.* Vienna: Edler von Kürzböck, 1779.

Rousseau, Jean Jacques. *Dictionnaire de la musique.* Paris: Suchesne, 1767.

Saint Lambert. *Nouveau traité de l'accompagnement du clavecin.* Paris: Ballard, 1707; facs. ed. Geneva: Minkoff, 1972.

————. *Les principes du clavecin.* Paris: Ballard, 1702; facs. ed. Geneva: Minkoff, 1972. English translation and edition by Rebecca Harris-Warrick, Cambridge: Cambridge University Press, 1984.

Samber, Johann Baptist. *Manuductio ad Organum.* Salzburg: J. B. Mayrs, 1704.

Speer, Daniel. *Grundrichtiger Unterricht der musicalischen Kunst.* Göppingen: Kühnen, 1687; 2d ed. Würtemberg: Erben, 1697.

Speth, Johann. *Vermehrter und zum zweytenmal in Druck beförderter kurtzer jedoch gründlicher Wegweiser.* Augsburg: J. Koppmayer, 1693.

Sulzer, Johann G., ed. *Allgemeine Theorie der schönen Künste.* Leipzig: Weidmanns Erben und Reich, 1771; Berlin: G. L. Winter, 1774; facs. ed. Hildesheim: Georg Olms, 1967-70.

Tomás de Sancta María. *Libro llamado arte de taner fantasia.* Valladolid: Francisco Fernandez de Cordoba, 1565; facs. ed. New York: Gregg, 1972.

Türk, Johann Daniel. *Klavierschule.* Leipzig: Schwickert, 1789; Halle: author, Hemmerde und Schwetschke, 1789. English translation by Raymond H. Haggh, Lincoln: University of Nebraska Press, 1982.

Walther, Johann Gottfried. *Musicalisches Lexicon.* Leipzig: 1732; facs. ed. Kassel: Bärenreiter, 1953.

SECONDARY SOURCES

Ahlgrimm, Isolde. "Current Trends in Performance of Baroque Music." Translated by Howard Schott. *Diapason* 73, no.4 (April 1982):1.

Aldrich, Putnam. " 'Rhythmic Harmony' as Taught by Johann Philipp Kirnberger." *Studies in Eighteenth-Century Music*, edited by H. C. Robbins Landon. London: Allen and Unwin, 1970.

————. *Rhythm in Seventeenth-Century Italian Monody*. New York: Norton, 1966.

Anderson, Emily, translator and editor. *The Letters of Mozart and His Family*. 2 vols. 2d ed., edited by A. Hyatt King and Monica Carolan. London: Macmillan, 1966.

Anthony, James R. *French Baroque Music from Beaujoyeulx to Rameau*. 2d rev. ed. New York: Norton, 1978.

Apel, Willi. *The History of Keyboard Music to 1700*. Translated and revised by Hans Tischler. Bloomington: Indiana University Press, 1972.

————. *The Notation of Polyphonic Music, 900-1600*. 5th ed. Cambridge: Mediaeval Academy of America, 1961.

Aranguren, Julia, and Ochse, Orpha. "Thomas de Sancta Maria, c. 1515-1570, How to Play with Complete Perfection and Excellence." *American Organist* 13, no.11 (1979):31.

Arnold, Franck Thomas. *The Art of Accompaniment from a Thorough-Bass*. London: Oxford University Press, 1931; reprint New York: Dover, 1965.

Barbour, J. Murray. *Tuning and Temperament*. East Lansing: Michigan State College Press, 1951.

Barford, Philip. *The Keyboard Music of C. P. E. Bach*. New York: October House, 1965.

Barnes, John. "Bach's Keyboard Temperament." *Early Music* 7 (1979):236.

Baron, John H. "A Seventeenth-Century Keyboard Tablature in Brasov." *Journal of the American Musicological Society* 20 (1968):279.

Boyden, David. *The History of Violin Playing from Its Origins to 1761 and Its Relationship to the Violin and Violin Music*. London: Oxford University Press, 1965.

Bradshaw, Murray. "Juan Cabanilles: The Toccatas and Tientos." *Musical Quarterly* 59 (1973):285.

Buelow, George J. "The Full-Voiced Style of Thoroughbass Realization." *Acta Musicologica* 30 (1958):159.

————. "The 'Loci topici' and Affect in Late Baroque Music: Heinichen's Practical Demonstration." *Music Review* 27 (1966):161.

————. "Music, Rhetoric and the Concept of the Affections: A Selective Bibliography." *Notes* 30 (1973-74):250.

————. "Rhetoric and Music." *The New Grove*, vol.15, p.793.

————. *Thorough Bass Accompaniment According to Johann David Heinichen*. Berkeley and Los Angeles: University of California Press, 1966.

Butler, Gregory G. "The Projection of Affect in Baroque Dance Music." *Early Music* 12, no.2 (May 1984):200.

Caswell, Judith. "Rhythmic Inequality and Tempo in French Music between 1650 and 1740." Ph.D. diss., University of Minnesota, 1973.

Clark, Jane. "Les Folies Françoises: Personalities in the Music of François Couperin." *Early Music* 8 (1980):163.

Cohen, Albert. "Symposium on Seventeenth-Century Music Theory: France." *Journal of Music Theory* 16 (1972):16.

Collins, Michael. "In Defense of the French Trill." *Journal of the American Musicological Society* 26 (1973):405.

Cooper, Kenneth. "The Clavichord in the Eighteenth Century." Ph.D. diss., Columbia University, 1971.

Cooper, Kenneth, and Zasko, Julius. "Georg Muffat's Observations on the Lully Style of Performance." *Musical Quarterly* 53 (1967):220.

Cortot, Alfred. *Rational Principles of Pianoforte Technique.* Translated by R. Le Roy-Metaxas. Paris: Salabert, 1930.

Curtis, Alan. *Sweelinck's Keyboard Music.* London: Oxford University Press, 1969.

————. "Unmeasured Preludes in French Baroque Instrumental Music." Master's thesis, University of Illinois, 1956.

Dart, Thurston. *The Interpretation of Music.* London: Hutchinson, 1954.

Devoto, Daniel. "De la zarabanda à la sarabande." *Recherches* 6 (1965):27.

Donington, Robert. *The Interpretation of Early Music,* rev. ed. New York: Saint Martin's Press, 1974.

Erig, Richard, and Gutmann, Veronika. *Italian Diminutions.* Zürich: Amadeus, 1979.

Ferand, Ernest T. *Improvisation in Nine Centuries of Western Music.* Cologne: Arno Volk Verlag, 1961.

Ferguson, Howard. *Keyboard Interpretation from the Fourteenth to the Nineteenth Century: An Introduction.* New York: Oxford University Press, 1975.

Fuller, David. "Dotting, the 'French style,' and Frederick Neumann's Counter-Reformation." *Early Music* 5 (1977):517.

————. *French Harpsichord Music.* Cambridge: Cambridge University Press, forthcoming.

————. "French Harpsichord Playing in the Seventeenth Century–after le Gallois." *Early Music* 4 (1976):22.

————. "Harpsichord Registration." *Diapason* 69, no.7 (July 1978):1.

————. "An Unknown French Ornament Table from 1969." *Early Music* 9 (1981):55.

Gát, Josef. *The Technique of Piano Playing,* 2d ed. Budapest: Corvina, 1965.

Goble, Elizabeth. "Keyboard Lessons with Arnold Dolmetsch." *Early Music* 5 (1977):89.

Green, Robert. "Annotated Translation and Commentary of the Works of Jean Rousseau." Ph.D. diss., Indiana University, 1979.

Guillet, Pierre. "Le livre de clavecin de Christophe Moyreau." *Recherches* 11 (1970):179.

Gustafson, Bruce. *French Harpsichord Music of the Seventeenth Century: A Thematic Catalogue of the Sources with Commentary.* 3 vols. Ann Arbor: UMI Research Press, 1980.

————. "A Letter from Mr. Lebègue Concerning His Preludes." *Recherches* 18 (1977):7.

Haar, James. "False Relations and Chromaticism in Sixteenth-Century Music." *Journal of the American Musicological Society* 30 (1977):391.

Harich-Schneider, Eta. *Die Kunst des Cembalospiels.* 2d ed. Kassel: Bärenreiter, 1958. Abridged English edition, *The Harpsichord.* Kassel: Bärenreiter, 1954.

Harnoncourt, Nikolaus. *Musik als Klangrede.* Salzburg: Residenz Verlag, 1982.

Harran, Don. "New Evidence for Musica Ficta: The Cautionary Sign." *Journal of the American Musicological Society* 29 (1976):77.

————. "More Evidence for Cautionary Signs." *Journal of the American Musicological Society* 31 (1978):490.

Helm, Eugene. "The 'Hamlet' Fantasia and the Literary Element in C. P. E. Bach's Music." *Musical Quarterly* 58 (1972):277.

Hill, John. "Realized Continuo Accompaniments from Florence *ca.* 1600." *Early Music* 11 (1983):194.

Hilton, Wendy. "A Dance for Kings: The Seventeenth-Century French Courante." *Early Music* 5 (1977):160.

————. *Dance of Court and Theatre: The French Noble Style 1690-1725.* Princeton, N.J.: Princeton Book Co., 1981.

Jackson, Roland. "The *Inganni* and the Keyboard Music of Trabaci." *Journal of the American Musicological Society* 21 (1968):204.

Jonckbloet, W. J. A., and Land, J. P. N., eds. *Corréspondance et œuvres musicales de Constantin Huygens.* Leyden: Brill, 1882.

Jorgensen, Owen. *The Equal-Beating Temperaments.* Raleigh: Sunbury Press, 1981.

————. *Tuning the Historical Temperaments by Ear.* Marquette: Northern Michigan University, 1977.

Kaufmann, Henry. "More on the Tuning of the Archicembalo." *Journal of the American Musicological Society* 23 (1970):84.

Keller, Hermann, *Thoroughbass Method.* Translated and edited by Carl Parrish. New York: Norton, 1965.

Kinkeldy, Otto. *Orgel und Klavier in der Musik des 16. Jahrhunderts.* Leipzig 1910; reprint Hildesheim: Georg Olms, 1968.

Kinsky, Georg. "Pedalklavier oder Orgel bei Bach?" *Acta Musicologica* 8 (1936):158.

Kirkpatrick, Ralph. "C. P. E. Bach's *Versuch* Reconsidered." *Early Music* 4 (1976):384.

————. *Domenico Scarlatti.* New York: Princeton University Press, 1953.

————. *Interpreting Bach's Well-Tempered Clavier.* New Haven: Yale University Press, 1984.

————. "On Playing the Clavichord." *Early Music* 9 (1981):293.

————. "On Re-reading Couperin's *L'Art de toucher le clavecin.*" *Early Music* 4 (1976):3.

Le Huray, Peter. "On Using Early Keyboard Fingerings: A Sequel." *Diapason* 60, no.6 (June 1969):14; no.7 (July 1969):10; no.8 (August 1969):10.

Le Huray, Peter, and Jenkins, Glyn. "Fingering," sections 1-5. *The New Grove,* vol.6, p.567.

Lee, Douglas A. "Some Embellished Versions of Sonatas by Franz Benda." *Musical Quarterly* 62 (1976):58.

Lenneberg, Hans. "Johann Mattheson on Affect and Rhetoric in Music." *Journal of Music Theory* 2 (1958):47, 193.

Leonhardt, Gustav. *The Art of Fugue: Bach's Last Harpsichord Work.* The Hague: Martinus Nijhoff, 1952.

————. "Johann Jakob Froberger and His Music." *L'Organo* 6 (1968):15.

Lindley, Mark. "Ammerbach's 1583 Exercises." *The English Harpsichord Magazine* 3 (1976):58.

————. "Instructions for the Clavier Diversely Tempered." *Early Music* 5 (1977):18.

————. "Temperaments." *The New Grove,* vol.18, p.660.

Lister, Craig L. "Traditions of Keyboard Technique from 1650 to 1750." Ph.D. diss., University of North Carolina, 1979.

Lloyd, L. S., and Boyle, H. *Intervals, Scales and Temperaments.* London: Macdonald and Jane's, 1978.

Little, Helen Meredith Ellis. "The Contribution of Dance Steps to Musical Analysis and Performance: *La Bourgogne.*" *Journal of the American Musicological Society* 28 (1975):112.

————. "Dance under Louis XIV and XV." *Early Music* 3 (1975):331.

————. "The Dances of Jean Baptiste Lully." Ph.D. diss., Stanford University, 1967.

————. "Inventory of the Dances of Jean-Baptiste Lully." *Recherches* 9 (1968):21.

Lohmann, Ludger. *Studien zu Artikulations-probleme bei den Tasteninstrumenten des 16.-18. Jahrhunderts.* Regensburg: Gustav Bosse, 1982.

MacClintock, Carol. *Readings in the History of Music in Performance.* Bloomington: Indiana University Press, 1979.

Marz, Hans. "Some Unknown Embellishments of Corelli's Violin Sonatas." *Musical Quarterly* 56 (1970):65.

Mather, Betty Bang. *The Interpretation of French Music from 1675 to 1775 for Woodwind and Other Performers.* New York: McGinnis and Marx, 1973.

Mellers, Wilfred. *François Couperin and the French Classical Tradition*. London: Dobson, 1949.

Mendel, Arthur. "Pitch in Western Music since 1500: A Reexamination." *Acta Musicologica* 50 (1978):1.

Mendel, Arthur, and David, Hans T. *The Bach Reader*. Rev. ed. New York: Norton, 1972.

Morey, Carl. "The Diatonic, Chromatic and Enharmonic Dances by Martino Pesenti." *Acta Musicologica* 38 (1966):185.

Moroney, Davitt. "The Performance of Unmeasured Harpsichord Preludes." *Early Music* 4 (1976):143.

Neumann, Frederick. *Essays in Performance Practice*. Ann Arbor: UMI Research Press, 1982.

———. *Ornamentation in Baroque and Post-Baroque Music: With Special Emphasis on J. S. Bach*. Princeton: Princeton University Press, 1978.

Newman, Anthony. *Bach and the Baroque: A Performer's View*. New York: Pendragon, 1985.

———. "Finger Exercises." *Contemporary Keyboard* 4, no.2 (March 1978):16.

———. "Strong and Weak in Baroque and Early Classical Music." *Journal of Performance Practice* 1 (1983):19.

O'Donnell, John. "The French Style and the Overtures of Bach." *Early Music* 7 (1979):190, 336.

Oldham, Guy. "A New Source of French Keyboard Music of the Mid-Seventeenth Century." *Recherches* 1 (1960):51.

Ortmann, Otto. *The Physiological Mechanics of Piano Technique*. New York: Dutton, 1929; reprint New York: Da Capo, 1981.

Parkins, Robert. "Cabezon to Cabanilles: Ornamentation in Spanish Keyboard Music." *Organ Yearbook* 11 (1980):5.

———. "Keyboard Fingering in Early Spanish Sources." *Early Music* 11 (1983):323.

Paulsmeier, Karin. "Temporelationen bei Frescobaldi." In *Alte Musik, Praxis und Reflexion*. Winterthur: Amadeus, 1983.

Pont, Graham. "Handel's Overtures for Harpsichord or Organ." *Early Music* 11 (1983):309.

Powell, Newman. "Kirnberger on Dance Rhythms, Fugues and Characterization." In *Festschrift for Theodore Hoelty-Nickel*. Valparaiso: Valparaiso University, 1967.

———. "Rhythmic Freedom in the Interpretation of French Baroque Music." Ph.D. diss., Stanford University, 1959.

Prevost, Paul. "Les preludes non mesurés chez les luthistes et les clavecinistes aux XVIIe et XVIIIe siècles." Ph.D. diss., University of Strasbourg, forthcoming.

Pruitt, William. "The Organ Works of Guillaume-Gabriel Nivers (1632-1714)." Ph.D. diss., University of Pittsburgh, 1969.

———. "Un traité d'interpretation du XVIIe siècle." *L'Orgue* 152 (October-December 1974):99.

Restout, Denise, ed. *Landowska on Music*. New York: Stein and Day, 1964.

Roche, Martine. "Un livre de clavecin français de la fin du XVIIe siècle." *Recherches* 7 (1966):39.

Rose, Gloria. "A Fresh Clue from Gasparini." *Musical Times* 106 (1968):28.

Sachs, Barbara, and Ife, Barry. *Anthology of Early Keyboard Methods*. Cambridge: Gamut, 1981.

Sadler, Graham. "Rameau's Harpsichord Transcriptions from *Les Indes Galantes*." *Early Music* 7 (1979):18.

Schott, Howard. "The Harpsichord Revival." *Early Music* 2 (1974):85.

———. *Playing the Harpsichord*. London: Faber, 1970.

———. "Wanda Landowska." *Early Music* 7 (1979):467.

Sheveloff, Joel L. "The Keyboard Music of Domenico Scarlatti." Ph.D. diss., Brandeis University, 1970.

Silbiger, Alexander. *Italian Manuscript Sources of Seventeenth-Century Keyboard Music.* Ann Arbor: UMI Research Press, 1980.

———. "Michelangelo Rossi and His *Toccate e Correnti.*" *Journal of the American Musicological Society* 36 (1983):18.

———. "The Roman Frescobaldi Tradition *ca.* 1640-1670." *Journal of the American Musicological Society* 33 (1980):42.

Smiles, Joan E. "Directions for Improvised Ornamentation in Italian Method Books of the Late Eighteenth Century." *Journal of the American Musicological Society* 31 (1978):495.

Soderlund, Sandra. *Organ Technique: An Historical Approach.* Chapel Hill: Hinshaw, 1980.

Steblin, Rita. *A History of Key Characteristics in the Eighteenth and early Nineteenth Centuries.* Ann Arbor: UMI Research Press, 1983.

Strunck, Oliver. *Source Readings in Music History.* New York: Norton, 1950.

Tagliavini, Luigi Ferdinando. "The Art of 'Not Leaving the Instrument Empty': Comments on Early Italian Harpsichord Playing." *Early Music* 11 (1983):299.

Taruskin, Richard; Leech-Wilkinson, Daniel; Temperly, Nicholas; and Winter, Robert. "The Limits of Authenticity: A Discussion." *Early Music* 12, no.1 (February 1984):3.

Troeger, Richard. "Buying a Clavichord." *Continuo* 7, no.2 (November 1983):7.

———. "Flexibility in Well-Tempered Tuning." *Diapason* 73, no.6 (June 1982):6.

———. "Metre and the Unmeasured Prelude." *Early Music* 11 (1983):340.

———. "Source Fingerings in Elizabethan Keyboard Music." *Performance Practice Journal* 1 (1983):47.

———. "Speculations on Bach's Clavichord Technique." *Diapason* 73, no.12 (December 1982):12

Valenti, Fernando. *The Harpsichord: A Dialogue for Beginners.* Hackensack: Jerona Music Corp., 1982.

Verlet, Columbe. "Les clavecins royaux au XVIIIe siècle." *Recherches* 3 (1963):159.

Walker, Paul. "Fingering, Bach and the *Wegweiser.*" *Early Keyboard Studies Newsletter* 1, no.3 (June 1985):1.

Williams, Peter. *Figured Bass Accompaniment.* 2 vols. Edinburgh: Edinburgh University Press, 1970.

———. "The Harpsichord Acciaccatura: Theory and Practice in Harmony, 1650-1750." *Musical Quarterly* 54 (1968):503.

———. "J. S. Bach's Well-Tempered Clavier: A New Approach," parts 1 and 2. *Early Music* 11 (1983):51, 332.

———. "Need Organists Pay Attention to Theorists of Rhetoric?" *Diapason* 73, no.4 (April 1982):3.

———, ed. *Bach, Handel, Scarlatti: Tercentenary Essays.* Cambridge: Cambridge University Press, 1985.

Witherell, Anne L. *Louis Pecour's 1700 Recueil de danses.* Ann Arbor: UMI Research Press, 1983.

Wolf, R. Peter. "Metrical Relationships in French Recitative of the Seventeenth and Eighteenth Centuries." *Recherches* 10 (1969):29.

INSTRUMENTS

Adlam, Derek. "Restoring the Vaudry." *Early Music* 4 (July 1976):255.

Bakeman, Kenneth. "Stringing Techniques of Harpsichord Builders." *Galpin Society Journal* 27 (April 1974):95.

Barnes, John. "Italian String Scales." *Galpin Society Journal* 21 (March 1968):175.

———. "Pitch Variations in Italian Keyboard Instruments." *Galpin Society Journal* 18 (March 1965):110.

Barry, Wilson. "The Keyboard Instruments of King Henry VIII." *The Organ Yearbook* 13:31.

Bedard, Hubert. "La restauration des clavecins anciens." *La Vie Musicale* 12 (1969):13.

Benton, Rita. "Hullmandel's Article on the *Clavecin* in the 'Encyclopedie Methodique.' " *Galpin Society Journal* 15 (March 1962):34.

Boalch, Donald. *Makers of the Harpsichord and Clavichord, 1440-1840.* 2d ed. New York: Oxford University Press, 1974.

Brauchli, Bernard. "Comments on the Lisbon Collection of Clavichords." *Galpin Society Journal* 33 (March 1980):98.

Clutton, C. "Arnault's Manuscript." *Galpin Society Journal* 5 (March 1952):3.

Doderer, Gerhard. *Clavicordios Portugueses do Seculo Dezoito/Portugiesische Klavichorde des 18. Jahrhunderts.* Lisbon: Gulbenkian Foundation, 1971.

Dowd, William R. "A Classification System for Ruckers and Couchet Double Harpsichords." *Journal of the American Musical Instrument Society* 4 (1978):106.

Dumoulin, P. "La Découverte de Bobines de Cordes de Clavecins du XVIII siècle." *Revue de Musicologie* 61 (1975):113.

Eisenberg, Jacob. "Virdung's Keyboard Illustrations." *Galpin Society Journal* 15 (March 1962):82.

Ernst, F. "Four Ruckers Harpsichords in Berlin." *Galpin Society Journal* 20 (March 1967):63.

Ferguson, Howard. "Bach's 'Lauten Werck.' " *Music and Letters* 48 (1967):259.

Germann, Sheridan. "The Harpsichord Decorators of Paris." *Early Music* 8 (1980):435; 9 (1981):192.

Gilchrist, H. "An Unusual Harpsichord." *Galpin Society Journal* 26 (May 1973):74.

Gough, Hugh. "Towards a Theory of the Design and Construction of Musical Instruments." *Brussels Museum of Musical Instruments Bulletin* 7 (1977):72.

Hardouin, Pierre J. "Harpsichord Making in Paris: Eighteenth Century." Translated by Frank Hubbard. *Galpin Society Journal* 10 (May 1957):10; 12 (May 1959):73; 13 (July 1960):52.

Henkel, Hubert. *Clavichorde.* Leipzig: Deutscher Verlag für Musik, 1981.

Hubbard, Frank. "The *Encyclopedie* and the French Harpsichord." *Galpin Society Journal* 9 (June 1956):37.

———. *Three Centuries of Harpsichord Making.* Cambridge: Harvard University Press, 1965.

———. "Two Early English Harpsichords." *Galpin Society Journal* 3 (March 1950):12.

Kastner, M. S. "Portugiesische und spanische Clavichorde des 18. Jahrhunderts." *Acta Musicologica* 24 (1952):52.

Kaufmann, Henry. "More on the Tuning of Archicembalo." *Journal of the American Musicological Society* 23 (1970):84.

Leipp, Emile. "Le Clavisimbalum d'Arnaut de Zwolle. Le Problème Acoustique." *G.A.M. Bulletin du Groupe d'Acoustique Musicale* 54 (February 1971):1.

Libin, Lawrence. "A Dutch Harpsichord in the United States." *Galpin Society Journal* 3 (March 1950):12.

McGeary, Thomas. "David Tannenberg and the Clavichord in Eighteenth-Century America." *The Organ Yearbook* 13 (1982):94.

Marcuse, Sybil. "Transposing Keyboards on Extant Flemish Harpsichords." *Musical Quarterly* 38 (July 1952):414.

Meer, John Henry van der. "Beitrage zum Cembalobau im Deutsche Sprachegebiet bis 1700." *Anziege des Germanischen Nationalmuseums* (1966):103.

———. "The Dating of German Clavichords." *Organ Yearbook* 6 (1975):100.

———. "An Example of Harpsichord Restoration." *Galpin Society Journal* 17 (March 1965):117.

———. "A Flemish 'Quint' Harpsichord." *Galpin Society Journal* 28 (April 1975):43.

———. "Harpsichord Building and Metallurgy: A Rejoinder." *Galpin Society Journal* 21 (March 1968):175.

Mould, Charles. "James Talbot's Manuscript (Christ Church Library Music Ms. 1187) VII: Harpsichord." *Galpin Society Journal* 21 (March 1968):40.

Neven, A. "L'Arpicordo." *Acta Musicologica* 42 (1970):230.

O'Brien, G. Grant. "Some Principles of Eighteenth-Century Harpsichord Stringing and Their Applications." *The Organ Yearbook* 12 (1981):160.

O'Brien, G. Grant; Thomas, Michael; and Rhodes, W. "A Clavichord, a Harpsichord and a Chamber Organ in the Russell Collection, Edinburgh." *The Organ Yearbook* 5 (1974):88.

Parsons, T. W. "Stiffness in Harpsichord Strings." *Galpin Society Journal* 23 (August 1970):164.

Paul, John. *Modern Harpsichord Makers.* London: Victor Gollancz, 1981.

Ripin, Edwin. "Clavichord." *The New Grove*, vol.4, p.458.

———. "The Early Clavichord." *Musical Quarterly* 53 (1967):518.

———. "Expressive Devices Applied to the Eighteenth-Century Harpsichord." *The Organ Yearbook* 1 (1970):65.

———. "A Five-foot Flemish Harpsichord." *Galpin Society Journal* 26 (May 1973):135.

———. "The French Harpsichord before 1650." *Galpin Society Journal* 20 (March 1967):43.

———. "A Reassessment of the Fretted Clavichord." *Galpin Society Journal* 23 (August 1970):40.

———. "A Three-Foot Flemish Harpsichord." *Galpin Society Journal* 23 (August 1970):35.

———. "The Two-manual Harpsichord in Flanders before 1650." *Galpin Society Journal* 21 (March 1968):33.

———, ed. *Keyboard Instruments: Studies in Keyboard Organology.* Edinburgh: Edinburgh University Press, 1971; Chicago: Aldine-Atherton, 1971.

Ripin, Edwin; Schott, Howard; Barnes, John, and O'Brien, G. Grant. "Harpsichord." *The New Grove*, vol.8, p.216.

Russell, Raymond. *The Harpsichord and Clavichord: An Introductory Study.* rev. 2d ed., by Howard Schott. New York: Norton, 1973.

Samoyault-Verlet, Colombe. *Les facteurs de clavecins parisiens.* Paris: Heugel, 1966.

Schott, Howard. "The Harpsichord Revival." *Early Music* 2 (1974):85.

———. "A Visit to the Adlam Burnett Workshop." *Early Music* 5 (1977):371.

———, ed. *The Historical Harpsichord.* New York: Pendragon, 1984.

Schütze, Ranier. "Die Akustische und klangliche Veränderung von Ruckers Cembali durch die späteren Erweiterungen im Tonumfang." *Musikinstrument* 19 (1970):891.

Skowroneck, Martin. "Das Cembalo von Christian Zell, Hamburg 1728, und seine Restaurierung." *The Organ Yearbook* 5 (1974):79.

———. "Problems of Harpsichord Construction from an Historical Point of View." *Diapason* 63 (December 1971):16; 64 (January 1972):14; 64 (February 1972):10.

Soehnlein, E. J. "French Harpsichord Reports at the American Musicological Society." *Diapason* 68 (January 1977):10.

Strack, Wolfgang. "Christian Gottlob Hubert and His Instruments." *Galpin Society Journal* 32 (1979):38.

Thomas, Michael. "Brass Strings on Italian Harpsichords." *Galpin Society Journal* 23 (1970):166.

————. "Making a Harpischord." *Music and Musicians* 18 (February 1970):35.

Val, J. L. "Une détermination de la taille des cordes de clavecin employées en France au XVIIIᵉ siècle." *Revue de Musicologie* 56 (1970):208.

Vodraska, Stanley L. "The Flemish Octave Clavichord: Structure and Fretting." *The Organ Yearbook* 10 (1979):117.

Wallon, S. "Harpsichord String Gauges in Seventeenth-Century Germany." *Galpin Society Journal* 13 (1960):89.

Zuckermann, Wolfgang Joachim. *The Modern Harpsichord*. New York: October House, 1969.

Index

RICHARD TROEGER teaches at King's College, in Edmonton, Alberta. He is the author of numerous articles on early performance practice and of a study of the French unmeasured harpischord prelude.